# THE LAST DAYS OF
# KIM JONG-IL

ALSO BY BRUCE E. BECHTOL, JR.

*Defiant Failed State: The North Korean Threat to International Security*

*Red Rogue: The Persistent Challenge of North Korea*

*Confronting Security Challenges on the Korean Peninsula* (editor)

*The Quest for a Unified Korea: Strategies for the Cultural
and Interagency Process* (editor)


RELATED TITLES FROM POTOMAC BOOKS

*Crisis on the Korean Peninsula*
—Christoph Bluth

*Korea on the Brink: A Memoir of Political Intrigue and Military Crisis*
—John A. Wickham, Jr.

*Building Six-Party Capacity for a WMD-Free Korea*
—Jacquelyn K. Davis, Charles M. Perry, and James L. Schoff

# THE LAST DAYS OF KIM JONG-IL

## The North Korean Threat in a Changing Era

BRUCE E. BECHTOL, JR.

**Potomac Books**
*Washington, D.C.*

Copyright © 2013 by Bruce Bechtol, Jr.
Potomac Books is an imprint of the University of Nebraska Press

**Library of Congress Cataloging-in-Publication Data**
Bechtol, Bruce E., 1959–
   The last days of Kim Jong-il : the North Korean threat in a changing era / Bruce E.
Bechtol, Jr. — First edition.
      pages cm
   Includes bibliographical references and index.
   ISBN 978-1-61234-611-3 (hardcover : alk. paper)
   ISBN 978-1-61234-612-0 (electronic)
   1. Kim, Chong-il, 1942–2011. 2. Korea (North)—Politics and government—1994– 3.
United States—Foreign relations—Korea (North) 4. Korea (North)—Foreign relations—
United States. 5. Korea (North)—Military policy. 6.  Security, International. I. Title.
   DS935.775.B43 2013
   951.9305'1092—dc23

                                                                        2012049626

Printed in the United States of America on acid-free paper that meets the American
National Standards Institute Z39-48 Standard.

Potomac Books
22841 Quicksilver Drive
Dulles, Virginia 20166

First Edition

10 9 8 7 6 5 4 3 2 1

*For Jung-eun, uncommon stress was a common virtue.*
*And for Sara Beth, the apple of my eye, the center of my life,*
*the youngest in our family, and the inspiration for this book.*

# CONTENTS

# ILLUSTRATIONS

# PREFACE

The Kim Jong-il era in North Korea began with the death of his father, Kim Il-sung, in 1994 and ended with his own death in 2011 after suffering from a variety of ailments. While the United States was never on friendly terms with North Korea, the Kim Jong-il era represented a time when relations were perhaps more tense than they had been since the end of the Korean Conflict in 1953. That said, North Korea has rarely, if ever, been at the top of Washington's national security priorities. Even today, as North Korea has a proven nuclear weapons capability, one of the largest militaries in the world, a potentially unstable dynastic government, and a record of proliferation that clearly identifies it as a rogue nation, other countries and issues play a more dominant role in the national security agenda of Washington. But North Korea went through some quite profound adjustments in both its domestic and foreign policy actions during Kim Jong-il's final years that will eventually bring Pyongyang (once again) to the forefront of Washington's foreign policy priorities.

North Korea exacerbated tension in the region and created questions for the international community during the last years of the Kim Jong-il era. The world watched as little information seeped out of Pyongyang following the leader's stroke, which left him bedridden for several months during 2008 and perhaps early 2009. The world—and the region—sat on edge as the North Korean military twice conducted violent provocations in 2010 that set relations with its neighbor to the south back significantly. North Korea (finally) admitted to a highly enriched uranium nuclear program, which, combined with its plutonium program, gave it the potential not only to strike targets in the region but also to proliferate elements of the program to other rogue states. And the dynastic succession process occurred in a way that had many analysts scratching their heads. Thus, the final years of the Kim Jong-il era rate analysis and lessons learned for policy priorities and planning today.

In this book I will address several key issues that arose during the final years of the Kim Jong-il regime. These issues are important because the Democratic People's Republic of Korea (DPRK), by its very nature, is a system and a government that cannot undergo extreme or sudden change. Thus these challenges and issues that North Korea presented as Kim Jong-il lived his final years profoundly affected—and continues to affect—what is happening on the Korean Peninsula today. What kind of a threat does the North Korean military present to the region, and how does its internal role influence the power of the new leadership in Pyongyang? Why has North Korea stepped up its violent military provocations, particularly in the Northern Limit Line area of the West Sea, and what is the strategy behind this move? How do advances in North Korea's nuclear program impact security and stability in the region, and how should nation-states with interests in Northeast Asia, particularly the United States, plan for a possible nuclear attack? How have North Korea's dealings with non-state actors that engage in terrorism, and the nation-states that support them, affected stability in other world regions, and what are North Korea's motivations for this activity? This book will address all of these issues and give the reader the opportunity to gain perspective and make assessments regarding the future of North Korea and the Korean Peninsula as a whole.

I have written this book for functional and regional specialists, international security specialists, military planners, scholars in the region, and anyone who has an interest in gaining perspectives about the great effect the final years of the Kim Jong-il era have had and will continue to have on events in the Korean Peninsula. The information in this book and its assessments will be of interest to analysts in the United States and in East Asia. As such, the goal of this book is to present a current and a recent historical picture that is both relevant and predictive. It is my hope that because of the style and method of writing this book, it will be of interest not simply to those who have a theoretical or scholarly interest in the region but also to those who have a practical interest in solving the complicated issues that the continued existence of the DPRK presents.

I am grateful to a number of people who have been helpful as I embarked on the journey to write this book. Dr. Doug Streusand at the Marine Corps University is both a scholar with a national security background and a friend who gave me profound context as I engaged in the writing of this work. Dr. Jerre Wilson, the vice president of the Marine Corps University, provided encouragement and engaged me with other scholars who were quite useful for this project. Carol-Anne Parker was invaluable in providing administrative support for my manuscript. I am also deeply indebted to Maj. Gen. Don Gardner, USMC (Ret.), the president emeritus of the Marine Corps University. His leadership and dedication to the faculty there will have a lasting effect on its success for many years to come.

A number of regional specialists have furnished invaluable insights to me as I pursued this project. David S. Maxwell, who is now at the Center for Peace and Security Studies at Georgetown University and is also a retired U.S. Army Colonel, provided useful collaboration for many aspects of my research. Dr. Chun Seong Whun of the Korea Institute for National Unification is a specialist with important insights on North Korea. Chuck Downs, the retired executive director of the Committee for Human Rights in North Korea, and Greg Scarlatoiu, the current executive director, were both helpful in sharing perspectives relating to human rights and society in North Korea. The specialist to whom I owe the most for this research and much of what I have done in my study of North Korea is Robert Collins, a retired senior staff officer in the Combined Forces Command, who has mentored not only me but also dozens of other action officers, international relations specialists, and senior military officers for many years. His perspectives and analyses regarding the way the North Korean government operates, the motivations for its policy goals, and the intent behind its often confusing actions were key contributions to the research I conducted for this work.

Though it would be impossible for me to acknowledge all of them, numerous other specialists provided important analysis and comments for this work. I would like to thank Dr. Hugo Kim, the president of the East-West Research Institute; Lt. Gen. Ray Ayres, USMC (Ret.); Gen. John

Tilleli, USA (Ret.); Dr. Patrick Morgan of the University of California– Irvine; noted military specialist Joseph Bermudez, Jr.; retired senior intelligence analysts John McCreary and Merrily Baird; journalists Don Kirk and Evan Ramstead; Dr. Richard Bush of the Brookings Institution; Charles (Jack) Pritchard of the Korea Economic Institute; retired Congressional Research Service analyst Larry Niksch; author Gordon Chang; Scott Snyder of the Council on Foreign Relations; and my good friend Dr. Lee Choong-mook of the Institute of Korean Studies. All of these individuals have unique knowledge regarding both the region and key related issues that added important context for my research.

It is important that I comment on the transliteration of the Korean language that I have used in this work. The written form of Korean (Hangul) has never been transliterated in one specific form. That said, until a few years ago, the most commonly used form by Westerners and some, but not all, Korean publications was the McCune-Reischauer system. In 2002, the South Korean government changed to a new system, but this system is not used by all (or even most) publications in South Korea—and some continue to use either the old system or one of the other means of transliteration. Thus, any South Korean government sources that were used before 2002 will be under the old system, sources after that time will be under the new system, and nongovernment sources from South Korea may have used a variety of different systems for transliteration. Because the McCune-Reischauer system is the one that I have been trained in, this is what I used for transliteration in the book whenever possible, with the notable exception of Kim Jong-il's name, which would have been transliterated as Kim Chong-il according to McCune-Reischauer (it is pronounced the same). When quoting sources using the new system, I quoted them exactly as written. When quoting sources that use a different system, I also quoted them exactly as written. Thus, it may appear that I sometimes use a different spelling for some of the names in this work, but in the interest of consistency, I believe the methodology described above will be the most practical for the reader. I used the Korean practice of placing family names first, not last, whenever possible, unless individuals requested otherwise or the sources used articulated the names in the Western style of placing family names last. The reader will also note that sometimes I refer to South

Korea as the Republic of Korea or as ROK. All these names are accepted in South Korea; in fact, many South Koreans refer to their country as simply Korea. While I most commonly refer to the Democratic People's Republic of Korea as North Korea, some sources refer to it as the DPRK. Either title is considered acceptable; thus, at times the reader will see both in this work.

The responsibility for the writing and research of this work is solely my own. Thus, the views that I express do not necessarily reflect the policy or position of any U.S. government agency or any university with which I have been affiliated. References to Internet sites were accurate at the time of writing. Neither the author nor Potomac Books is responsible for websites that have expired or changed since this book was prepared.

# 1

# INTRODUCTION

---

North Korea is a nation-state that has been a thorn in the side of several American presidents since the Korean Conflict. Coming up with a foreign policy that effectively deals with North Korea while still ensuring stability and security on the Korean Peninsula—and in Northeast Asia as a whole—continues to be a priority that has been met with mixed success.[1] With Kim Jong-il's death at the end of 2011, a great deal of discussion has ensued in the international press, on radio and television shows, and in some short "think pieces" published by scholars and other experts on both sides of the Pacific. But perhaps precisely because Kim Jong-il's death is so recent, almost no books have been published that specifically discuss the impact that Kim Jong-il's last years as the leader of the Democratic People's Republic of Korea (DPRK) will have on the future of North Korea. In fact, the last years of the Kim Jong-il regime will likely have a profound effect not only on how the nation moves on now that he is gone but also on the security and stability of the Korean Peninsula and ultimately all of Northeast Asia.

The Kim Jong-il era (1994–2011) consisted of threatening state behavior, the complete collapse of much of the country's economic infrastructure, and a defiant foreign policy toward the United States. Pyongyang's often confusing (to Westerners) nation-state behavior only exacerbated the "engagement versus containment" argument among scholars and policymakers, many of whom continued to believe that by engaging North Korea, it would somehow begin to conduct itself in accordance with international

norms.[2] In fact, it has not done so. Since Kim Jong-il assumed power following his father's death, no matter who was president of the United States
and no matter what foreign policy he followed—Democrat or Republican
and engagement or containment, respectively—North Korea has routinely
engaged in rogue behavior that has created a variety of threats to the national
security interests of the United States.[3] Thus, the title of this book reflects
the importance of the final years of Kim Jong-il's rule. The era saw the continued brinkmanship and provocations, a proven nuclear weaponization
capability, the proliferation of both weapons of mass destruction (WMD)
and conventional weapons to fellow rogue states and non-state actors, and
perhaps as important, a flurry of activity designed to promote his son Kim
Chong-un as the next leader in an effort to ensure the third generation of the
Kim family regime—and the DPRK government—would survive.[4]

The objective of this book is to show how the Kim Jong-il government
in North Korea used foreign and domestic policies to pose a multifaceted
threat to the national security of the United States and several of its key
allies, and to maintain the Kims' power once the "Dear Leader" passed from
the scene. Despite having a basket-case economy and lacking suppliers for its
conventional weapons needs, North Korea and its conventional military
were—and continue to be—able to create violent and deadly provocations
that threatened its neighbor to the South and to maintain its hostile posture in a manner that forces the U.S.–South Korean alliance to prepare for
a full-scale force-on-force conflict. In addition to the proliferation that
North Korea has facilitated with various states in the Middle East, Africa,
and South Asia, Pyongyang has also engaged in perhaps even more disturbing activity by providing weapons—of course, for a price—to non-state actors
that choose to engage in acts of terrorism as part of their policy. During the
last years of the Kim Jong-il era, North Korea continued to advance its two-
track nuclear weaponization program and refused either to allow transparent inspections or to dismantle its nuclear programs. As Kim Jong-il grew
older and physically weaker, the succession process became a top priority for
the regime. All of these issues presented grave threats not only to the United
States but also to its key allies in the region and elsewhere. Further, the continued development—and, in most cases, advancement—of these threats
served to lay the groundwork for the younger generation that was to follow.

## Framework of Analysis

This volume is designed to analyze how the final years of the Kim Jong-il regime exacerbated the threats that North Korea has and continues to pose to the region and the nation-states that have an interest in it. As such, the book also explores how these threats present important challenges to the ROK-U.S. alliance as it goes through a period of flux and changing roles and responsibilities militarily. While this book does not address every issue involving the DPRK, it does focus on several key issues that will remain important for the region and for the United States as long as North Korea continues to exist as an independent nation. Thus, the book analyzes, and offers assessments and policy recommendations pertinent to, the key issues of (1) North Korea's evolving conventional military threat; (2) North Korea's strategy in the Northern Limit Line (NLL) area and how it ties into the DPRK's foreign and domestic policy (examined through a case study); (3) North Korea's nuclear capabilities and intentions and how the United States and its allies would respond to an actual nuclear attack; (4) North Korea's support for terrorism—an evolving history that continues to bring money into the coffers of the elite and to support Pyongyang's foreign policy goals; and (5) the North Korean succession process and its projected chances for success. By analyzing these five key factors, the reader will be able to understand how Kim Jong-il's government in its final years was able to continue to function, to present a threat to its neighbors, and attempt to guarantee its continued existence through the regime succession process.

## Research Strategies and Sources

There has been no shortage of scholarship written about North Korea in recent years. Much of this scholarship has served to inform and add to the debate regarding both North and South Korea policy and its importance to the national security goals of the United States. Scholars have also developed a variety of approaches to analyzing North Korea and the U.S.–South Korea alliance that has served to deter the threat from Pyongyang since 1953. Among the many examples, they have most frequently analyzed the following issues: North Korea's nuclear program, largely through a purely political science prism; the inner workings of the North Korean government;

North Korea's foreign policy, from a largely political science perspective; the North Korean economy; the U.S.–South Korea alliance, largely from a non-military perspective; and the North Korea–South Korea relationship.[5]

All of these issues have been written on extensively—and have been important for the scholarship relating to the Korean Peninsula—both in a historical and contemporary context. While all of these works are important, they often do not focus on these issues in the specific context of how they present a threat to the security of the United States and its allies. This book is decidedly different. The North Korean military has many challenges and issues, but what kind of threat (in detail) can it actually present? North Korea's nuclear program has been analyzed and reanalyzed from nearly every political science perspective available. But what is the actual threat that this two-track program presents not only to South Korea but also to the region and to the United States? At the end of the George W. Bush administration in 2009, the U.S. State Department had a great debate about removing North Korea from its list of nations that support terrorism. Other published works have offered almost no analysis on this issue, but chapter 5 of this book discusses it in depth.[6] And, of course, many observers now consider the internal workings of the North Korean government to be extremely important as Kim Jong-il's son has attempted to consolidate the power base that his father built (many would say way too quickly to be truly effective) to "carry on the Kim family regime."[7] This issue, too, is very important, but equally as important is a study of what security challenges this presents for the world and specifically for the United States.

As the United States looks to an uncertain economic future and a shrinking military, its presence on the Korean Peninsula will almost certainly become a matter of debate. Together, the United States and South Korea have deterred the North Korean threat since 1953. Many would say the relationship between Barack Obama and Lee Myung-bak was as good as any between an American president and a Korean president.[8] Yet many questions remain about the future of this long-standing alliance and the role that America will play in Asia in coming years. The two governments have experienced flux in both their North Korea policy and their overall goals in Asia. Because elections occurred in both nations during 2012, more change is likely. Exacerbating the uncertainty is the ongoing evolution of the North Korean threat, particularly as uncertainty regarding the status and power of the Kim Chong-un regime will likely continue for the foreseeable future.

This book is unique because it specifically addresses the end of the Kim Jong-il era from a national security perspective. For the first time, it combines the key issues discussed in this chapter with an eye on how the recent past can influence a very uncertain future. Few serious studies about North Korea's conventional military forces have been published in the United States.[9] Indeed, almost no one has published studies regarding the support North Korea provides to non-state actors that engage in terror. As in any autocratic dictatorship, these issues are directly related to North Korea's two-track nuclear program and are considered an important aspect of survival for the regime. By addressing how North Korea posed challenges in all of these issues at the end of the Kim Jong-il era, this work presents the reader with evidence that will lead to important assessments about what to expect for the future of a North Korea without the Dear Leader.

The research involved in writing this book comes from a variety of sources in order to put current history into context. The sources used in this work include but are not limited to interviews with academics, policymakers, and military experts on both sides of the Pacific. Other important sources include scholarship and books regarding the issues that widely acknowledged experts from both sides of the political spectrum address, in order to give the reader a realistic perspective on the challenges faced. Also consulted were papers and presentations from conferences and symposia (again, from many sides of the political spectrum), and an analysis of speeches from policymakers and government officials on both sides of the Pacific. Finally, a great deal of research in this book covers such sources as press releases, press reports, and press conferences; U.S. and South Korean government reports, white papers, and legislative testimony; declassified defector reports; speeches and statements by policymakers in the United States and East Asia; and a study of papers, reports, and special releases by important think tanks, government agencies, public policy institutes, and universities. The reader can gain insight on the diverse sources used in this book by consulting the bibliography.

I wrote this book in the hope that it will be of use to those with an interest in national security policy; international relations; U.S., South

Korean, and North Korean foreign and defense policy; and Korean security issues. This work is intended to show how the last years of the Kim Jong-il era left a profound impact that will influence events on the Korean Peninsula in the years to come. The evidence presented will give readers on both sides of the Pacific insights into North Korea's foreign, military, and internal policy. As such, they will glean lessons from recent events that will have applicability to planning, policy, and statecraft.

## Outline of Chapters

Chapter 2, "Maintaining a Rogue Military: North Korea's Military Capabilities and Strategy at the End of the Kim Jong-il Era and South Korea's Ability to Counter the DPRK Threat," addresses the DPRK's non-nuclear military capabilities. North Korea's obvious lack of hesitance to use violent military force raises many national security questions—not the least of which, how has North Korea's strategy for use of its military forces changed in recent years? North Korea with its very large army is facing a variety of sustainment and modernization issues. Indeed, I would also contend that the North Korean military confronts (and has for a number of years) an array of morale and welfare issues that continues to have an impact on its preparedness to conduct warfare. In this chapter, I will address how and why the military has adjusted to these issues. I also review how North Korea has changed the focus of its forces to meet the challenges of sustainment, aging equipment, and a prosperous, militarily well-equipped neighbor to the south. Perhaps as important, I will look both at how North Korea has made advances since the mid-2000s in its military forces that directly threaten the U.S.-ROK alliance and at the alliance's ability to defend the South Korean landmass. While North Korea's nuclear weaponization capabilities and intent are important, I will address these issues in chapter 4.

The succession process has played a key role in the North Korean governmental infrastructure, particularly since Kim Jong-il's health issues began in earnest during the summer of 2009. The DPRK government's power structure is tied to the military in ways that make it far different from those of most nation-states. I will look at and analyze how the process of the planned handover of power from the father to the third son occurred and how it played out in the early tenure of the Kim Chong-un regime. I will also examine and analyze how it will affect military readiness and the stability of the military command structure now that Kim Jong-il is dead. Finally, I will analyze how the U.S.-ROK alliance has addressed the changes in the North Korean threat that became exacerbated during the final years of his regime and remain unpredictable in many ways today.

Chapter 3, "The Sinking of the *Cheonan* and the Shelling of Yeonpyeong Island: A Case Study of North Korea's Asymmetric Northern Limit Line Strategy," will analyze the implications behind the North Korean sinking of the South Korean naval ship *Cheonan* on March 26, 2010, and the artillery attack on Yeonpyeong Island that occurred within the NLL confines several months later. First, however, I will review events that occurred prior to the *Cheonan* sinking and address how the North Korean planning process probably evolved, based on leadership and organizational changes that took place before the incident. These important changes probably affected the way it was conducted. Chapter 3 will also examine (in chronological order as much as possible) the events that ensued immediately after the sinking of the South Korean corvette. This chapter will consider dissenting views on the evidence regarding the *Cheonan*'s sinking (though the evidence is overwhelming) and the responses of other responsible analysts as their views arose in the press and at some levels in academia. I will also address the courses of action that South Korea and its allies took as the investigation's final results came to light and what the likely implications for future security issues on the Korean Peninsula will be as a result. Finally, I will cover the North Korean violent, unprovoked surprise artillery attack against South Korea's Yeonpyeong Island that occurred on November 23, 2010; the response from the South Koreans; and to a lesser extent, the American reaction to the attack.

In chapter 4, "Planning for the Unthinkable: Countering a North Korean Nuclear Attack and Management of Postattack Scenarios," I will outline how the U.S.-ROK alliance should prepare for a North Korean nuclear attack. Such an attack is most likely to be staged either against South Korea or against another key American ally, namely, Japan. Thus, I will first describe North Korea's known and potential nuclear capabilities and include the type and number of possible weapons that it could use in a nuclear attack. Second, I will address several key scenarios that the North Koreans could use to initiate a nuclear attack. A nuclear attack would create such horror and destruction—no matter how or where it occurred—that a preemptive strike is an option many analysts have discussed in the past.[10] Thus, I will analyze the viability of a first strike by U.S. or South Korean forces, the way in which it would or could occur, its probable effectiveness, and North Korea's likely reaction. One of the most important questions many have asked is how much damage a North Korean nuclear attack could cause. Along those lines, I will analyze the expected damage from a nuclear attack, the military countermeasures that the United States and its allies could take, and how consequence management might work. Finally, I will make a judgment on the level of current U.S.-ROK military readiness to deter and defend against a North Korean nuclear attack. This chapter will conclude with some assessments and implications for the future.

Chapter 5, "North Korea and Support for Terrorism: An Evolving History," will follow with an analysis of North Korea's support for terrorism and how it has evolved since the beginning of the Cold War. Its backing of terrorism, terrorist groups, and insurgents did not begin overnight, not even during the Cold War. Thus, first I will discuss how Kim Il-sung built his power base, with his rise to power having started as the leader of a partisan group fighting against the Japanese (some would say the early activities of Kim's partisan group bordered on terrorism).[11] For the reader to appreciate an important aspect of Pyongyang's support for terrorist groups, I will provide a brief history of the DPRK and the kind of support that Kim Il-sung received from both the Union of Soviet Socialist Republics (USSR) and the People's Republic of China. I will also address how Kim Il-sung accumulated his power, because Kim's power consolidation during the 1950s directly affected North Korea's foreign policy and the way that Pyongyang worked with its sponsors and allies during the Cold War. As a result, chapter 5 will summarize North Korea's role in supporting terrorism in the Cold War years, as well as many of the specific terrorist groups it backed and why.

By the time the Cold War ended, the North Koreans had built an international network with ties to a number of state and non-state actors.

Unfortunately, while the end of the Cold War meant an end to non-state actors engaging in terrorism and those who supported them for much of the globe, it also meant rogue state regimes that were motivated by financial gain, as North Korea was, could step in to fill the void. Chapter 5 will address how North Korea's support to terrorist groups adjusted to geopolitical paradigms that radically changed during the 1990s and beyond during the Kim Jong-il (and now Kim Chong-un) regime. North Korea is widely known as a rogue state, willing to proliferate both conventional weapons and WMD to any country that will buy them. This international security issue, which I have analyzed in the past, rates serious discussion, but in this book I will deal specifically with North Korea's support for terrorist groups (and those who back them), its reasons for doing so, the goals it has reached, and the implications for American foreign policy.

Chapter 6, "Conclusion: The Impact of the Last Years of the Kim Jong-il Regime on the Future of North Korea," will summarize the analysis of the key national security issues that North Korea at the end of the Kim Jong-il era represents for the United States. As the United States moves into a new era of foreign policy shaped by a smaller military and daunting economic challenges, the threat from a defiant and/or unstable North Korea is quite compelling. To make this security challenge all the more daunting, North Korea also presents an evolving and unpredictable military threat to both South Korea and Japan, which are arguably America's two most important allies in Asia. Because of its support for non-state actors that engage in terrorism in the Middle East, North Korea also poses national security problems for America's closest ally there, Israel. And finally the (as yet unfinished) Kim Jong-il succession process to his son Kim Chong-un leaves us with a variety of scenarios—many of which end in collapse or implosion—that can occur should it not go smoothly. The instability that now exists in North Korea because it has an inexperienced leader with a tenuous power base is a concern for all nations with an interest in the region. The final chapter will conduct assessments and offer policy recommendations regarding all of these issues.

## 2

# MAINTAINING A ROGUE MILITARY

*North Korea's Military Capabilities and Strategy*
*at the End of the Kim Jong-il Era and South Korea's*
*Ability to Counter the DPRK Threat*

———

N orth Korea was a constant source of news from 2009 through 2011 and into 2012 after the death of the Dear Leader. Kim Jong-il's health issues in 2009 led to a plethora of pondering press pieces all over East Asia and in the United States. Indeed, questions about how long the Dear Leader would continue to live also led to international curiosity about the regime succession process in North Korea and about the apparent plans for Kim to be succeeded by his third and youngest son, Kim Chong-un. But while these questions caught the fancy of the international press and of scholars who focus on East Asian issues, the issues that truly made North Korea a constant and focused source of news and concern for not only East Asia but also the rest of the world were associated with Pyongyang's violent military provocations against its neighbor to the south. Twice in 2010 North Korea's unprovoked acts of military violence against South Korea not only brought the Korean Peninsula into the headlines all over the world but also raised concerns over both the capabilities of the North Korean military and the strategy that Pyongyang uses and plans to use for its very large—the world's fifth largest—and often unpredictable military.[1]

North Korea's aggressive use of violent military force raises many national security questions and not the least of which is, how has North Korea's strategy for using its military forces changed in recent years? It is my belief, based on the evidence, that North Korea and its large army are facing various sustainment and modernization issues. Indeed, I would also assess that the North Korean military faces morale and welfare issues that continue to have an impact on its readiness to conduct warfare. But this chapter addresses exactly how the military—which in North Korea operates in more of a state of flux than most people realize—has adjusted to these issues. North Korea has gradually but quite clearly changed the focus of its forces to meet the challenges of sustainment, aging equipment, and a prosperous, militarily well-equipped neighbor to the south. Along those lines, I examine recent (since the mid-2000s) advances North Korea has been able to initiate in its military forces that directly threaten the U.S.-ROK alliance and the alliance's ability to defend the South Korean landmass.

Because the succession process has played such a major role in the North Korean governmental infrastructure and because the government's power structure is so tied into the military in North Korea, I review the often unpredictable and highly unusual process of the planned handover of power from father to third son in Pyongyang and how it will affect military readiness and the stability of the military command structure now that Kim Jong-il is dead. Finally, I will show how the South Korean military and its American allies have reacted to and planned for changes occurring in the North Korean military and government.

## Issues Facing the North Korean People's Army

Always in the background of any discussion about the readiness and capabilities of the North Korean military are serious questions about North Korea's long-standing economic problems, and East Asian analysts often cite them as a reason why the army would not be able to fight effectively in a war with South Korea.[2] The North Korean military has not been able to add as many upgrades to its forces as Pyongyang would prefer, and this situation has existed since 1990, when the Soviet Union cut off subsidies of military equipment and fuel.[3]

North Korea is struggling to feed its people and simply provide fuel and power nationwide, and it is against this backdrop that the issues for the North Korean military should be addressed. The military is the best-fed, most efficient institution in North Korea, but in recent years, reports have begun to seep out about morale, efficiency, and readiness issues in some military units. According to a Chinese source that visited North Korea and reported to the South Korean press in early 2011, a new issue that has arisen is the illicit proliferation of South Korean movies and dramas among North Korean officers and troops. Reportedly, the army is taking this discovery seriously and is cracking down on those who are caught watching these films largely because of the morale problem that they create.[4] In other reports from 2011, soldiers are seen stealing food from local villagers, and some units are said to be getting less than normal rations even by North Korean standards.[5] Recent testimony from defectors also alleges that in some units—sometimes even key units like tank battalions—malnourishment exists.[6] And an ongoing lack of fuel has reportedly led some units located in the country's northern section (which is not where the most important units are stationed and perhaps influences this important issue) to suffer from extreme cold in the wintertime and sometimes from a lack of food.[7]

It is important to note that all reports coming out of North Korea about isolated incidents of food or fuel shortages in the military are anecdotal. Indeed, no evidence indicates that these reports are anything other than isolated incidents in units (at least for the most part) that are not of high military significance. Nevertheless, these reports do lead one to ask how a military with more than a million men on active duty has been able to maintain its military readiness and capabilities in the face of food and fuel shortages that have lasted in one form or another for more than twenty years. How is a military that no longer receives free supplies of the latest military equipment and systems (as it did from the Soviet Union during the Cold War) able to present a credible, threatening stance against its neighbor to the south? And perhaps as important, has the North Korean military made the necessary adjustment in strategy that will allow it to go toe-to-toe with the U.S.-ROK alliance in combat?

## North Korea's Strategy in the Late Kim Jong-il Era: Focus on Asymmetric Forces

As analysts and policymakers discussed the decline of the North Korean military's capabilities because of economic woes in the 1990s, the North Koreans were making a focused, highly involved transition to asymmetric forces.[8] This transition began in the mid- to late 1990s and has evolved to the point that it can be judged as complete though still evolving. In fact, as articulated earlier, North Korea continues to engage in violent acts of provocation, displays of brinkmanship (such as missile tests), and bombastic rhetoric that have resulted in Americans placing the isolated rogue state at the top of the list of those posing the greatest threat to their security. According to a *Christian Science Monitor* and TechnoMetrica Market Intelligence poll released in December 2010, Americans rated only Al Qaeda as a higher threat to the United States.[9]

This asymmetric strategy continues to be a credible, deadly threat, even as North Korea struggles to maintain the capabilities of its slowly declining, though large and well-armed traditional conventional forces. In fact, in his confirmation hearings before the ROK National Assembly, South Korean defense minister Kim Kwan-jin remarked that North Korea's asymmetrical forces—strategic weapons, submarines, Special Operations Forces (SOF)—"were increasingly becoming a serious threat to the South Korean military." He further stated, "An additional attack by the North using its asymmetrical strengths is the most serious threat as of now."[10]

In compelling congressional testimony given during 2010, Assistant Secretary of Defense for Asian and Pacific Affairs Lt. Gen. Wallace "Chip" Gregson, USMC (Ret.), stated, "As North Korea's conventional military capability slowly deteriorates, the unconventional threat it poses only increases, posing new challenges to the U.S.-ROK Alliance." Commenting on how resource constraints have affected North Korea's strategy, General Gregson said,

> Other nations possess material capabilities that match or exceed what North Korea possesses, but North Korea poses a unique threat because of its proven willingness to match resources and capabilities with provocative, unpredictable behavior, and its continued export of illicit items to other states that seek to harm the United States and our allies and friends around the world. The danger posed by North Korean weapons and military strength are [*sic*] amplified greatly by the regime's willingness to dedicate its meager resources to maximizing its lethality.

General Gregson made perhaps the most cogent, accurate assessment ever in recent times regarding the North Korean military strategy and the threat that it presents when he stated, "North Korea's decline in conventional military terms has led to an evolution in the nature of the North Korea threat, not a diminution of it. North Korea has adapted to the U.S.-ROK Alliance's conventional military superiority by developing tactics and weapons systems that equip them with offensive capabilities that avoid confronting the greatest military strengths of the alliance, in an attempt to compete on what it likely perceives as a more favorable playing field."[11]

High-level officials in both the United States and South Korea have made statements that reflect a concern for a North Korean strategy that has evolved to a degree of lethality that is extremely threatening to security in Northeast Asia. But this observation leads one to ask, what forms the asymmetric threat? Further, if North Korea has faced serious constraints on making military acquisitions, what advances has Pyongyang made? I believe these questions have easy answers. North Korea's evolving asymmetric threat comprises three key components: long-range artillery, SOF, and ballistic missiles. While North Korea also uses asymmetry in other aspects of its armed forces, these three key columns form the hub of a threat that it has developed, honed, and maintained since the mid- to late 1990s.

When analyzing the first component of the "tripod" that forms the North Korean multiheaded asymmetric threat, long-range artillery, the results are quite interesting. U.S. and South Korean estimates state that North Korea has more than 13,000 artillery and multiple rocket launcher (MRL) systems.[12] A thousand of these systems or more fall into the long-range category and consist of long-range 170mm self-propelled guns that are augmented by long-range 240mm MRLs. Somewhere between 250 and 400 of these systems have the ability to hit Seoul with their ordnance, and many are located in hardened artillery sites (HARTS) that have been constructed close—often within five kilometers—to the demilitarized zone (DMZ). Estimates show as many as 500 of these HARTS are positioned in locations from which they could hit Seoul or surrounding areas with little to no warning (the locations are within the North Korean II and V Corps along the DMZ). The artillery deployed to these locations mostly sits in the main invasion corridors into South Korea through the Kaesong-

Munsan corridor and the Chorwon Valley corridor (see figure 1). Perhaps as important, an estimated 5–20 percent of rounds provided to forward artillery units would be equipped with chemical munitions, thus quite literally turning North Korean long-range artillery systems along the DMZ into weapons of mass destruction.[13] Press reports based on released South Korean government data assess that North Korea has approximately five thousand tons of chemical agents—and could contaminate an area up to four times the size of Seoul—meaning the long-range artillery North Korea has deployed along the DMZ presents a planning nightmare for ROK and U.S. military staffs.[14]

Reports from 2010 and 2011 indicate that North Korea has deployed more artillery systems along the DMZ. According to multiple sources, Pyongyang has added perhaps as many as a hundred MRL systems along the DMZ. Some are shorter-range systems that would target smaller cities and towns in Kyonggi Province, but at least some of these systems are likely the long-range 240mm MRLs, indicating that in recent years Pyongyang has actually added to the lethality of the weapons systems it has deployed along the DMZ that are capable of causing panic and mass casualties in Seoul. (North Korea may now have two hundred or more of the long-range MRL systems deployed where they can hit Seoul, and two hundred more of the 170mm guns deployed where they can do the same.) In addition, Pyongyang has recently increased the survivability of its artillery systems deployed along the DMZ. Press reports citing ROK Ministry of National Defense officials state that the North Koreans have built tunnels into hills and mountains at several artillery sites. The systems would fire their ordnance from behind the hill or mountain and then scoot back into the tunnel, thus making it more difficult for ROK or U.S. counter-battery fire and ground-attack aircraft to destroy them.[15]

Reviewing the second part of the tripod of North Korea's asymmetric threat—ballistic missiles—shows an evolving, ever-improving threat. North Korea's ballistic missiles threaten not only South Korea and Japan but also regions much farther away (as I will describe later). North Korea received its first ballistic missiles in the form of the Scud B from Egypt as early as 1976.[16] Pyongyang was able to build on technology from the Scud B to later develop the Scud C and, in following years, the Scud D, which has a range

FIGURE 1: KOREAN INVASION ROUTES

| KAESONG-MUNSAN | CHORWON VALLEY | EAST COAST |
|---|---|---|
| Kaesong-Munsan North | Kumwha Valley Chorwon West (MSR 3) | Taedong Mountains |

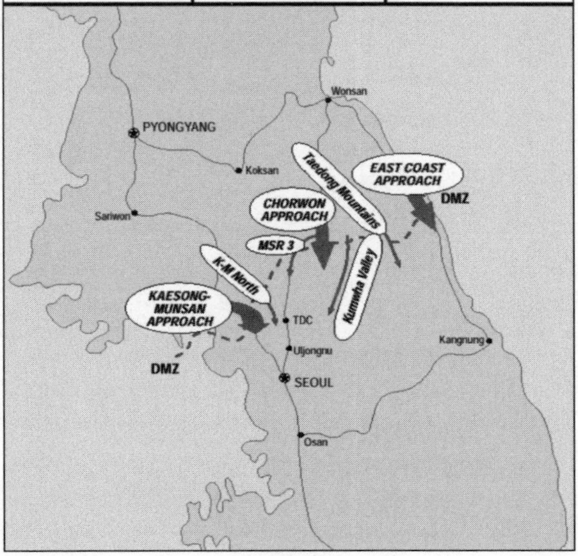

*Source:* U.S. Department of Defense, North Korean Country Handbook (Washington, DC: Defense Department, May 1997), http://www.dia.mil/publicaffairs/foia/nkor.pdf.

of more than 700 kilometers.[17] In 2006 the North Koreans conducted missile tests, and expert analysis showed that they had also apparently built and deployed an extended-range (ER) Scud with a range of 850 kilometers.[18] The North Koreans have also developed, deployed, and successfully test launched at least twice the No Dong missile, which has a range of 1,300 to 1,500 kilometers and can hit Japan. The No Dong missile is believed to have been developed from Scud technology.[19] The development of the missiles just described means that with Scuds, North Korea can literally target every single inch of the South Korean landmass. With the No Dong missile, North Korea can target key areas in Japan, including Tokyo. Further, North Korea continues to hone the capabilities of the Scud and No Dong missile systems.

North Korea also has other short-range missiles that rate discussion. Key among these missiles is the North Korean version (with an extended range) of the Soviet SS-21. North Korea probably acquired this missile from

Syria in the late 1990s. Soon after acquiring the missile, which is well known for having been deployed against allied forces in Europe during the Cold War, the North Koreans engineered their own indigenously produced version of the system, identified as the KN-02. The tactical, mobile missile has a range of at least 120 kilometers and can target U.S. and ROK bases south of Seoul.[20] The KN-02 is "road mobile," which means it is on a truck-mounted, transporter-erector-launcher (TEL). The North Korean version of the SS-21 uses solid fuel; thus, it can be deployed faster and loaded and fired more rapidly than other less modern systems can.[21] Pyongyang has conducted several test firings of this missile, and analysts have stated that they appeared to be successful.[22]

Another missile that the North Koreans have developed successfully in the past ten years and that has received far less publicity than the Taepo Dong missiles is the Musudan, which sometimes is also known as the Taepo Dong X. The North Koreans built the Musudan based on SS-N-6 technology, one of the former Soviet Union's submarine-launched ballistic missiles. Pyongyang does not have submarines capable of launching such a missile; thus, the North Koreans converted the missile so that they could deploy it from mobile land-based launchers or TELs. The Musudan also is reportedly deployed at fixed sites. Perhaps its most ominous specification is its range. At up to 4,000 kilometers, it gives North Korea the ability to hit Guam.[23] The pubic had its first look at the Musudan in 2010, when it was included in a military parade in Pyongyang.[24] Equally disturbing, some analysts reportedly believe that the Musudan is capable of carrying a nuclear warhead.[25] By 2010, the North Koreans had apparently deployed so many Musudan missiles that they decided to form a new, independent missile division to keep up with this latest capability.[26] Their deployment of these missiles appears to have changed the South Koreans' assessment of the number of North Korean ballistic missiles. In March 2010, the South Korean minister of national defense reportedly stated that North Korea had about a thousand ballistic missiles—an increase over previous estimates of eight hundred ballistic missiles—and this estimate was apparently a direct reference to an appraisal regarding the Musudan missile.[27] U.S. intelligence officials reportedly also have determined that North Korea is developing a road-mobile intercontinental ballistic missile (ICBM) and that it may be a variant of the Musudan.[28]

Thus, the Scud missiles can target all of South Korea; the No Dong, key nodes in Japan; and the Musudan, American sovereign territory in Guam. All of these systems have been test launched in one form or another successfully. (The Musudan has not been test launched from North Korea, but Iran, which acquired the missile in 2005 from North Korea, and then reportedly successfully tested it in 2006.[29]) The North Koreans continue to develop the Taepo Dong 1 and Taepo Dong 2 systems, these three-stage missiles have not proven to be successful in test launches conducted in 1998, 2006, and 2009. (I will discuss the attempted missile launch of 2012 later.) Now that these missiles have proven to be successful, they will potentially have the capability to target the continental United States (or at least Alaska and Hawaii).[30] The map in figure 2 shows some examples of the ranges of North Korea's ballistic missiles. Of course, as North Korea continues to develop its short-range, medium-range, and long-range ballistic missiles, it also builds and expands the facilities from which the test launches of these missiles will occur. A facility at Tongchang-ni, which is a significant upgrade over facilities where other missile launches have occurred, principally those at Musudan, is now ready to go and was the site of North Korea's missile launches in 2012.[31]

FIGURE 2: NORTH KOREAN BALLISTIC MISSILE CAPABILITIES

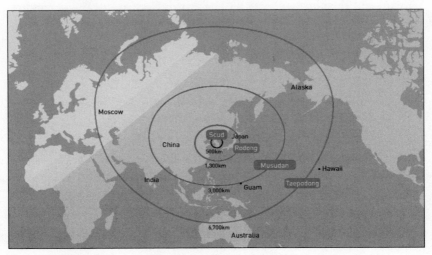

*Source:* Ministry of National Defense, Republic of Korea, "Defense White Paper," 2008, http://www.mnd.go.kr/.

Pyongyang's state-sponsored propaganda outlet, Korea Central News Agency (KCNA), formally announced that the North Koreans would conduct a "satellite launch" on March 16, 2012. They called the launch platform the Unha-3, when in reality it was the three-stage, long-range ballistic missile platform commonly known as the Taepo Dong 2. Pyongyang informed the International Civil Aviation Administration and the International Maritime Organization that the first stage of the rocket would land in the water approximately 140 kilometers west of the Byeonsan Peninsula in South Korea and that the second stage would land approximately 190 kilometers east of the Philippines. It also declared that the launch would be from the new North Korean facility (not used to this point) at Tongchang-ni.[32] The North Koreans formally communicated that the launch would occur sometime during a five-day period from April 12 to April 16, 2012, anytime between seven in the morning until noon.[33]

The site at Tongchang-ni near the west coast is interesting because it is an upgrade from the Musudan facilities on the east coast that North Korea has used for long-range missile launches in the past. The facilities at Tongchang-ni have some similarities to the Iranian launch facility at the Shahid Hemat Industrial Complex east of Tehran. Reportedly, the static rocket motor test stand at Tongchang-ni closely resembles the one located in Iran, indicating probable collaboration on launch facilities between the Iranians and the North Koreans. (The North Koreans had been building the site at Tongchang-ni for at least ten years and may have aided the Iranians in some of their construction as well.) Missiles launched from the site at Tongchang-ni also can achieve a higher altitude before passing maritime ballistic missile defense (BMD) platforms (like the American Aegis-equipped ships), thus increasing their survivability in a potential conflict. The site has other advantages as well, such as an underground pipeline equipped with a fuel tank next to the launch pad that can hide fueling operations from potential satellite coverage.[34]

On March 19, 2012, South Korean and American officials revealed that they planned to search for debris from the missile's first stage after it fell into the waters west of South Korea, though these quite muddy waters would be difficult to hunt for debris.[35] South Korean and U.S. officials also reportedly believed that the North Koreans had been planning the launch since 2011. North Korean officials told U.S. administration officials during bilateral talks held days before Kim Jong-il's death that Pyongyang intended to launch a satellite in commemoration of Kim Il-sung's hundredth birthday. During the bilateral talks, U.S. special envoy Glyn Davies warned Kim Kye-gwan, the North Korean first vice foreign minister, that such a launch—which the United States and South Korea consider a missile test in reality—would be a violation of bilateral agreements. Following this exchange, the North Koreans reached an agreement with the United States in which U.S. food aid would go to North Korea in exchange for a moratorium on missile launches and an opening of nuclear facilities for inspection (among other things). Despite this agreement, several days after it was reached and proclaimed on February 29, 2012, the North Koreans announced the upcoming launch of a satellite, thus breaking the agreement and creating puzzlement in diplomatic circles on both sides of the Pacific.[36]

On March 21, 2012, aircraft flying routes between the Philippines and Japan—specifically from the Philippine east coast of Mindanao to the Kyushu island chain of Japan—were cautioned for the days that the North Korean Taepo Dong 2 (or Unha-3) launch was scheduled. Seoul also announced that South Korean flights would be affected, specifically aircraft leaving Cheju Island bound for Beijing.[37] Of note, North Korea announced that its upcoming missile launch (in reality a test of the Taepo Dong 2) was supposed to launch a satellite called Kwangmyongsong-3 into orbit. It said that the "satellite" would broadcast remote data in the ultra-high frequency (UHF) band and video in the X band, according to the International Telecommunications Union.[38] In an apparent response to North Korea's intentions to carry out the launch, South Korea initiated efforts to deter Pyongyang's launch of the Taepo Dong 2 missile, and South Korean government officials stated they would refer it to the United Nations Security Council (UNSC) if the launch went forward.[39] Japan also took action quickly. The Japanese government declared that it would mobilize both Patriot advanced capability-3 (PAC-3) BMD forces and deploy three Aegis-equipped ships in reaction to the launch, because falling debris from the missile was a key concern. If the launch were to go as planned, it would fly over Okinawa Prefecture.[40]

By March 26, 2012, North Korea had moved the missile by special train from the factory to the launch site at Tongchang-ni. According to a statement by Col. Lee Bung-woo of the South Korean Joint Chiefs of Staff Office, "North Korea has transported the body of its long-range missile to Dongchang-ri and is making preparations inside a building for the blastoff."[41] The reactions of the international community by this time were starting to mount. A senior American official reportedly stated that debris from the rocket could cause casualties, thus raising concerns for both the South Koreans and the Japanese.[42] By March 29, 2012, the North Koreans had reportedly begun several key preparations. According to 38 North, a website run by the U.S.-Korea Center at the Johns Hopkins University School of Advanced International Studies (whose report was based on commercially available imagery),

> The mobile launch pad is seen sitting on tracks next to the gantry tower. All the work platforms have been folded back and the crane on top is at a 45 degree angle relative to the pad, indicating that equipment is being loaded onto the gantry. At the base of the gantry there are numerous small objects on the pad and several people. There is also a plate under the mobile launch stand to cover the entrance into the flame trench that is still in place and will be removed prior to launch. A crew appears to be cutting brush away from the concrete in the brown dirt area that extends from in front of the pad up the right side.

The report further stated, in part, "At the two largest propellant storage buildings to the right of the launch pad, containing large tanks to supply the Unha-3's first stage, trucks can be seen delivering fuel and oxidizer to small tanks."[43]

By March 30, 2012, the North Koreans had begun assembly work on the first- and second-stage rocket for the long-range missile, according to South Korean officials. North Korea announced that the Kwangmyongsong-3 satellite to be mounted on the top of the three-stage missile would weigh 100 kilograms. In an unprecedented move, the North Koreans also said that they would invite international observers to the launch. Both South Korea and the United States declared that they would decline this invitation.[44] Also on March 30, the Obama administration announced that it would no longer provide 240,000 metric tons of food aid to North Korea because of Pyongyang's plans to conduct a long-range missile launch in direct violation of the February 29, 2012, agreement. President Obama stated that the launch could also lead to further economic sanctions against North Korea.[45] In a likely reaction to North Korean refusal to halt launch preparations, the United States dispatched the sea-based X-Band radar to track North Korean operations.[46] The first of three Japanese Aegis-equipped destroyers left port on March 31, and PAC-3 ballistic missiles systems left their home bases on the same day, bound for deployment in anticipation of the North Korean missile launch.[47]

By April 1, 2012, a mobile radar trailer with a dish antenna (likely radar-tracking equipment) was detected at the Tongchang-ni site. The radar-tracking equipment was identified using analysis from imagery of March 28. The mobile trailer and its accompanying equipment were likely brought to the site to recover important telemetry data from the missile's engines and guidance system and to ensure that it remained on the correct trajectory.[48] The technology the North Koreans have used thus far in attempting to perfect a three-stage missile appears to be rather primitive when compared to that of those other nation-states that have already launched a similar platform. While some disagree regarding the actual makeup of the missile, many analysts agree that the first stage (the bottom), which needs the most power as the missile is launched, appears to be a "cluster" of No Dong engines. The second stage appears to be made up of a Musudan missile (or key parts and the engine of a Musudan missile). The third stage is unknown. Some analysts have said that it seems similar to the top stage of the Iranian Safir-2 platform, which the Iranians likely designed with a great deal of help from the North Koreans. The first Taepo Dong 2 launched in 2012 was approximately 32 meters long, though some analysts have assessed it to be slightly longer or slightly shorter.[49]

By April 2, 2012, the Pentagon had activated its global missile defense shield in reaction to North Korea's imminent long-range missile launch. According to national security reporter Bill Gertz, "The measures include stepped-up electronic monitoring, deployment of missile interceptor ships, and activation of radar networks to areas near the Korean Peninsula and western Pacific." Gertz also reported in part that "current US missile defense systems include networks of radar and space tracking gear, including ground- and sea-based radar, Aegis ships, and long-range interceptor missiles based in Alaska and California. A total of 30 three-stage interceptors are deployed." He also commented that according to U.S. officials, "the initial phases of the US missile defense activation include stepped-up intelligence gathering by spy satellites and RC-135 Cobra Ball aircraft based at Kadena Air Base in Okinawa, Japan."[50] By April 4, 2012, the South Korean government had also confirmed that it intended to send at least two Aegis-equipped ships to the waters near the west and south coasts of the Korean Peninsula. By this time South Korea, the United States, and Japan had all dispatched Aegis-equipped ships to waters where they could track the missile or possibly shoot it down if necessary.[51]

On April 8, 2012, South Korean press sources confirmed that media from around the world had arrived in Pyongyang. KCNA confirmed that more than twenty media outlets had arrived in the isolated country, including the Associated Press, Cable News Network, Reuters, Agence France-Presse, British Broadcasting Corporation, Kyodo News, and Japan Broadcasting Corporation (NHK).[52] On the same day, in full view of the foreign news agencies, North Korea had moved all three stages of the missile into position on the launch pad.[53] Meanwhile, North Korea's announced plans for an imminent missile launch prompted several Asian airlines to further adjust their routes during the time window it was scheduled to occur. Philippine Airlines announced that about a dozen of its flights would fly routes away from the missile's flight path, as did two South Korean airlines. Japan Airlines and All Nippon Airways announced that they would alter flight paths on routes between Tokyo to Manila, Singapore, and Indonesia.[54] On April 10, Ryu Kum-chol, the deputy director of North Korea's space development department, announced that the scientists were ready to complete the assembly of the missile by adding the satellite payload. He also announced that debris from the missile in its flight path posed "no danger to countries in the region."[55] On April 11, North Korean engineers were observed pumping fuel into the missile, which was mostly covered with a green tarp.[56]

According to press reports, days before North Korea actually conducted the test launch of the Taepo Dong 2, a secret U.S. delegation made a one-day trip to Pyongyang. The delegation apparently made the trip to convince the North Koreans to cancel the test launch of the long-range missile. When reporters asked about the last-minute secret trip, American special envoy for North Korea policy Davies stated, "I don't have anything for you on that. I understand your need to ask those questions, but I can't help you."[57] According to a diplomatic source quoted in the press, Sydney Seiler, a member of the White House National Security Council staff, and another senior official departed on April 7, 2012, aboard a U.S. Air Force 737 and flew from Guam to Pyongyang.[58] If the purpose of the trip was to convince North Korea not to launch the missile, it was unsuccessful.

On April 13, 2012, the North Koreans conducted their fourth test of a long-range ballistic missile. The Taepo Dong 2 (called "Unha-3 by the North Koreans) was launched at 7:39 a.m. Korean time. The missile launch did not go well. The platform apparently exploded approximately two minutes after launch, and the missile broke into about twenty pieces, all of which fell into the ocean approximately 165 kilometers southwest of Seoul. The cause of the failure may have been a fuel leakage or a flawed engine in the first-stage rocket. Some analysts believe the North Koreans may have intentionally aborted the flight because of a problem with the staging system. Other possibilities also exist. The missile launch may have failed because the first-stage propellant did not separate from the rest of the system. Most analysts agree that the failure was possibly a result of a flaw in the first stage of the missile. By April 17, 2012, South Korean ships searching for debris from the missile off the west coast of the Korean Peninsula were ready to shut down operations, reportedly not having found any debris. Lt. Gen. Patrick J. O'Reilly, commander of Washington's BMD program, remarked later that month that he saw little progress in North Korea's program. Meanwhile, another (apparently duplicate) missile remained near Tongchang-ni at an assembly plant.[59]

Immediately following North Korea's failed launch of the Taepo Dong 2, the UN Security Council condemned the action. According to U.S. ambassador to the United Nations Susan Rice, "Members of the Security Council deplored this launch which is in violation of Security Council resolutions 1718 and 1874. Members of the Security Council agreed to continue consultations on an appropriate response in accordance with its responsibilities given the urgency of the matter."[60] The United States also immediately announced that it was nullifying its previous deal with North Korea to provide food aid in return for a moratorium on ballistic missile launches (in addition to other actions).[61] In response to the UNSC condemnation, the North Korean Foreign Ministry defiantly issued a statement that said in part, "Firstly, we resolutely and totally reject the unreasonable behavior of the UNSC to violate the DPRK's legitimate right to launch satellites." The North Korean statement also tersely dismissed the Americans' actions and claimed, "We have thus become able to take necessary retaliatory measures, free from the agreement. The US will be held wholly accountable for all the ensuing consequences."[62]

According to sources in the Japanese press, the United States sought to gain more sanctions against Pyongyang as a result of the launch and, seeking asset freezes, submitted a list to the UNSC of at least seventeen North Korean entities (though the list reportedly grew to forty entities).[63] On May 3, 2012, the UNSC imposed sanctions on three North Korean state-owned companies—Green Pine Conglomerate, Korea Heungjin Trading Company, and Amroggang Development Banking Corporation—after China insisted on drastically shortening the list.[64] In my view, though much less than what Washington would have preferred, the sanctions were an important international action and added to the U.S.-imposed sanctions during 2010 (which I will address later).

The results of North Korea's so-called satellite launch on April 13, 2012, are important and should be addressed. First of all, contrary to the North Koreans' claims, it was not simply a satellite launch. The technology for a three-stage ballistic missile or a platform for a satellite is exactly the same, and only the payload is different (satellite or warhead).[65] Thus, the nature of the event was threatening and provocative and provoked the negative international reaction. Another important aspect of the launch was that it was the first to occur from the facility at Tongchang-ni, though this improved facility does not yet apparently give the North Koreans the ability to conduct a covert long-range missile launch, which would cut the warning time of U.S. BMD systems. This launch, when compared to those in 1998, 2006, and 2009, differs in that North Korea invited the international press to attend the event and openly, or publicly, admitted that the launch was unsuccessful.

The political aspects of the context surrounding the launch are important as well. This launch showed that Kim Jong-il's son would continue policies that were planned before the Dear Leader's death; indeed, the test launch is one of the first examples that this would happen. According to former acting assistant secretary of state Evans Revere, during July 2011 the North Koreans informed him, "We have the sovereign right to launch a satellite and we will never give up that right no matter what."[66] This assertion probably indicates that Pyongyang had begun plans to conduct a long-range missile launch at least as early as the middle of 2011. Other political aspects of this launch indicate issues dealing with the transition of power from father to son and of policy being carried forward. As I said in a press piece March 26, 2012,

> There may still be some confusion within the "new" government in North Korea with Kim Jong-un as its leader. Reportedly, during bilateral talks just days before Kim Jong-il's death, U.S. officials, when notified of plans for a test-launch, told the North Koreans that a ballistic missile launch (no matter what the "purpose") would violate U.N. Security Council Resolution 1874 and breach agreements.
>
> And yet the North Koreans went ahead with a new deal for inspections and a moratorium on ballistic missile testing—and then announced the "satellite test launch" soon thereafter (showing either obvious confusion in the decision-making process or a sudden decision reversal). Perhaps the North Korean succession process is not proceeding as "smoothly" as many have assumed.[67]

While assuming the launch would have occurred if Kim Jong-il were still alive (since it was a carryover of his policy) is reasonable, the diplomatic confusion that ensued under his son's regime would not have occurred under the elder Kim.

The last—and perhaps most compelling—factor concerning the test launch conducted in April 2012 is related to proliferation. According to press sources, a twelve-member Iranian delegation went to North Korea to observe the launch. The Iranians were engineers from the Shahid Hemat Industrial Group and arrived in North Korea to watch all of the pre-launch and launch activities. The engineers reportedly acquired information regarding the high-thrust engines and separation technology for a three-stage missile. In keeping with past exchanges between Iran and North Korea, Tehran is said to have helped fund the launch in exchange for valuable data that can be used for the Iranians' own programs. The industrial group is in charge of Iran's Shahab-3 program (among others)—Iran's version of the North Korean–built No Dong missile—and has long been under U.S. sanctions.[68] A successful launch of the Taepo Dong missile system will now mean hundreds of millions of dollars (or more) in sales from North Korea to Iran; but before that happened, the sale of development technology between Pyongyang and Tehran continued to be mutually beneficial for both nations.

By late November 2012, the North Koreans were again showing signs that they intended to conduct a long-range missile test of the Taepo Dong system from their site at Tongchang-ni. The first two stages of the missile were imaged sitting near the launch site. In addition, several vehicles and fuel tanks were noted involved in activity that was assessed (correctly) as preparations for a test launch. The Pentagon immediately began activating global missile defenses in close collaboration with South Korea and Japan.[69] In early December, North Korean officials announced that a "satellite" launch would occur mid-month, and that issues with the April launch had been analyzed and fixed. The North Koreans announced later that the launch would occur between December 10 and 22, and parts from the rocket would not be a danger to countries in the region or elsewhere.[70] According to South Korean officials who were quoted in the press, the North Koreans may have used foreign scientists to help resolve some of the problems of previous long-range missile test launches—problems such as weak engine thrust. North Korea may have used smuggled technology and/or rogue scientists from the Ukraine and other former Soviet republics to fix problems that had plagued previous test launches of their long-range ballistic missiles.[71]

By December 3, 2012, North Korean technicians had placed the first of three stages of the Taepo Dong missile on the rocket pad. According to data released by North Korean officials, the missile's first stage would fall into the Yellow Sea (West Sea), close to where the first stage was scheduled to fall from the missile during the April 2012 launch. It was announced that the second stage of the missile would come down in the ocean about 190 kilometers east of the Philippines. U.S. and South Korean forces immediately increased their airborne and seaborne surveillance, including Aegis-equipped ships and reconnaissance aircraft missions.[72] By December 4, 2012, the second of three stages had been placed on the launch pad, and by December 5, all three stages had been placed there. By December 6, the United States had deployed a floating, sea-based "X-Band Radar" from Hawaii to the area, in order to track the North Korean test launch. The large, sophisticated radar is a key component of the U.S. BMD system.[73] By December 9, North Korea appeared to be experiencing "difficulties" with preparations for the launch. The North Koreans may have swapped out components of the missile that were on the launch pad during this time frame—and even announced that the launch might be delayed (which it apparently was not).[74]

On December 12, 2012, North Korea once again conducted a test-launch of the Taepo Dong 2 missile system. This time the test launch of a three-stage ballistic missile appears to have been successful, as the rocket went through all three of its stages and launched a small satellite into space. Despite the successful launch, many pundits were skeptical of the North Korean technology. The success of the satellite was called into question by many (though in my view the satellite means nothing; it is all about the success or failure of a three-stage ballistic missile platform), and some even called into question the "re-entry" capability of North Korea's long-range missiles. It should be pointed out that North Korea has had "re-entry" technology for its other ballistic missiles for more than thirty years now and thus probably has the same capability for its Taepo Dong 2 platform. At a press conference soon after the successful test launch, White House spokesperson Jay Carney indicated that the North Koreans could still not hit the continental United States with a ballistic missile, though he did not mention Alaska or Hawaii.[75]

In an interesting—though completely predictable—development, several press sources revealed that an Iranian team arrived in North Korea several weeks before launch preparations began. The Iranians have observed all of the Taepo Dong test launches the North Koreans have conducted and were almost certainly there to observe the launch to see if Tehran would purchase technology and/or actual missiles. Iran did not (at the time) have three-stage ballistic missile technology (none of Iran's missiles or satellite platforms at the time had three-stage capability). Thus, any reports that Iran was there to "assist" North Korea with their launch can only be described as being written by those who had not done their research. When it comes to ballistic missiles, North Korea is the seller, and Iran is the buyer. There is no evidence to indicate any other possible assessment. In fact, according to press reports, Iran was not even informed of the launch until October 2012.[76]

There is much that can be learned from North Korea's first successful test launch of a three-stage ballistic missile. North Korea has now proven that it has the technology and the will to launch a three-stage missile capable of hitting targets in Alaska and Hawaii—and perhaps even the continental United States (depending on what one's assessment is based on the data from the launch). North Korea has also shown that it is more than willing to proliferate this technology (and perhaps the actual missiles as well) by inviting a team of Iranians to observe the launch. There is no doubt that Tehran will pay a great deal of money for three-stage ballistic missile technology. Even more was learned when South Korean experts retrieved and analyzed components of the rocket's first stage after it fell into the ocean during the launch on December 12. After examining what turned out to be the Taepo Dong 2 first stage in detail, experts reported several interesting facts. One of the experts reporting to the press after the missile components had been examined stated, "Because it used red fuming nitric acid as an oxidizer, which can be stored for a long time at normal temperature, the team concluded that (the rocket) was intended for testing (the North's) ICBM technology, rather than developing a space launch vehicle." The expert further stated, "It used four Nodong missile engines for the first stage booster, while utilizing one Skud missile engine to make the second stage propellant in a bid to save time and cost." Perhaps among the most important things revealed during the analysis was the data produced from a simulation, which showed (based on size and propellant) that the missile was assessed to have a capability of flying 10,000 kilometers carrying a war-head weighing 500 kilograms.[77] A senior South Korean military official further confirmed the technology behind North Korea's Taepo Dong program when he stated, "They efficiently developed a three-stage long-range missile by using their existing Rodong and Scud missile technology."[78]

North Korea's missile programs have all proved to be successful—and have been widely deployed and proliferated—and this now also includes the long-range missile program (the Taepo Dong series). North Korea is apparently developing yet another long-range missile that is perhaps capable of being deployed and launched from a mobile TEL. In December 2011, national security reporter Bill Gertz broke the story that North Korea was developing a new intercontinental ballistic missile, which was perhaps a variant of the already developed, deployed, tested, and proliferated Musudan missile (which has a range of 4,000 kilometers). Secretary of Defense Robert Gates may have first alluded to it in his speech given June 2011 in Singapore: "With the continued development of long-range missiles and potentially a road-mobile intercontinental ballistic missile and their continuing development of nuclear weapons, . . . North Korea is in the process of becoming a direct threat to the United States."[79]

The missile previously described was apparently the model put on display in a parade in Pyongyang during April 2012. While many analysts said that the missile on display appeared to be a mock-up, North Korea has only included missiles in parades that were either in development or already deployed. The missile is rumored to have boosters that would give it a maximum range of 6,200 miles—which means it could hit the continental United States—and appears to be longer than the Musudan missile on which it may have originally been modeled. Arguments remain about whether the missile displayed was actually a medium-range ballistic missile, like the Musudan, or in fact an intercontinental ballistic missile. Of interest, the TEL that towed the missile appeared to be of Chinese design, which would put Beijing in violation of UNSC-imposed sanctions. The design of the sixteen-wheel TEL appears to be consistent with the one produced by the Ninth Academy of China Aerospace Science and Industry Corporation. A Chinese firm (suspected to be Hubei Sanjiang) may have sold the designs or the chassis for the vehicle to the North Koreans, "not realizing" it was dual-use technology. The Chinese government denied allegations that it had violated UN sanctions. According to press reports, a Chinese firm sold North Korea eight of the vehicles, which are equipped with U.S.-manufactured diesel engines and have German-made transmissions. American officials have reportedly voiced their concerns about the unconfirmed proliferation to Chinese officials.[80] In congressional testimony, Defense Secretary Leon Panetta commented on Chinese assistance to North Korea's missile program, stating in part, "I'm sure there's been some help coming from China. I don't know, you know, the exact extent of that." He continued, "But clearly there's been assistance along those lines," while declining to give more details because of "the sensitivity of that information."[81]

The third and perhaps most ominous (to South Korea) component of the North Korean asymmetric threat is the country's Special Operations Forces. North Korea's SOF is the best trained, best fed, and easily the most indoctrinated of all DPRK military forces. North Korean SOF undertakes different missions and thus has a wide variety of units. Organized by brigade or battalion, all the way down to special two- or three-man teams, most SOF units fall under various commands that often work closely together during exercises or live operations. Units are subordinate to the Light Infantry Training Guidance Bureau (sometimes called the XI Corps), the Reconnaissance General Bureau, army corps and divisions, and the Korean People's Navy and Air Force. Most official estimates place strength at more than twenty-five brigades and five independent reconnaissance battalions, though those numbers have probably grown significantly since 2006.[82]

North Korean SOF can be inserted into South Korea in several ways. They can "para-drop" from one of the three hundred AN-2 biplanes in North Korea's air inventory (or via helicopter), use maritime insertion means—submarines, air-cushion vessels, and semisubmersibles—and enter the south via tunnels dug under the DMZ.[83] A defector report attributed to a former North Korean military officer (now defected) states that between 2004 and 2007, the DPRK built eight hundred or more bunkers close to or right on the DMZ. According to the former North Korean military officer, the contents of the bunkers include sufficient military equipment to arm up to two thousand men. The defector also stated that South Korean military uniforms and name tags were stocked in the bunkers so that North

Korean forces could disguise themselves prior to infiltration. They also contained small arms, such as 60mm mortar shells, that would be effective at the tactical level.[84] Evidence at least partially confirming the former North Korean officer's assertions came to light in late 2010, when North Korean SOF troops were spotted training in military uniforms that featured the same camouflage pattern that South Korean troops wear.[85]

According to a report by Brig. Gen. Lee Won-seung, ROK Army (Ret.), of the Korea Advanced Institute of Science and Technology that was released to the South Korean press, North Korea's SOF units have been trained to infiltrate and strike important targets in South Korea. At least partially based on defector testimonies of former North Korean SOF (and based largely on the military drills the defectors participated in), the report states, "After witnessing the drills, the North's defectors concluded that North Korean special forces could infiltrate more than 90 percent of important facilities in South Korea." The South Korean Ministry of National Defense now places the numbers for SOF in North Korea at around 200,000 men. General Lee also stated that North Korean SOF units "have been trained to conduct composite operations, such as major target strikes, assassinations of important figures and disruptions of rear areas in South Korea."[86] High-ranking North Korean defector Hwang Jang-yop stated in testimony that "each North Korean special forces unit has been assigned a specific target in South Korea, usually strategic objectives such as missile bases and airfields. The units will be delivered to their targets by parachute or hovercraft."[87] SOF military training during the winter of 2010–2011 was at typically high levels. According to press reports, "Light infantry soldiers march 20km for 10 hours with a 35kg gear bag. On the way to the mountains, they train attacking, ambushing, infiltrating and camping. When they arrive at the assembly place, they would have a martial arts match between units to have actual experience."[88]

Interesting developments in the command and control of North Korean SOF have occurred in recent years. According to several reports, Kim Jong-il's longtime friend and close confidant Gen. O Kuk-ryol was moved from his position as head of the Operations Department (an organization that was roughly similar to a combination of the Russians' Committee for State Security [known as the KGB] and the military's Main Intelligence

Directorate [or GRU]) to a key position on the National Defense Commission (NDC). When he moved, his organization apparently moved with him and combined with the elite Reconnaissance Bureau (a military SOF organization). To quote one of the press sources, "The General Bureau of Reconnaissance which Oh was placed at the head of is a gigantic organization, the result of a merger between the former Reconnaissance Bureau, the Operations Department, of which Oh was formerly in charge, and the No. 35 Office, which previously carried out overseas spy and international terrorist operations." The press piece further summarizes the significance of the change by stating, "Combining the Reconnaissance Bureau of the People's Army with the Operations Department and the No. 35 Office of the Central Committee unifies spy operations, undercover and direct military attacks in one office."[89] General O is thus now (either directly or indirectly) in control of all North Korean SOF. According to North Korean defector Kim Seong-min, North Korea's 200,000 SOF troops are trained and equipped to "damage South Korea's reputation by creating an internal commotion, and paralyze the country's command structures to facilitate a (Pyongyang-led) forced unification of the Korean Peninsula."[90]

Since 2006, North Korea has also been able to augment the troop strength of its SOF by converting several conventional divisions to light infantry divisions (and thus SOF units are presumably subordinate to either their geographical corps or the XI Corps). According to a South Korean military source in 2008, "The North Korean military recently activated several light infantry divisions that are affiliated with frontline and rear corps."[91]

In discussing how North Korea's asymmetric capabilities would be used in an actual full-scale conflict, it is useful to turn to the analysis of Capt. Duk-Ki Kim of the South Korean Navy. Kim assesses key aspects of a likely scenario (and believes Pyongyang can apply these tactics on a more limited scale to provocations) when he states, "The North will launch an offensive with its diverse collection of missiles (including the recently developed KN-01 and KN-02) and long-range artillery against the strategic center of the ROK, inflicting terror and realizing its threats to make Seoul an ocean of flames." Kim further develops the scenario by pointing to Pyongyang's thinking that it can win a victory simply by taking Seoul: "The North Korean regime will conduct a rapid front-and-rear combined operation to seize and conquer the Greater Seoul Metropolitan Area while carefully monitoring the ROK's and international community's response. Furthermore, it will infiltrate the South by deploying special operations units by land, sea, and air in multiple ways not only to disturb and disperse ROK forces but also to conquer Seoul and use it for bargaining leverage."[92]

## Other Recent Military Developments in North Korea

As articulated earlier, North Korea has focused on modernizing, resourcing, and training its three-headed asymmetric military forces' capability of long-range artillery, ballistic missiles, and SOF. (North Korea's nuclear capabilities will be addressed in chapter 4.) The evidence is clear. Each one of these forces has increased in numbers, improved its command and control, and modernized its equipment in recent years. Thus, even as some of North Korea's conventional capabilities have slowly eroded because of resource constraints, its asymmetric forces have actually grown in capability.

But even as North Korea has increased the capabilities of its asymmetric forces, the DPRK has also made some important upgrades and acquisitions that improve the capabilities of other forces and create a real threat to the U.S.-ROK alliance. One example is the recently confirmed fielding and deployment of the Storm Tiger tank, the North Korean variant of the Soviet T-72 system, that is a significant upgrade over the T-62 tank that the North Koreans had previously fielded in key units.[93] Another important development has been the fielding of infrared antiaircraft missiles that can potentially shoot down fighter aircraft, transportation aircraft, and helicopters. In 2011, the South Korean Ministry of National Defense Board of Audit and Inspection revealed that North Korean Igla ground-to-air and AA-11 air-to-air missiles use medium-range infrared waves that are not easily diverted by South Korean flares or chaff. The new antiaircraft missiles can even threaten South Korea's most advanced aircraft, the F-15K strike fighter.[94] And North Korea's newest long-range antiaircraft missile, known as the KN-06, has a longer range (possibly 150 kilometers) and is more advanced than previous systems.[95]

North Korea has also made important advances in its naval capabilities that particularly will enhance its ability to threaten South Korea in waters off the west coast. Pyongyang has reportedly now deployed a new version of its most advanced mini sub, the Sango. The newer version has better performance, higher underwater speed, and a body that is five meters longer than the previous version. North Korea has enhanced its mini-sub fleet with the addition of these newer versions and has conducted drills with them off both coasts of the Korean Peninsula. According to recent reports, another mini sub, known as the Daedong-B, is an advanced infiltration submarine equipped with a special ramp to offload SOF and has torpedo launch tubes. This submarine was also noted training during 2010.[96]

Perhaps the most ominous new naval development in North Korea is the construction of a hovercraft base at a port near the town of Koampo, located less than thirty-five miles from South Korean islands off the west coast of the Korean Peninsula. The base reportedly can accommodate up to seventy hovercraft, and each hovercraft is capable of traveling at speeds of up to 90 kilometers per hour with a full platoon of elite naval infantry commandos aboard. Once the base is complete, North Korean troops could reach South Korean sovereign territory on the hovercraft in thirty to forty minutes. The high speed of the naval craft will make reaction by South Korean forces a difficult proposition. North Korea has approximately 130 Kongbang class hovercraft, but they have never before been deployed so close to border areas with South Korea.[97]

In a development that was likely directly related to the construction of the new Koampo Naval Base, reports in September 2011 indicated that the North Koreans had also deployed approximately three thousand elite troops from one of their amphibious sniper brigades at nearby Pipagot Naval Base. During 2011, the troops were detected in combined arms training with both air and naval units while conducting large-scale landing exercises on Cho Island (also located near the west coast of the Korean Peninsula). The exercises apparently consisted of both amphibious landings using hovercraft and para-drop drills using AN-2 aircraft.[98] Of note, the amphibious troops (naval infantry), which were deployed in 2011 to a location where they could easily marry up with the hovercraft that would deploy to Koampo

Naval Base, are exactly the kind of troops that would be used in an attack on one of the five ROK-occupied islands that sit in or near the Northern Limit Line. Thus, the threat of a future North Korean SOF attack on one of these islands is very real.

While not commonly thought of as an "asymmetric capability," cyber warfare is a new sphere in which the North Koreans have now apparently decided to dab their toes. In 2011, the North Koreans were confirmed to have been behind massive cyber attacks that targeted dozens of South Korean government agencies and military entities. In 2012, United States Forces Korea Commander General James Thurman commented on this significant and growing capability during Congressional testimony.[99] The attacks have been so effective that the South Korean government has actually been compelled to chart out a national cyber security strategy. Reportedly South Korea's most prominent intelligence organization, the National Intelligence Service, will lead the effort.[100] North Korea has also been pinpointed as being responsible for the jamming of global positioning systems (GPS)—both military and civilian—in South Korea during 2011. North Korea has also reportedly offered to sell its GPS jammer system to nations in the Middle East.[101]

During 2012, North Korea once again stepped up its GPS jamming operations against targets in South Korea. Beginning as early as April 30, North Korea once again began GPS jamming operations that were reportedly conducted from near the border. By May 3, the jammers had interfered with at least 250 civilian aircraft flights. The North Koreans reportedly purchased the GPS jamming equipment from the Russians, and the systems are said to be effective to a range of up to 150 miles.[102] By May 4, North Korean GPS jamming systems had also interfered with the navigation systems of at least 120 ships, including South Korean Coast Guard craft, fishing boats, and passenger vessels. Unclassified order of battle indicates North Korea has an electronic warfare regiment in Pyongyang and several battalions with the same mission near the DMZ. North Korea may have as many as five thousand personnel engaged in electronic warfare operations. According to Lee Sang-wook of South Korea's Electronics and Telecommunications Research Institute, the interference that North Korea caused during the spring of 2012 was more advanced and on a larger scale than its 2011 operations.[103] By May

10, the GPS jamming systems had affected at least 687 aircraft, including aircraft from several foreign countries transiting into South Korean airspace. Typically, civilian aircraft simply switched to alternate navigation systems when the jamming occurred. Civilian aircraft were likely targeted because their equipment is targeted rather easily, with military navigation systems being far more difficult to jam. The disruption of civilian aircraft and ships, however, can have a profound impact on both commerce and, in wartime, support to military operations.[104]

North Korea apparently ceased its GPS jamming operations against the south approximately May 14. While the jamming operations did not affect military operations and no casualties or damage was confirmed, it did have an impact both on civilian flight patterns in and around Seoul and, to a greater extent, on maritime civilian craft (particularly craft operating near the west coast), which are more reliant on GPS systems for navigation. South Korea at the time was essentially unable to stop the electronic warfare attacks on GPS navigational systems operating in its territory except to file an official protest letter with the International Civil Aviation Organization.[105] While unconfirmed, the North Korean GPS jamming operations may have resulted in the crash of an unmanned aerial vehicle (UAV) near Inchon on May 10. When the UAV's GPS went out that day, it crashed into a control van, killing an engineer and two "remote pilots."[106]

Jamming operations in 2012 proved that military cyber and electronic warfare operations that occurred under Kim Jong-il are likely to continue under his son Kim Chong-un. North Korea's electronic warfare and cyber warfare capabilities have the potential to present a significant threat during a conflict with South Korea. As Capt. Duk-ki Kim explains when describing a likely scenario of attack during a large-scale north-south conflict, "It is expected that the North Korean regime will first conduct a simultaneous and multifarious cyber offensive on the Republic of Korea's society and basic infrastructure, government agencies, and major military command centers while at the same time suppressing the ROK government and its domestic allies and supporters with nuclear weapons. If the North succeeds in developing and deploying its EMP [electromagnetic pulse] weapons, it will be able to paralyze electronic functions as well."[107]

## The North Korean Regime Succession Process: Its Impact on the Military

Four key institutions dominate the North Korean government: the military establishment, the party, the security services, and the inner circle of the Kim family regime. In fact, when one examines the government of North Korea and the power brokers within it, it is prudent not to think of a hierarchical system of power sharing such as one sees in democracies or even in other communist governments like China's. Rather, one should regard the power system in North Korea as that of several key institutions all feeding into what has always been one man in power—until December 2011, Kim Jong-il (see figure 3). While Kim took advice from trusted leaders in each institution, he wielded absolute power over them. Thus, as North Korea goes through the important process of succession from Kim Jong-il to his third son, Kim Chong-un, it is important to analyze the impact that this process is having and will continue to have on the military.

In the North Korean system, Kim Jong-il was the chairman of the National Defense Commission, which in many ways is the de facto most

### FIGURE 3: KIM'S POWER CIRCLE

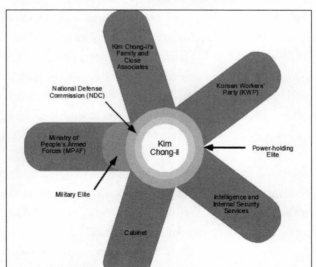

*Source:* Joseph S. Bermudez, Jr., "North Korea's Strategic Culture," Defense Threat Reduction Agency, Advanced Systems and Concepts Office, Fort Belvoir, Virginia, October 31, 2006.

powerful decision-making body in the country.[108] Kim was also head of the party and ran it through a key entity known as the Organization and Guidance Department, whose offices even control promotions in the military.[109] The security services in the country are highly redundant (precisely for security reasons) and, as I will discuss later, hold a key position in the power broker process in North Korea. Finally, the Kim family's inner circle, dominated by Kim relatives and old-time, absolutely loyal family friends, plays an integral role. Kim Jong-il conducted a focused effort to bring his third son to power within all of these governmental power-broking institutions.

The power process in North Korea received a substantial jolt when Kim Jong-il died in December 2011. North Korean television formally announced his death on December 19.[110] North Korean media also immediately reported that the military and the people pledged to follow Kim Chong-un's leadership to "carry on the legacy" of the DPRK.[111] Before the announcement of his father's death, Kim Chong-un reportedly issued his first "military order"—instructing military units to cease exercises and return to base—thus signaling his control of one of the key institutions in North Korea (even though Kim Chong-un was not yet officially designated the "Supreme Commander").[112] In an important follow-up to Kim Chong-un's first military order, state-run outlets then announced he was the supreme commander of North Korea's military at the end of December 2011. The official report said in part, "The dear respected Kim Jong-Un . . . assumed the supreme commandership of the Korean People's Army at the behest of leader Kim Jong-Il on October 8."[113] It is important to consider how the process of Kim Chong-un's taking over from his deceased father in December 2011 evolved before Kim Jong-il's death and what it means for North Korea's future.

The succession process in North Korea has occupied a hugely important aspect of North Korean activity since at least 2009 and until Kim Jong-il's death in December 2011. At the center of the storm sat Kim Chong-un, the heir apparent and the man whom propaganda frequently refers to as the "young general." In fact, a defector-based nongovernmental organization reported in 2010 that a key museum in Pyongyang had even opened a permanent exhibition on Kim Jong-il's third son in one move of many that was designed to promote his cult of personality (as already existed around his father).[114] Kim Chong-un was appointed to the powerful post of vice chairman of the Central Military Commission in 2010, and some analysts believe that his quick rise to an important military post moved much more rapidly than did his father's promotion during the previous succession process from Kim Il-sung to Kim Jong-il.[115]

Kim Jong-il in some ways "militarized" the party by placing key military figures in powerful positions within it.[116] Thus, his placing Kim Chong-un in a crucial military position is extremely important. Military units reportedly initiated propaganda campaigns designed to tout the "glories" of Kim Jong-il's third son.[117] Kim Chong-un was also appointed to an essential position within the party in 2009.[118] As in many communist societies, group photos show who is in major positions of power. In an official group photo that the North Korean media published in 2010, Kim Chong-un—along with his aunt Kim Kyong-hui and principal military and party members— was placed close to his father (see figure 4).[119]

### FIGURE 4: NORTH KOREAN LEADERSHIP, SEPTEMBER 2010

*Source:* KCNA.

Key appointments during 2010 to positions all over the North Korean government point to those who would both mentor Kim Chong-un and will be loyal to him. Not the least among these appointments were U Dong-chuck, who is the first deputy director of the powerful State Security Department (one of the key security services), and Chu Sang-song (who leads the arguably equally powerful Ministry of People's Security, another one of the key security services). Chu was appointed as a full member of the Politburo, and U was assigned to the Central Military Commission, where he will sit with Kim Chong-un. Both individuals were considered to be mentors of Kim Chong-un's before his father's death and were absolutely loyal to his father. Kim Jong-un's aunt Kim Kyong-hui and her husband, Chang Song-taek, also received important, additional new positions during 2010. Again, both are considered mentors and loyal guardians of Kim Chong-un's in the succession process.[120]

Further evidence of the ongoing propaganda campaign supporting Kim Chong-un's military leadership abilities was revealed in 2011, when a military document proclaiming his role in the planning of the attacks on South Korean forces—the sinking of the naval ship *Cheonan* and the artillery attack on Yonpyeong Island—was discovered in China and given to the South Korean press.[121] And in an important development that was reportedly revealed during an intelligence briefing to the South Korean National Assembly in 2011, Kim Chong-un was said to be occupying a key position of power within the State Security Department—one of several key security services (as discussed earlier), and serving as a key player among the institutions that wield power in North Korea.[122] Meanwhile, Kim Chong-un's supporters were said to be filling mid-level posts in the government in order to help smooth the transition of power. According to South Korean press reports, South Korean National Intelligence chief Won Sei-hoon said, "Kim Jong-un took the director position of the North's Ministry of Public Security and others, including the son of O Kuk-ryol, vice chairman of the National Defense Commission, are filling up positions under Jong-un. They are Jong-un's core of power."[123] An elite group of the children of North Korea's highest leadership are said to occupy key areas of the North Korean government. This new, younger group is known as Bonghwajo and is said to have positions in the General Bureau of Reconnaissance, the

Ministry of People's Armed Forces, the Central Prosecutors' Office, and other key entities.[124]

The disruptions and shuffling of positions of power have equally affected—and perhaps even more so—the military in North Korea. As has been the case for the entire span of the North Korean regime, one's family name means everything. The sons of well-known and powerful former or retired leaders in the North Korean military continued to be appointed to powerful positions within the military infrastructure during 2010 and 2011.[125] Top military officers in 2010 and 2011 also dominated the security services, another vital institutional power base for controlling the government. Gen. Lee Myong-su—a member of the NDC, which is the most powerful military entity in the country—was selected to lead one of the central security services and was also seen with Kim Jong-il conducting on-site inspections a few months before the latter passed away.[126]

Meanwhile, in August 2011 North Korea's defense minister at the time, Kim Yong-chun, was sidelined in the father-to-son succession process, according to members of the South Korean government who reported the results of an intelligence briefing to the press. An official (who declined to be named) commented, "I believe Minister Kim's weakening position is due to generational conflicts and rivalries between his forces and Kim Jong-un's younger loyalists within the military."[127] Key figures believed to have supported Kim Chong-un's succession (and later his leadership) are Gen. Ri Yong-ho, former chief of staff of the North Korean People's Army, and Gen. Kim Yong-chol of the SOF who probably answers directly to O Kuk-ryol (who sits in the NDC). Generals Ri and Kim were said to have been personally close to Kim Chong-un during the late years of his feather's reign.[128] Kim Chong-gak, who until early 2012 was the first vice director of the powerful General Political Bureau (GPB), also reportedly helped Kim Chong-un to consolidate his power base.[129]

It is important to note that the North Korean military has not one but two separate organizations that are political in orientation. As shown in figure 5, the first is the GPB, which operates in a separate chain of command and has political officers in units at every level in the North Korean People's Army, from corps all the way to battalion. The second (also see figure 5) is the Military Security Command, which comes directly under the State

Security Department and has military officers monitoring activities in nearly every military unit in North Korea.[130] Thus, the North Korean military literally has three separate chains of command, and commanders in every unit have not one but two political officers looking over their every move.

Professor Toshimitsu Shigemura of Waseda University in Japan explains this highly controlled, very rigid system of monitoring everything that every North Korean officer does. Shigemura states, in part, "North Korean military personnel are divided into two groups: field soldiers that engage in combat operations and political soldiers that supervise field soldiers. Political soldiers are tasked with providing ideological education to field soldiers as well as detecting a planned coup d'etat."[131] Cheong Seong-chang, a scholar at the Sejong Institute in South Korea, expands on this description: "Military commanders are not even allowed to congregate in small numbers of threes or fours, lest they plan for factional power."[132] This constant shuffling of officers in key military positions, however, brings about the possible scenario of eventual instability. It should be noted, however, that one main component, the Bodyguard Command, essentially acts as the palace guard and answers directly to the NDC.[133]

As the disruptions and shuffling of military positions occurred in the military during 2010 and 2011, they also took place throughout the government and again raised the potential for instability in the future as the leadership was forced to change because of Kim Jong-il's death. Executions

### FIGURE 5: NORTH KOREA'S MILITARY COMMAND ORGANIZATION

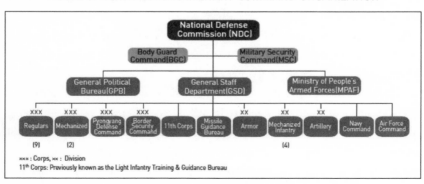

*Source:* Ministry of National Defense, Republic of Korea, "Defense White Paper," 2010, http://www.mnd.go.kr/.

in 2010 tripled in number over the previous year, and at least sixty of them were public executions. Border guards were reportedly given orders to shoot to kill as defectors tried to cross into China, and those caught reading South Korean propaganda leaflets, which South Korean nongovernmental organizations routinely send over the border via balloon, were punished to the extreme and even by execution.[134]

Several senior North Korean officials began dying under mysterious circumstances in 2010. Park Jung-sun, the first vice minister of the Organization and Guidance Department—the party's most powerful entity—was reported to have died of lung cancer in 2011, though he was not previously known to have been ill. Lee Yong-cheol, another high-ranking party official, died in a mysterious car crash in 2010, as did Lee Jeh-gang, another powerful party official. Lee Jeh-gang was noted for having been in a power struggle with Kim Jong-il's brother-in-law, Chang Song-taek, thus adding to the mystery of Lee's death.[135] Two senior officials—Kim Yong-sam and Mun Il-bong—were executed in 2010, both appearing to have been used as "fall guys" for failed economic and security policies. In 2011, Ryu Kyong, a high-ranking official in the powerful State Security Department, was also purged—again perhaps because of succession issues and because of the perception that he was not absolutely loyal to those who backed Kim Chong-un. Finally, in a move that also appears to be related to the succession process, at least thirty officials who participated in talks between the two Koreas were either executed or killed in so-called traffic accidents during 2010 and 2011.[136] Some of these forcible removals appeared to be related to putting younger men in key positions in the security services, the military, and the party.[137]

In the early months of 2012, the North Korean government showed that it would continue to carry out Kim Jong-il's policies, and sometimes in rather grisly ways. Reportedly, when Kim Chong-un found out that the assistant chief of staff of the Ministry of the People's Armed Forces had been drunk during the mourning period for Kim Jong-il, he ordered that the individual be executed and "to leave no trace of him behind down to his hair." The official was then executed using a mortar round, literally blowing him to pieces. During this early mourning period for Kim Jong-il, dozens of military officers were reportedly purged.[138]

The North Korean government moved quickly during early 2012 to consolidate Kim Chong-un's power and to surround him with hand-picked individuals who were absolutely loyal. In April, Kim Chong-gak, the first vice director of the all-powerful GPB, was named defense minister.[139] The GPB monitors military activities, so the move was likely made to ensure the military officers' loyalty to Kim Chong-un. (That Kim Jong-il personally chose Kim Chong-gak to look after his son is also well known.) Of all the titles bestowed on Kim Chong-un during April 2012, the following were the most important. Kim Chong-un was named first secretary of the Korea Workers' Party, with Kim Jong-il being deemed the "eternal" general secretary of the party. Kim Chong-un was also (in quick order) officially named the chairman of the Central Military Commission and the "first chairman" of the de facto most powerful ruling body in the country, the NDC. His deceased father was named the "permanent chairman" of the NDC.[140] By that April, Kim Chong-un had most of the titles bestowed on him that his father had needed several years to acquire officially. The question that remained, of course, was if these titles carried real power, for his need to consolidate power in order to truly control the country's vital institutions remained a key concern.

Other shuffling of important positions occurred during April 2012 as well. Two chief players under the Kim Jong-il regime who had been closely associated with the Dear Leader were promoted to the title of vice marshal— Choe Ryong-hae and Hyon Chol-hae. Choe is directly descended from a man who fought with Kim Il-sung as a partisan, while Hyon Chol-hae was a vice director of the GPB and a principal player in keeping the military loyal to Kim Chong-un.[141] Along with Gen. Kim Won-hong, Choe was also appointed to the NDC, where they joined Lee Myong-su and other existing members in ensuring that the NDC was manned by individuals from all of the major institutions in the country—the military, the party, the security services—and, of course, by loyal Kim family members.[142] The shuffling in the NDC was likely intended to ensure that the new regime carried on the policies and wishes of the Kim Jong-il regime and kept his son in power.

In another key move, Kim Chong-un's uncle, Chang Song-taek, was placed in charge of the Bodyguard Command, according to sources reporting from inside North Korea. If true, this move is unprecedented. As noted earlier, the command serves as the palace guard for the leadership in North Korea and, as such, is manned by elite troops.[143] Its previous commanding general had answered directly to Kim Jong-il. Thus, Chang Song-taek's control over the Bodyguard Command may be a temporary move until the younger Kim can consolidate his power; yet (if true), it also shows that in early 2012 this power still needed to be consolidated and protected by those around him.

The apparent and surprising purge of NKPA Chief of Staff Yi Yong-ho occurred in July 2012. Yi was widely reported to be a member of the inner circle of the Kim Family regime, and in the opinion of many analysts, had been a mentor of Kim Chong-un before his father's death.[144] Though unconfirmed, there are reports that gunfire erupted when Yi was relieved of his post.[145] Not long after this occurred, Kim Chong-un was named a marshall, as his father and grandfather had been, and little known Vice Marshall Hyon Yong-chol was named as Yi's replacement. The July surprise led some to opine that this was yet another example of a "generational shakeup," and proof that Kim Chong-un was striving to gain control of the military.[146]

The shuffling of officials and apparent purges continued into the fall of 2012. Hyon Yong-chol was apparently demoted to the rank of four-star general (from the rank of vice marshal)—perhaps because of defections that involved several young but influential members of the elite.[147] By November, Kim Chong-gak had reportedly been replaced as defense minister by the longtime Kim Jong-il confidant, Kim Kyok-sik. The reshuffling may have come because Kim Chong-gak's son defected—and thus loyalty issues came into play.[148] It is ironic that at the time of Kim Jong-il's funeral, of the eight people who walked alongside the hearse carrying his body, four were military officials who were trusted by the elder Kim and expected to mentor his son as he led the DPRK. Of the four, Yi Yong-ho has now been purged, Kim Yong-chun has now been replaced as defense minister (and holds—at least on paper—a very minor post now), Kim Chong-gak has also been replaced as defense minister, and U Dong-chuk (who was running the State Security Department) was not sighted at all during the last six months of 2012.[149] Purges are certainly nothing new in North Korea. They have occurred since the beginning of the regime, and thus, during 2012, Kim Chong-un was simply following the same template as his father and grandfather.[150] The new leader of North Korea has reportedly ordered frontline commanders to sign a loyalty oath. In addition, checks on senior officers were reportedly implemented during October 2012.[151] In a move to step up his personal security, Kim Chong-un's several luxurious homes are now also protected by armored vehicles, and all cell phones in Pyongyang are said to be jammed during his public appearances.[152] Much of the activity described above appears to be a result of moves to gain strong control over the military.

Any hopes that Kim Jong-il would hang on for several years—and thus enhance the succession process—have been dashed. Because of the shuffling of positions, the purges, and the appointments of younger officials to leadership positions throughout the North Korean government, the potential for instability—including in the military—now that Kim Jong-il is dead is very real. In fact, Sohn Kwang-ju, a scholar at the Kyonggi Research Institute in South Korea, assessed that the succession process by 2011 was far inferior to the one that had occurred when Kim Jong-il inherited power from his father. Oh Gyeong-seob of the Sejong Institute addressed the military's role in the succession process—and stability—when he stated, "Kim Jong-eun's most important political foothold will be the military, and it will only be through reliance on military force in the same manner as his father that his regime will be stabilized."[153] But most analysts see Kim Chong-un's power (at least for now) as being far weaker than his father's. Thus, now that Kim Jong-il is dead, his son's chances of holding onto power—or even maintaining stability in the country—are at best questionable. As Yoo Ho-yeol, a professor of North Korean studies at Korea University, states "The abrupt emergence of Kim Jong-un is directly linked to Kim Jong-il's health, and chances are that a situation that the 27-year-old successor cannot cope with will soon develop."[154] This statement was made in October 2011. Now that Kim Jong-il has in fact passed away, hopes that he would hang on for several years—and thus enhance the succession process—have faded away.

So what does all of this uncertainty mean for the future of North Korea and ultimately the North Korean threat? In the summer of 2011, South Korean defense minister Kim Kwan-jin told reporters in South Korea,

"Inner society is not in a normal condition and anything could happen."[155] According to a source in North Korea reporting to a nongovernmental organization in the south, the recent purging of many high-level officials (and others) has caused unrest in the DPRK's "cadre society." Sections of the elite have felt increasingly betrayed because of the large number of purges and executions that have occurred, presumably because of succession issues.[156] Many analysts agreed that the North Korean government's ability to bring about a stable succession process depended on Kim Jong-il's health and how long he was able to survive. Kim suffered a stroke in 2008, had chronic renal failure from diabetes, and was believed to also suffer from cardiovascular disease. His death in 2011 brought about even more uncertainty.[157]

As long as Kim was alive, many expected that he would rule even if bedridden (not a sound formula for stability). As Kim Yong-hyun, an expert at Dongguk University in South Korea, has been quoted as saying, "Should Kim Jong-il be able to maintain his health and continue to lead the state affairs for the next three to five years, chances are that the succession scheme will become quite stable." Kim Yong-hyun's statement continued in scope and detail by adding, "But, should his health deteriorate rapidly, there could be instability which stems from the possible conflict within the elite group in the North and other influence from outside to shake up the succession process."[158] Now that the leader has died, despite the public showing of Kim Chong-un as the next absolute leader, some experts expect a ruling combination of Kim Jong-il's third son; his brother-in-law, Chang Song-taek; his sister, Kim Kyong-hui; and perhaps the military.[159] Whether establishing a ruling combination or making a gradual move to absolute rule by Kim Chong-un is the plan, undoubtedly the transition to power for Kim Chong-un is much more difficult than it was for his father following the death of Kim Il-sung in 1994. Indeed, that previous succession was no cakewalk, with Kim Jong-il not actually assuming all positions of leadership formally until 1997, but his power was fully consolidated.[160]

In fact, Kim Chong-un may be able to maintain his position for a few years, but the chances are very good that the country could collapse as the military splinters from purges and resource constraints and as the party and security services vie for power because of a lack of strong central authority. Thus, when one considers the threat from North Korea as it stands at the end of the Kim Jong-il era, it is important to regard it as a two-headed threat—with a military that has clearly managed to adjust to resource constraints, to "re-invent itself," and to focus on asymmetric forces and with a government (including the military) that in many ways has been fighting to stave off instability, collapse, and ultimately absorption by South Korea. The U.S.-ROK alliance has had to prepare for these two threats—an attack from the north and a collapse of the DPRK—and both present compelling challenges for military planners.[161]

## Defending against North Korean Aggression: U.S.-ROK Alliance Capabilities

South Korea has not been idle in its response to North Korean aggression and military developments. While the previous Roh Moo-hyun administration of South Korea instituted many cuts and reforms that were both unrealistic—and, in my view, dangerous for the national security of South Korea—under President Lee Myung-bak in 2009, the Ministry of National Defense focused on responding effectively to the threats that North Korea posed. In 2011, the Defense Ministry called for a 6.6 percent increase in its budget for 2012 because of capabilities that North Korea exhibited. The Defense Ministry also began constructing a war gaming center, drawing up plans to increase its annual weapons imports from the United States to $4 billion and doubling the Defense Ministry's workforce by 2020, with the goal of becoming more self-reliant. The focus on maintaining a strong military, on being able to answer to North Korea's asymmetric capabilities, and on acquiring weapons and programs necessary for a more self-reliant national defense (while still maintaining a close relationship with South Korea's key ally, the United States) are important pillars of Lee's defense policy, which aimed to reinvigorate South Korea's defense infrastructure.[162]

In response to the asymmetric and the traditional conventional forces' capabilities from North Korea that threaten the South, Seoul in the fall of 2010 finalized plans to develop an advanced tactical communications and data system for its military that is scheduled to be fielded by 2014. The military also planned to develop a medium-altitude UAV to be deployed by 2014, with thirty units scheduled to be distributed at the division level. And the first of four E-737 advanced early warning and control aircraft arrived in South Korea and was placed into service in August 2011.[163] By March 2011, the ROK Air Force had acquired and placed into service forty-seven advanced F-15K strike fighter aircraft. Further, the Pentagon approved plans for South Korea to acquire the stealth version of the F-15 (in 2010). These moves were important, because the ROK Air Force has warned that a shortage of fighter aircraft will occur in coming years as it is forced to replace decades old F-4 and F-5 jets with newer, more advanced aircraft.[164]

By 2011, the two members of the U.S.-ROK alliance had developed new, more effective plans and countermeasures to North Korean asymmetric threats, particularly SOF-generated attacks and provocations, according to former commander of U.S. Forces, Korea (USFK) Gen. Walter Sharp.[165] They planned to respond to North Korea's growing SOF presence near the DMZ by strengthening guard posts near the border area with sound tracking devices and sniper rifles (among other improvements). South Korea also initiated plans for deploying elite special warfare troops near the border with a primary mission of countering North Korean SOF.[166] During April 2012, the ROK Army I Corps and the U.S. Army Second Infantry Division signed a pact that will increase interoperability in joint and combined drills. The signed memorandum of understanding advances intelligence sharing between these two key combat units through the use of UAVs and mobile radar systems.[167] In a related earlier development—particularly regarding command and control of key forces—in March 2011, Seoul and Washington agreed to delay the planned move of most American troops to a base south of Seoul until 2016.[168]

In recent years South Korea has also made a concerted effort to address shortfalls relating to its ability to combat another North Korean asymmetric capability, namely, ballistic missiles. In 2011, the United States and South Korea signed an agreement to engage in bilateral cooperation in developing Seoul's ballistic missile defense system. South Korea is looking to complete its own BMD system by 2015; however, perhaps for sensitive political reasons, South Korea continues to oppose joining the U.S.-led global missile defense system, as other nations have done. Many of the systems and updates that the South Koreans plan to initiate are also inferior in both technology and numbers to those of Japan. Their neighbor to the east has already initiated plans for advanced Patriot BMD systems near key bases and population centers all over the country. In addition, Japan will be equipping all six of its Aegis-equipped destroyers with more of the advanced SM-3 missile interceptor systems. The PAC-3 and SM-3 BMD systems are designed to go after incoming missiles at different levels and altitudes. Of utmost importance, Japan has also joined in the U.S.-led global BMD system.[169] South Korean policymakers would be wise to consider the Japanese example because North Korea presents far more of a missile threat to South Korea than it does to Japan (as discussed earlier, North Korea's ballistic missiles can reach every inch of the South Korean landmass).

An alternative to upgraded indigenous BMD—or to joining the U.S.-led BMD system currently in place—is for South Korea to increase the range of its missiles so that they can strike targets deep in North Korea. Using this school of thought, South Korea would be able to ensure it struck targets deep in North Korea if Pyongyang attacked using Scuds and other missiles. In fact, the government in Seoul has put this plan forward, and some South Korean think tanks have embraced it. Government officials and others in South Korea stated during 2012 that a range of 800 kilometers is needed for South Korean missiles in order to meet the North Korean threat. Under an agreement with the United States (signed in 1979 and revised in 2001), South Korea was limited to 300 kilometers in range for its ballistic missiles.[170] Unfortunately, this plan would still not protect South Korea's military bases and population centers from a North Korean ballistic missile attack; however, reports have circulated that the United States and South Korea reached a compromise on this range.[171] In fact, now that this plan has been adapted—and South Korea neither acquired its own advanced BMD systems capable of shooting down DPRK missiles nor joined the U.S.-led BMD system—the potential for hundreds of thousands of casualties in major South Korean cities from a missile attack continues to exist. Currently the only advanced PAC-3 systems on the Korean Peninsula protect U.S. bases.[172] South Korea and the United States agreed during the fall of 2012 that Seoul's new missile range would be eight hundred kilometers.[173]

South Korea's best answer to the North Korean ballistic missile threat is to acquire advanced PAC-3 BMD systems to protect its bases and cities and

SM-3 BMD systems for its Aegis-equipped ships. Unfortunately, at least for now (as of the writing of this manuscript), while South Korea and the United States have agreed to cooperate on BMD, the details remain mired in ambiguity, and to date, Seoul has not yet formally joined the U.S.-led BMD system (as Japan has done). While South Korea may acquire the advanced BMD systems it truly needs in the future, at least for now, it has a Patriot system (PAC-2) that recent studies show is only effective in hitting its target less than 40 percent of the time.[174] Of course, predictably, soon after the extended South Korean missile range was announced formally, North Korea announced that the U.S. mainland was within range of its missiles—something Pyongyang came very close to proving during December 2012.[175]

As of 2012, the South Korean response to the third pillar of North Korea's asymmetric capability—long-range artillery—continued to face many challenges. Before 2005, the counterfire mission against North Korean long-range artillery fell primarily to the U.S. Second Infantry Division. The Americans manned and maintained thirty multiple rocket launcher systems and thirty M109A6 Paladin self-propelled howitzers. In 2005, as part of the transferring of several defense responsibilities on the Korean Peninsula between South Korean and U.S. forces, the responsibility for this key mission shifted to the South Korean Army.[176] South Korean radar systems used to respond to North Korean long-range artillery attacks, however, are reportedly both too small in number and susceptible to numerous breakdowns. South Korea had twenty U.S.-made artillery radar systems and six imported from Sweden as of 2011, but the Swedish systems broke down 78 times between late 2009 and 2010, and the American-made systems had malfunctioned more than 150 times over a five-year time period. Experts in 2011 said that the South Korean Army needs at least ten more radar systems to be truly effective against a North Korean attack. The radars are extremely important because, as noted previously, the North Koreans have enhanced the survivability of their artillery by putting artillery positions near caves and tunnels. Thus, speedily locating the source of DPRK artillery fire is essential to any counterfire mission. While airpower can make up for some of these deficiencies, improving South Korea's artillery counterfire capability— and soon—is a vital aspect of improving enhancing its national defense against one of North Korea's key asymmetric threats.[177]

The U.S.-ROK alliance has taken careful steps to ensure that it is also ready for a possibility that is quite different than an attack from North Korea led by Pyongyang's asymmetric forces—that is, the collapse or instability of the DPRK. In October 2010, plans were made public for responding to a sudden change (reflected in a variety of scenarios) in North Korea owing to the instability caused by the regime succession process, and these plans, of course, included responding to collapse of the DPRK's government. An unidentified ROK official told the press, "South Korea and the United States assessed that uncertainty in the North has grown higher during the course of the power succession to Kim Jong-un [from his father Kim Jong-il]." The official continued, "It is my understanding that Seoul and Washington have decided to specify scenarios of sudden changes in the North due to the leadership succession and reflect them in Conplan 5029."[178] "Conplan" refers to a conceptual plan drawn up between the two allies for facing a variety of crises. In a joint communiqué issued following high-level talks between defense officials from Washington and Seoul, instability was specifically mentioned as a scenario to which their combined militaries must be "prepared to effectively respond."[179]

In 2011 in Key Resolve/Foal Eagle, one of two large-scale annual exercises, South Korea and the United States reportedly conducted drills designed to prepare for both a sudden change in North Korea and provocations. Scenarios that are said to have been addressed included a civil war in North Korea, instability due to Kim Jong-il's death, and issues relating to his third son's inability to maintain control.[180] Reports from later exercises in 2011 indicated that specially trained American and South Korean units participated in drills designed to detect and destroy North Korean WMD capabilities. These skills would also likely be key when responding to collapse or instability scenarios.[181] During an exercise dubbed Key Resolve in the winter of 2012, South Korean and U.S. forces again conducted drills designed to prepare for sudden change in North Korea, according to sources in the South Korean press.[182] Further, some reports (to date unsubstantiated) say that South Korea and the United States have drawn up plans to deal with potential interference from China (and avoiding a clash) in the event of North Korean collapse or instability.[183]

## Conclusions

In the last days of Kim Jong-il, North Korea certainly presented significant challenges to the U.S.-ROK alliance. These challenges became even more compelling with Kim Jong-il's death. North Korea's concerted (and largely successful) efforts to build up its asymmetric capabilities presented threats that called for the alliance to upgrade its military systems, improve planning, and make personnel changes. Indeed, while the alliance acknowledged the danger and took countermeasures, the North Korean military menace continued to create a climate of a "Cold War in miniature" on the Korean Peninsula, with the DPRK continuing to use its asymmetric forces for provocations and brinkmanship designed to terrorize and intimidate the South Korean populace. As IHS (Information Handling Services) *Jane's* senior armed forces research analyst Alexander von Rosenbach has said, "The South Korean Army is half the size of North Korea's million-man army, whose soldiers would be determined fighters despite being poorly trained and equipped. While nuclear capabilities are often on the spotlight, it is their inventiveness and the sheer size of the military and traditional capabilities that are the bigger threat."[184] Of course, the risk of instability, leading to such scenarios as civil war, collapse, or even an explosion that could trigger a war, remains an equally ominous threat and one for which the South Korean and U.S. militaries needed to plan. As one considers the complicated North Korean problem, in my view it is also important to review a key component in North Korean strategy—that is, its violent provocations in the Northern Limit Line area near the west coast of the Korean Peninsula.

# 3

# THE SINKING OF THE CHEONAN AND THE
# SHELLING OF YEONPYEONG ISLAND

## A Case Study of North Korea's Asymmetric
## Northern Limit Line Strategy

O n March 26, 2010, a North Korean mini sub snuck across the
Northern Limit Line (NLL), the de facto sea border on the west
coast that separates the two Koreas, and launched what an investigation has
now determined was a CHT-02D, indigenously produced, wake-homing
torpedo at the ROK Navy ship *Cheonan*. The torpedo produced a bubble
effect, causing an explosion that split the ship in half. Forty-six naval personnel (out of a crew of 104) perished in the attack.[1] At the time of the
attack, the *Cheonan* was sailing in waters south of the NLL that even North
Korea recognizes as being within South Korean sovereignty (see figure 6).

FIGURE 6: LOCATION OF *CHEONAN* SINKING

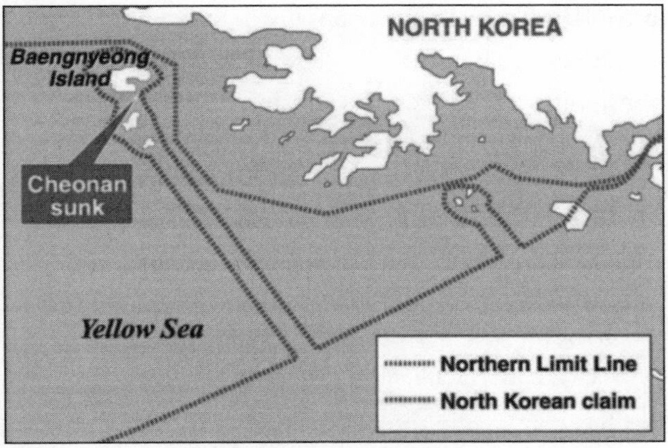

Sources: Republic of Korea Ministry of National Defense, and *Stars and Stripes*.

57

This chapter will examine the implications behind the North Korean sinking of the South Korean naval ship *Cheonan* and the artillery attack that also took place within the confines of the NLL several months later. In order to do so, I will first analyze events that occurred prior to the March 26 incident. I will also explore the likely planning process and the leadership and organizational changes that happened before the incident and probably affected the way it was conducted. I will then examine (in chronological order as much as possible) the events that ensued immediately following the sinking of the South Korean corvette. Of course, I will also consider dissenting views on the evidence regarding the sinking of the *Cheonan* (though the evidence is overwhelming), keeping an eye on the responses of other responsible analysts as their views arose in the press and at some levels in academia. Then I will discuss the actions of South Korea and its allies as the investigation's final results came to light and all of the information's implications for the future. Finally, I will address the North Korean artillery attack on Yeonpyeong Island on November 23, 2010, and the actions that the South Koreans (and, to a lesser extent, their American allies) took as a result of the attack.

Before I begin my analysis, I must point out that the sinking of the *Cheonan* was a provocation. While this detail might seem minor, it is relevant. As I have written in previous publications, most of North Korea's provocations "have had four things in common: 1) they are intentionally initiated at moments when they have the likelihood of garnering the greatest attention on the regional and perhaps even the world stage; 2) they initially appear to be incidents that are relatively small, easily contained, and quickly "resolved;" 3) they involve continuously changing tactics and techniques; and 4) North Korea denies responsibility for the event."[2] Certainly these factors were present for the sinking of the *Cheonan*. But before going into exact details of the incident (and of the artillery attack on November 23, 2010), I believe it is important to first examine the context of the events leading up to March 26, 2010.

## Events Leading to the *Cheonan* Incident: Rhetoric and Brinkmanship

North Korea has truly made the NLL a high-priority issue—and one that often involves violent acts of provocation—since 1999, when a short naval battle resulted in the sinking of a North Korean ship.[3] In 2002, North Korea was able to "exact revenge," when in an act of cunning and well-planned violence, one of its ships sank a South Korean patrol craft that was sailing south of the NLL and engaged in non-provocative behavior.[4] The incident in 2002 raised alarm in South Korea and caused its allies, such as the United States, to speak out against the action, but it did not end North Korea's provocative acts in the NLL. (See figure 7 for a map of the North Korean maneuvers during the 2002 provocation.)

Other tensions in and around the NLL arose after the 2002 incident and leading up to the sinking of the *Cheonan*, but the latest spate of North Korea's brinkmanship and building tension in the NLL began in January 2009. At that time a member of the North Korean military was displayed on Pyongyang's state-run television "demanding" that South Korea stop its "hostile posture" in the NLL. The broadcast further relayed that the North would "preserve" the sea border. Of course, the natural implication was that North Korea would use military force to do so. Seoul took the remarks—intended for both South and North Korean ears—seriously and placed its military on full alert for the first time since North Korea conducted a nuclear test in 2006.[5] The North Koreans also threatened an "all out confrontational posture" in the NLL, blaming the South Koreans for what Pyongyang called violations of the de facto sea border that separates the two nations.[6] In reaction to what Beijing likely perceived as increased tensions along the

**FIGURE 7: NORTH KOREAN NLL PROVOCATION, 2002**

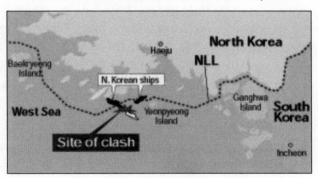

*Source:* Map courtesy of the Republic of Korea, Ministry of National Defense, 2002, http://www.mnd.go.kr/.

west coast of the Korean Peninsula, China ordered all of its fishing boats out of the area, warning that possible violence could occur there.[7]

North Korea made key leadership moves that enhanced its ability to conduct provocations in the NLL and that placed Kim Jong-il's most trusted generals at the center of the planning process for any moves that the leadership might make. Only weeks after the rhetoric began in January 2009, Gen. Kim Kyok-sik, formerly chief of the General Staff, was named the new commander of IV Corps of the North Korean People's Army. The IV Corps borders the NLL. Kim Kyok-sik was well known as one of Kim Jong-il's most trusted generals.[8] Thus, he likely was put in his new position because Kim Jong-il trusted him and because he could help plan for activities in the NLL area.[9] On paper, it would appear that a move from Chief of the General Staff to corps commander is a demotion—when in fact, it was likely a move made because of the importance of the mission at hand (conducting provocations in the NLL).

Soon after the shift involving Kim Kyok-sik was made, another important general's position was shuffled. Gen. O Kuk-ryol, the head of the Operations Department (which at the time was under the authority of the Korean Workers' Party), was transferred to a senior position on the National Defense Commission, the chief command and control organ of the DPRK's armed forces.[10] Next, the Operations Department (which has often conducted many of North Korea's clandestine operations) was removed from under the umbrella of the Korean Workers' Party and placed under the control of the Reconnaissance Bureau, the DPRK's military organization that controls everything from Special Operations Forces and intelligence to clandestine infiltrations into South Korea. The Reconnaissance Bureau also comes under the NDC's control.[11] Based on the evidence, clearly O Kuk-ryol was also likely involved (at all levels) in the planning of the NLL provocations and brinkmanship, as it appears the mini sub that attacked the *Cheonan* was probably a Reconnaissance Bureau vessel and was not subordinate to the North Korean People's Navy. Thus, in early 2009, the appointments of key people who would plan the provocations in the NLL coincided with an uptick in rhetoric regarding the disputed border area. Key shifts in these leadership positions of essential personnel in the party and the military helped enable operations that took several months to build up for, as everyone would see from events that occurred in the late fall and winter of 2009 and in 2010.

Once the chief players were in place, two major events happened prior to the attack on the *Cheonan*. The first was a naval skirmish on November 10, 2009, when a North Korean patrol boat violated the NLL near Daecheong Island, one of the five islands in the NLL area that the ROK Navy craft patrolled and ROK Marines protected ashore. The North Korean ship fired at a South Korean craft, which returned fire immediately. The South Korean ship reportedly pumped more than forty-nine hundred rounds into the North Korean ship in less than two minutes, leaving it badly damaged and limping home. According to reports that leaked out of North Korea and were discussed in the South Korean press, Kim Jong-il vowed to military officers that he would seek revenge for the small defeat.[12] The altercation received little attention in the South Korean press or in the United States at the time.

The second event that occurred prior to the attack on the *Cheonan* was a large-scale artillery live-fire exercise that North Korea conducted off its west coast at the end of January 2010. Its army engaged in what appeared to be "time on target" drills. In other words, different types of artillery were used and fired at different times and from different ranges, with the goal being simultaneous volleys of rounds landing on a single target. The drills took place almost right next to the NLL. The North Korean artillery involved reportedly consisted of coastal artillery pieces, multiple rocket launchers, and self-propelled howitzers. Over a period of three days, North Korea pounded the waters near the NLL, with some shells said to have fallen less than two kilometers from the de facto sea border. The army fired close to four hundred live rounds in an event that was obviously meant to intimidate Pyongyang's neighbor to the south. Unlike the short sea skirmish that occurred the previous November, this act of provocation received a great deal of attention in South Korea.[13] This drill, however, would prove to be a practice run for a later provocation.

The context and focus of the events that transpired before the *Cheonan*'s sinking on March 26, 2010, are important. In my view, they show a deliberate, gradual process that began with North Korea's rhetoric and gradually built up with escalating types of brinkmanship or provocations meant to intimidate and disturb its neighbor to the south. These episodes were enhanced by a leadership change that meant generals who had the absolute trust and confidence of Kim Jong-il oversaw the planning and operations process. But these events paled in comparison to the destruction that the sinking of the *Cheonan* caused.

## The Sinking of the *Cheonan*: How Did It Occur?

The sinking of the *Cheonan* occurred before 9:45 p.m. on the night of March 26, 2010. The *Cheonan*, a 1,200-ton corvette equipped with missiles and torpedoes that had been in service in the South Korean Navy since 1989, was on a routine mission south of the NLL at the time.[14] Reportedly, an unusual North Korean scout plane formation flew near the area immediately after the sinking of the ship.[15] Initial statements from the ship's captain indicated that it split in half five minutes after an explosion occurred.[16] At a briefing session with the South Korean press, Cdr. Choi Won-il stated, "Suddenly, I heard a loud 'bang' sound from the rear of the vessel, and it started to list toward the right side. Then all power and communication means were lost." One of the other officers, Lt. Park Yeon-su, added, "I don't think the ship was wrecked on a rock, and neither by an explosion inside. That's not possible. I'm almost sure. So there's a possibility that the ship was attacked. But I don't have proof at the moment."[17]

By March 30, 2010, the ROK Navy had tentatively concluded that the sinking of the *Cheonan* was not from an internal explosion.[18] Survivors from the sinking testified that the ship broke in two after the ship shot up into the air and that it was broken in half from an external explosion.[19] Soon thereafter, it was revealed that the corvette *Sokcho* fired more than 130 shots at what crewmembers thought was a North Korean target in the area. The *Sokcho* rushed to the scene after the *Cheonan* explosion.

By March 31, 2010, press sources had disclosed reports that before the ship sank a North Korean submarine had left its base on the west coast, the most likely place from which one of the DPRK's underwater vessels would deploy.[20] But according to reports at the time, the ROK Navy did not initially detect any submarines near the *Cheonan* on the night of the sinking.[21] By early April it began to appear—with some clarity—that North Korea may have been responsible for the ship's sinking. A senior military officer was quoted as saying that there was a 60 to 70 percent chance that a torpedo sank the Cheonan.[22] South Korea's defense minister, meanwhile, cautioned that salvage operations must first occur, and until then all possibilities must be considered.[23] He also stated, however, that the seismic wave detected at the time of the explosion was consistent with what a North Korean torpedo would cause.[24] In a move designed to show deliberate investigation techniques and transparency, during the first week of April, South Korea announced that it intended to request help from American experts in determining what caused the sinking of the Cheonan.[25]

Initial efforts to salvage the remains of the ship—and the valuable evidence that they would reveal—began the first week of April. On April 3, the South Korean Coast Guard recovered the bodies of two fishermen from the Kumyang 98, a small vessel with a nine-man crew that the ROK government had employed to help search for clues in the West Sea. The small ship had collided with a Cambodian-registered freighter in the area that South Korean authorities had briefly detained.[26] By April 4, the South Korean Navy had preparations for salvage operations in full swing, but the weather hampered deployment of naval craft.[27] By April 5, navy divers' observations of the hull revealed that the Cheonan was probably hit from below.[28]

Even before the ship's remains were lifted out of the water, evidence continued to mount that North Korea had in fact launched an attack on the Cheonan, and experts once again voiced their belief that the likeliest weapon that sank it was probably a torpedo.[29] In a statement that showed any premeditated attack had to have been ordered from the top, National Intelligence Service director Won Sei-hoon testified to National Assembly members that "a project of this scale could not be carried out by a single unit commander without the approval of National Defense Commission Chairman Kim Jong-il."[30] To strengthen the assessment that the North Korean military and leadership carried out and sanctioned this operation, Radio Free Asia reported that North Korea's armed forces went on alert after the sinking of the Cheonan.[31] On April 7, South Korean prime minister Chung Un-chan released to the press information that Seoul planned to invite naval experts from several nations to help conduct the investigation into the Cheonan's sinking.[32]

During the second week of April 2010, the South Korean government announced that it had won agreement from four nations—the United States, the United Kingdom, Australia, and Sweden—to take part in the investigation.[33] All four nations sent experts who were involved in all aspects of the investigation.[34] By April 12, after several days of unsuccessful salvage operations, military divers were well on their way to linking chains and hoisting up the hull of the *Cheonan* above the water's surface for examination.[35] By April 13, after part of the ship had been lifted out of the water and moved to a better location, analysis revealed that it had been ripped apart, thus removing the possibility of a wreck from impact with a rock or from metal fatigue.[36] In addition, because the weapons on the ship remained intact, an internal blast causing the wreck was rendered nearly impossible.[37] Yoon Duk-yong, one of the leaders of the South Korean investigation team, was quoted as saying, "The results of the investigation into the waters where the vessel submerged and the probe into the inside of the ship show a low possibility of a collision with a reef or metal fatigue of the ship." He continued, "The hull and steel plates of the bottom of the stern were bent inward due to pressure from the left, and the right side of the stern was damaged and bent outward."[38]

By April 20, recovery crews were able to move the wreckage of the sunken ship to land, where they planned to take three-dimensional pictures of it and conduct computer simulations. Meanwhile, South Korean and U.S. divers continued to search the debris field between the bow and stern in the tumultuous waters of the West Sea.[39] U.S. and South Korean intelligence agencies also reportedly exchanged intelligence regarding the movement of North Korean submarines in the area on the day the *Cheonan* was sunk.[40] That same day, President Lee Myung-bak announced that the team of foreign experts would jointly sign the official report on the assessments regarding the sinking.[41] As if on cue, the North Koreans publicly announced that they had nothing to do with the sinking of the *Cheonan*, called the South Koreans "warmongers" and accused Seoul of trying to "build an international consensus" against them.[42]

Meanwhile, as details from the evidence recovered in the investigation began to be revealed, it became obvious that the attack had come from a torpedo launched by a North Korean submarine, specifically a Reconnaissance

Bureau submarine and not a submarine subordinate to the navy. On April 9, 2010, an unidentified government official alleged to the press that not only was a North Korean torpedo the cause of the *Cheonan*'s sinking, but also the torpedo had been launched by an SOF craft subordinate to the Reconnaissance Bureau.[43] Two days earlier, Kim Hak-song, the chairman of the National Assembly's Defense Committee, claimed to the press that North Korean mini submarines had disappeared from military surveillance between March 23 and 27.[44] Ha Tae-keung, who operates Open Radio for North Korea, cited sources in North Korea (in a report that came out in May 2010) that two submarines had conducted a planned intrusion into South Korean waters. A larger sub supported a smaller mini sub, which he said was carrying two torpedoes.[45] (A map of the bases that support submarines on North Korea's west coast is shown in figure 8.)

During May 2010, the South Korean Defense Ministry confirmed that the Reconnaissance Bureau was in fact the most likely suspect in the sinking of the *Cheonan*. Government sources also reported to the press that the likeliest culprit in the torpedo launch and the sinking of the *Cheonan* was a

FIGURE 8: NORTH KOREA'S SUBMARINE CAPABILITY

*Source: Korea Times.*

130-ton Yeoneo class submarine.[46] Reportedly, intelligence agencies also acknowledged during May that North Korea had purchased underwater radio communications equipment from China and Russia.[47] Former North Korean submarine crew member Lee Kwang-soo was the lone member of a Sango class submarine crew who was captured alive in 1996. In a rare interview, he had described some of the capabilities of the Yeoneo class submarine: "I received helmsman training for submarines from Romeo-class down to midget subs; the Yeoneo-class sub is a modified version of the Yugo-class." He further stated, "Yugo-class submarines have a torpedo tube, but the Yeoneo-class does not. Yeoneo-class subs have a medium-sized torpedo fitted to both sides and are launched by applying an electrical charge."[48] North Korea has also proliferated the Yeoneo class submarine to Iran, a country that probably finds the submarine quite useful in its shallow coastal waters, which are similar to those off the west coast of the Korean Peninsula.[49] Despite North Korean denials that the Yeoneo class submarine even exists, the *Daily NK* was able to use Google Earth satellite imagery to show pictures of the twenty-nine-meter-long naval craft in port at a naval base on North Korea's west coast.[50]

Returning to the chronological examination of how events unfolded after the *Cheonan* sinking, the investigation team reported in mid-April that it had tentatively concluded that an external explosion caused by a water shock wave, known as the bubble jet effect, had sunk the ship.[51] Officials also confirmed that North Korea had increased training designed to launch a provocation during 2010.[52] Later in the month, a North Korean party cadre leaked (probably via cell phone) to sources in South Korea that the sinking of the *Cheonan* was proudly being discussed in party lectures. Quoting one such lecture, the North Korean said that the secretary of a party cell announced, "Since our heroic Chosun People's Army took revenge on the enemy, all South Chosun has been in fear of our defensive military ability."[53] During the same time frame, Kim Jong-il publicly visited Unit 586, a unit designator widely believed to refer to the Reconnaissance Bureau. (Perhaps he wanted to congratulate the personnel on their successful infiltration and attack on an ROK naval craft.)[54] Also near the end of the month, South Korea's defense minister publicly stated that a torpedo exploding under the hull of the *Cheonan* likely caused the ship to sink.[55] The team of investigators also confirmed at this time that it was likely a "non-contact explosion" from a torpedo had caused the sinking.[56] And in perhaps one of the month's more important developments, the Defense Ministry's investigative team ruled out any possibility that an "old South Korean mine" had caused the sinking of the *Cheonan*, eliminating any speculation that an old mine placed near the de facto sea border may have caused the tragedy.[57] During the same time frame, Seoul announced that it would brief both Chinese and Russian officials on the results of the investigation.[58]

At the end of April 2010, Bae Myung-jin of Soongsil University led a team of scientists in South Korea and disclosed that they had reached a conclusion regarding the type of torpedo that hit and sank the *Cheonan*. Bae told the press, "As a result, we presume that the torpedo ran at the *Cheonan* at the speed of 65.7 km/h and exploded underwater 2.3 m from the ship with power equivalent to 206 kg of TNT."[59] That same day government officials also said that the wrecked hull itself would provide much of the evidence on what type of external explosion sank the *Cheonan*.[60] In a meeting with Chinese leader Hu Jintao, President Lee informed him that the South Korean government would apprise China of the results of their efforts and asked for Beijing's interest and cooperation.[61] Though South Korean officials had still stopped short of blaming North Korea for sinking the ROK naval ship, by May 4, reportedly several officials had privately acknowledged that there was little doubt that North Korea was responsible for the tragic event.[62] In a speech that President Lee gave to the top commanders of the ROK armed forces, he stated, "What is clear as of now is the fact that the sinking of the *Cheonan* was not simply an accident. As soon as I received the first report, I knew by intuition that it would escalate into a grave international issue involving inter-Korean relations."[63] Defense Minister Kim Tae-young made a public statement that South Korea would strive to improve its intelligence and antisubmarine capabilities, thus imparting another clue about how Seoul's officials were leaning as the investigation progressed.[64]

By mid-May reports indicated that the joint investigating team had found in the wreckage of the South Korean ship traces of explosive that had been used in the former Soviet bloc, providing further proof that the likely torpedo that caused the explosion came from North Korea.[65] And as the evidence continued to mount, a group of American senators led by Joe

Lieberman called for the international community to abide by UN sanctions imposed on North Korea in the wake of the *Cheonan* sinking.[66] Meanwhile, Choi Moon-soon of South Korea's National Assembly cited remarks by Chinese foreign official Zhang Xinsen that North Korea had met with Chinese officials and denied any involvement in the deadly sinking of the *Cheonan*.[67]

By May 18, 2010, the evidence regarding the type of weapon used to sink the South Korean ship was becoming even clearer. Investigators disclosed publicly that they had discovered pieces of a torpedo's propeller in the wreckage of the *Cheonan*.[68] Investigators also revealed that traces of explosive residue recovered from the wreckage were identical to that contained in a North Korean torpedo.[69] Investigators soon thereafter announced that the investigation's initial results would be completely divulged to thirty major nations and the international press.[70] Seoul invited envoys from dozens of countries to attend the hours-long briefing.[71] In a rather stunning disclosure, investigators also explained that North Korean fonts were found on fragments of the torpedo. The torpedo was said to be powered by two propellers rotating in opposite directions.[72]

## Initial Investigations Results and the Aftermath: Sanctions and Denials

The initial results from the Joint Civilian-Military Investigative Group (JIG) were both compelling and well documented in a large—and quite long (several hours)—briefing that was broadcasted live on South Korean television. The JIG comprised twenty-five experts from South Korea and twenty-four foreign experts who constituted four support teams from the United States, the United Kingdom, Australia, and Sweden. The report stated, "The JIG assesses that a strong underwater explosion generated by the detonation of a homing torpedo below and to the left of the gas turbine room caused Republic of Korea Ship (ROKS) *Cheonan* to split apart and sink." The investigators addressed the torpedo as follows;

> The evidence matched in size and shape with the specifications on the drawing presented in introductory materials provided to foreign

countries by North Korea for export purposes. The marking in Hangul, which reads "1 (or No. 1 in English)", found inside the end of the propulsion section, is consistent with the marking of a previously obtained North Korean torpedo. The above evidence allowed the JIG to confirm that the recovered parts were made in North Korea.

The report also addressed the type of submarine used in the attack: "The North Korean military is in possession of a fleet of about 70 submarines, comprised of approximately 20 Romeo-class submarines (1,800 tons), 40 Sango-class submarines (300 tons) and 10 midget submarines including the Yeoneo-class (130 tons)." It continued, "Given the aforementioned findings combined with the operational environment in the vicinity of the site of the incident, we assess that a small submarine is an underwater weapon system that operates in these operational environment conditions. We confirmed that a few small submarines and a mother ship supporting them left a North Korean naval base in the West Sea 2-3 days prior to the attack and returned to port 2-3 days after the attack." The final assessment was also unambiguous: "Based on all such relevant facts and classified analysis, we have reached the clear conclusion that ROKS Cheonan was sunk as the result of an external underwater explosion caused by a torpedo made in North Korea. The evidence points overwhelmingly to the conclusion that the torpedo was fired by a North Korean submarine. There is no other plausible explanation."[73]

The results of the investigation as revealed in the televised report were very interesting and left no doubt that a North Korean submarine was responsible for the sinking of the ROK ship Cheonan. (For a map of where the submarines and perhaps the "mother ship" supporting them deployed from and the route that they likely took to the Cheonan, see the map in figure 9.) A question-and-answer session following the briefing was also important. Lt. Gen. Kang Won-dong stated that the team was able to conclude that a Yeoneo class submarine had conducted the attack and that the craft infiltrated South Korean waters via the fringes of international waters—which helped it to avoid detection in the murky waters off the west coast of the Korean Peninsula. The JIG team also noted that one Sango class submarine and one Yeoneo class submarine had departed port before the attack.[74] Immediately following the formal open briefing, the United States condemned the North Korean attack and supported the results of the probe, with White House press secretary Robert Gibbs calling the North Korean attack unacceptable.[75] Predictably, the North Korean government immediately denied any involvement in the attack and called the investigation a fabrication.[76]

As the results of the JIG investigation became public, the U.S. House of Representatives took action. Republican congresswoman Ileana Ros-Lehtinen of Florida presented a bill titled "North Korea Sanctions and Diplomatic Non-recognition Act of 2010."[77] Also immediately following the public briefing of the JIG investigation's results, on May 21, President Lee Myung-bak called an emergency meeting of the ROK National Security Council to address what punitive measures Seoul would take against its neighbor to the north for the violent, unprovoked act on March 26.[78] Seoul announced that action would be sought with the UN Security Council.[79] Meanwhile, in a Korea Research Center poll taken two days after the JIG briefing, 72 percent of respondents agreed that the JIG had presented a convincing case that North Korea had caused the *Cheonan*'s sinking.[80] UN Command in Seoul announced that it planned to investigate whether the torpedo attack was a violation of the armistice from the Korean Conflict (a question easily answered in my view).[81]

FIGURE 9: ESTIMATED NORTH KOREAN SUBMARINE INFILTRATION ROUTE

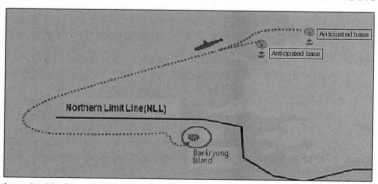

*Source:* Republic of Korea, Ministry of National Defense.

In a speech on May 24, 2010, President Lee addressed many of the punitive actions that South Korea planned to take against the North. He outlined a key move: "From this moment, no North Korean ship will be allowed to make passage through any of the shipping lanes in the waters under our control, which has been allowed by the Inter-Korean Agreement on Maritime Transportation. The sea routes meant for inter-Korean exchanges and cooperation must never again be used for armed provocations." He further noted,

> Trade and exchanges between the Republic of Korea and North Korea will also be suspended. We still remember the killing of an innocent South Korean tourist by a North Korean armed guard at the Mt. Kumgang resort. More recently, North Korea unilaterally confiscated South Korean assets at this same resort. Worse yet, the North sank the Cheonan taking the precious lives of our young sailors. Under these circumstances, any inter-Korean trade or other cooperative activity is meaningless.
>
> However, we will continue to provide assistance for infants and children. Matters pertaining to the Kaesong Industrial Complex will be duly considered, taking its unique characteristics into consideration.

Finally, he referred to the United Nations when he said, "In close consultations with the nations concerned, the Government will refer this matter to the UN Security Council, so that the international community can join us in holding the North accountable. Many countries around the world have expressed their full support for our position."[82]

On May 24, 2010, South Korea announced a ban on travel for all of its citizens going into North Korea except for the minimal number of individuals required for the operations at the Kaesong Industrial Complex.[83] The South Korean government resumed anti-Pyongyang radio broadcasts, which had been suspended for the past six years.[84] The North Koreans, never ones to sit idle, announced that all relations with South Korea would be severed and all inter-Korean dialogue frozen during the rest of Lee Myung-bak's term as president.[85] South Korean government–imposed sanctions on North Korea in the aftermath of the Cheonan sinking (and the resulting investigation) were reportedly expected to cause a loss of around 10 percent of the North's legal income.[86] The South Korean government also announced the resumption of loudspeaker broadcasts into North Korea along the DMZ.[87] In a move that showed South Korea was serious, the first North Korean merchant vessel attempting to travel a route through the NLL since the punitive measures were announced was forced to retreat and take a detour route along the west coast of the Korean Peninsula.[88]

In late May, the U.S. Congress passed a resolution 411 to 3 that condemned "North Korea in the strongest terms for sinking the ROK Ship *Cheonan*; calls for an apology by North Korea for its hostile acts and a commitment by North Korea never to violate the Korean War Armistice Agreement again."[89] In a poll taken the last week of May 2010, six out of ten (60.4 percent) South Koreans stated that they approved of the sanctions their government had imposed on Pyongyang.[90] Predictably, at the end of May 2010, the North Korean National Defense Commission again publicly disputed the results of the JIG investigation, denying that the torpedo was North Korean (even though the torpedo was marked in Hangul) and that it even had a 130-ton Yeoneo class submarine in its inventory. In an announcement to the ROK press, the Ministry of National Defense countered the highly unusual and easily disputable North Korean claims.[91] As stated earlier, satellite imagery on Google Earth had already revealed North Korea's Yeoneo class submarines sitting in port.

## The *Cheonan* Sinking Is Referred to the UNSC: Results and Disappointments

On June 4, 2010, President Lee announced that Seoul would formally refer the case of the *Cheonan* sinking to the UN Security Council.[92] South Korea's ambassador to the UN, Park In-kook, presented a letter to Mexican diplomat Claude Heller, the rotating head of the UNSC, asking for appropriate action to be taken. The United States supported South Korea's move. Of course, at the time, the wild card was how much China and Russia would go along with any UNSC punitive action (and blame) directed at North

Korea. In a press briefing, U.S. State Department spokesman Philip Crowley said, in part, "I don't think anyone's necessarily got a specific idea of exactly what the response should be." He further commented, "I don't think that South Korea called, necessarily, for a specific response. We'll consider this within the Security Council, and I think, as South Korea's indicated, it wants the Security Council to act appropriately, given the severity of the North Korean sinking of the *Cheonan*."[93] On June 7, in what appeared to be a good sign, the UNSC adopted a resolution that extended for another year existing sanctions on North Korea. These sanctions had originally been introduced after North Korea conducted nuclear and ballistic missile tests in 2009.[94]

On June 10, Professor Yoon Duk-yong and Lt. Gen. Park Jung-yi led a ten-member South Korean team that traveled to New York and presented their findings from the JIG investigation to the UNSC.[95] According to South Korean government officials, the UNSC raised no objections to the investigation results that the South Korean experts and experts from five other countries submitted in mid-June.[96] In July, the fifteen-member UNSC issued a formal statement, but reportedly on China's insistence it had been diluted from what South Korea and the United States (among others) had requested.[97]

In fact, the UNSC statement fell short of Seoul's and Washington's hopes, but no one was surprised, given Beijing's close relationship to Pyongyang.[98] Former U.S. State Department official Mark Fitzpatrick was quoted as saying, "The compromise came out entirely because China would not accept a condemnation, . . . [and] it is likely to defuse tensions for the time being."[99] The formal statement from the UNSC was obvious in its assessment that the ship's sinking came from an attack while stopping short of formally blaming North Korea for the attack. But the UNSC did express alarm based on the JIG findings: "In view of the findings of the Joint Civilian-Military Investigation Group led by the Republic of Korea with the participation of five nations, which concluded that the Democratic People's Republic of Korea was responsible for sinking the *Cheonan*, the Security Council expresses its deep concern." The UNSC also denounced the attack on the *Cheonan*, stating, "Therefore, the Security Council condemns the attack which led to the sinking of the *Cheonan*."[100]

## Events Surrounding the UNSC Statement and the Aftermath: Action and Defiance

As the many events following the initial results of the JIG investigation (and the UNSC procedures) ensued, the Russians sent an investigation team to South Korea.[101] Seoul had invited both China and Russia to send investigation teams to evaluate (in detail) the evidence from the *Cheonan* sinking, but the Chinese declined.[102] By June 11, North Korean ships had been commanded to leave South Korean waters on more than twenty occasions since President Lee had issued his official orders regarding the passage of North Korean ships on May 24.[103] It was also revealed that North Korea actually had a marketing catalog for the type of torpedo that hit and sank the *Cheonan*. The torpedo even came with a quality assurance guarantee in the catalog.[104] Meanwhile, despite the incidents and the overwhelming evidence that links North Korea to proliferation and support for terrorist groups, the Obama administration decided not to reinstate North Korea on the State Department's list of state sponsors of terrorism.[105]

While the events that occurred during June and July were both compelling and relevant to geopolitics in East Asia, in mid-July more evidence became available regarding North Korea's actions on March 26, 2010. In late June (and reported in mid-July), a Chinese businessman visiting Pyongyang photographed a poster (see figure 10) showing a helmeted North Korean sailor smashing in two a ship that appears to be a South Korean corvette like the *Cheonan*. The businessman, speaking on terms of anonymity, told Radio Free Asia, "It's hard to understand how high-ranking officials can adamantly deny North Korea's responsibility for the sinking of the *Cheonan* while propaganda posters showing a ship being broken in half by a fist are in circulation."[106] Whether the ship shown in the poster is the same class as the *Cheonan* or not, and whether it is an older picture that was simply being recirculated in July, the timing and the message it carried—the North Korean sailor smashing the ROK Navy ship in half—are important.

At the end of July, the United States announced that it would put a new package of sanctions into effect against North Korea that would include targeting weapons proliferation and other criminal activities that bring profits into the North Korean elite's coffers. Such illicit activities include

but are not limited to counterfeiting U.S. hundred-dollar bills, selling counterfeit cigarettes, and trafficking illegal drugs such as heroin and metham-
phetamines.[107] The U.S. State Department also reaffirmed its assertion that
North Korea was responsible for the torpedo attack on the *Cheonan*, despite
the lukewarm support the UNSC statement received from the Russians
and particularly from the Chinese.[108] Coincidentally, at the beginning of
August, the Russian government announced that it would not make public
the results of its investigation into the sinking of the South Korean ship.[109]
By early September, a poll showed that only three in ten South Koreans
completely trusted the JIG's finding.[110] But in the week of September 13, the
final results of the JIG investigation were released to the public. The overwhelming results in the evidence chain that the JIG used point to North

FIGURE 10: NORTH KOREAN POSTER IN PYONGYANG
"READY TO CRUSH ANY ATTACK WITH A SINGLE BLOW!"

*Source: Radio Free Asia.*

Korea as the attacker on March 26. The JIG's final 313-page document clearly shows exact details of how the ship was sunk, of the intelligence surrounding the deployment of the DPRK submarines, of diagrams and simulations of the torpedo used to sink the *Cheonan*, and of numerous other pieces of evidence.[111]

As a result of the JIG investigation, the ROK Navy announced that it would focus more on littoral warfare with an understanding that the North Korean maritime threat had not declined.[112] In addition, in a rather revealing breaking news story, Russia's state-run television network reported that the *Cheonan* was in fact sunk by a North Korean torpedo, though the Russian government still declined (and continues to do so, as of this writing) to publicly release the results of its investigation.[113] In October Shin Hak-yong, a member of South Korea's National Assembly, revealed to the press that the South Korean Navy had knowledge of the movement of North Korean submarines on the day of the attack, but the ROK military did not raise the alert level. If the statement is true, it makes a compelling charge about the readiness of Seoul's naval forces at the time. The Defense Security Command, meanwhile, announced that it would investigate Mr. Shin for leaking military secrets.[114]

Finally, in October 2010, a new poll was released. Conducted by the Asian Institute for Policy Studies, it showed that 68.7 percent of South Koreans believed the North Koreans were responsible for torpedoing the *Cheonan*. Only 8.5 percent said they disagreed, while 22.8 percent had no opinion.[115] By March 2011, even more South Koreans placed the blame squarely on the North Koreans. According to a Hankook Research poll commissioned by the Ministry of Culture, Sports, and Tourism, 80 percent of South Koreans surveyed believed the North Koreans sank the *Cheonan*.[116] The polls may reflect the findings of the final JIG investigation results and the many compelling pieces of evidence pointing to North Korea as the culprit. Of course, North Korea officially continued to deny the accusations regarding the sinking at all seven rounds of talks with military officers from UN Command that began in July and continued through October 2010 at Panmunjom.[117]

Despite the overwhelming evidence, even with several evidence chains available, a few naysayers disputed the JIG investigation. Professors Seunghun Lee of the University of Virginia and Professor J. J. Suh of the Johns Hopkins University School of Advanced International Studies claimed that the evidence was not compelling enough. For example, to quote Professor Lee, "To begin, the 'No. 1' could logically have been written by South Koreans as well, and thus could not be adopted as evidence in the courtroom of a democratic society."[118] In referring to the North Korean markings on a North Korean–manufactured weapon, Lee's assertion assumes that an international team consisting of South Korea, the United States, the United Kingdom, Australia, and Sweden would conspire to do such a thing. (Ironically, almost the exact same type of markings showed up on the remains of an artillery shell that the North Koreans fired on November 23, 2010, and was recovered on Yeonpyeong Island.[119])

Lee and Suh published a paper on July 15, 2010, and their many assertions simply made little sense from an evidentiary stance when compared to the assessments of the JIG investigation. For example, among many other points that they make, the two write, "First, the JIG failed to produce conclusive, or at least convincing beyond reasonable doubt, evidence of an outside explosion."[120] Again, their statement simply is incorrect. Both the initial and the final JIG reports clearly show how the bubble jet effect occurred from the North Korean torpedo. At a press conference that the two professors held in Japan, Lee reportedly said, "Some of the data produced by the investigative team may have even been fabricated to justify its claim."[121] Again, his accusation is completely unsupportable and assumes highly qualified teams from five democratic nation-states intentionally conspired to build false evidence. To quote Rear Adm. Thomas Eccles, USN, who led the American team that helped conduct the investigation, those who do not agree with the investigation's results, which showed the North Koreans were responsible for the attack, are "those who are unfamiliar with the mechanics of torpedoes."[122]

Lee and Suh's assertions gained some traction in the press but little traction with real experts or policy people. Their contentions are both lacking in credibility and dangerous to the national security of South Korea. While one would hope that their assertions were not politically and ideologically motivated, they both have been outspoken critics of President Lee Myung-bak and all of his policies. As conservative scholar Bruce Klingner has stated, "Despite overwhelming evidence, there are those determined to remain unconvinced because it is inconvenient for them to admit North Korean culpability."[123]

During March 2012, a North Korean defector who had arrived in South Korea in May 2011 gave quite compelling testimony. The defector, known as Choi Young-pil, testified that the attack on the *Cheonan* was carried out as revenge for the Battle of Daecheong in November 2009, when South Korean ships nearly destroyed a North Korean navy craft. He also explained, "In April 2010, the month after the Cheonan incident occurred, the Organizing Secretary for the Musan County branch of the Party commented proudly in one particular event, 'The hero who destroyed the South Chosun naval vessel received a vacation in honor of his work, so he has [*sic*] back to his house in Musan.'"[124] While this defector's testimony became public nearly two years after the JIG investigation, it further supports the multinational team's findings. Thus, in my view, those who claim the JIG investigation did not prove North Korea planned a deliberate attack and sank the *Cheonan* cite weak evidence that completely lacks credibility. Further, making such assertions is potentially dangerous to the security of the U.S.-ROK alliance because it attempts to undermine what is probably the most transparent, deliberate, and internationally cooperative maritime investigation ever conducted in East Asia.

## U.S.-ROK Military Responses to the Sinking of the *Cheonan*

Soon after it became apparent that North Korea was responsible for the sinking of the *Cheonan*, the South Korean government began making important moves to counter both possible future North Korean provocations in the NLL and proliferation of WMD that provides cash for the North Korean elite and military forces. Washington also played a major role in this renewed emphasis on readiness for countering provocations, not only as a vocal supporter of these moves, but also as a participant in what would prove to be important military exercises. In June 2010, South Korea announced that for the first time, it would be the host nation for a Proliferation Security Initiative (PSI) exercise simulating interdiction of ships carrying illegal weapons.[125] Officials in Seoul stated that South Korea was looking to become one of the twenty nations (out of ninety-five participating countries) that hold membership in PSI's Operational Experts Group.[126] In June the U.S.

and South Korean Navies also formally agreed to work closer together in joint antisubmarine exercises. Admirals from the two navies also assented to bolster sharing of intelligence (some of it likely very sensitive) on North Korean submarines.[127]

Several examples of stepped-up readiness and military drills occurred that were meant to send a strong message to North Korea following the sinking of the *Cheonan*. During the last half of June, South Korea and the United States planned eventually to stage joint and combined naval drills off the west coast of the Korean Peninsula in what would be a show of force for North Korea.[128] In July, South Korean and U.S. naval forces, as well as smaller units from other forces, conducted a joint and combined exercise off the east coast of the Korean Peninsula that involved about twenty ships and two hundred aircraft and included antisubmarine simulations.[129] The exercise included the aircraft carrier USS *George Washington* in what was also seen as a major show of force; however, some condemned the exercise for not being staged off the west coast, where the provocation initiated by North Korea occurred. Of course, North Korea predictably also publicly criticized the exercise.

In an even stronger demonstration of its capabilities in August, South Korea conducted a large antisubmarine exercise near the west coast of the Korean Peninsula that involved naval, air, and ground forces. All four services participated in live-fire drills, antisubmarine simulations, and troop landings.[130] During October, South Korea hosted the multinational PSI exercise simulating the interdiction of WMD. Fourteen nations, including the United States, took part in the exercise, which was obviously aimed at stopping WMD proliferation from countries like North Korea (and others).[131] While all of these actions were important, on November 23, 2010, North Korea decided to conduct another violent and deadly provocation. This time it launched an artillery attack on one of the islands that sits near the NLL.[132]

## The North Korean Artillery Attack on Yeonpyeong Island: A Violent NLL Provocation

Following the sinking of the *Cheonan*, the South Korean government took prudent and balanced action. While the Lee Myung-bak administration did not pursue violent retaliatory measures, which some would have thought appropriate, neither did it take a soft line with North Korea. In the past, North Korea had been able to use provocations to advance its national security goals. That did not prove to be the case following the sinking of the *Cheonan*; instead, South Korea took steps to impede the North Koreans' efforts to carry out such an act in the future. For their part, instead of attempting to ease tensions, the North Koreans decided once again to create a violent provocation in the Northern Limit Line. On November 23, 2010, the North Koreans launched another attack in the NLL area, this time shelling with artillery an island that sits in the de facto border area. The attack resulted in deaths and injuries for both military and civilian personnel.[133]

On the afternoon of November 23, 2010, at 2:34 p.m., the North Koreans began an artillery barrage against Yeonpyeong Island (the Koreans refer to Yeonpyeong Island as Yeonpyeong-Do, for *do* means "island" in Korean). They used 122mm multiple rocket launchers from a battalion (three batteries) that had been moved to the west coast in previous days and hours and deployed to positions about 10 kilometers north of the island that would give their soldiers optimum firepower capability as they targeted the island. The barrage consisted of approximately 170 rounds, 80 of which reportedly hit the island and 20 of which failed to detonate. The initial barrage was apparently a "time-on-target" attack, one that the North Korean army previously had practiced off the west coast near the NLL in January 2010 (as discussed earlier). The practice run may have been to help the soldiers hone their skills for the deadly attack that occurred on November 23. South Korean troops initially returned fire at 2:47 p.m., using a battery of six K9 155mm self-propelled howitzers. The artillery exchange continued until about 3:47 p.m. Two South Korean Marines and two South Korean civilians were killed in the attack. A total of nineteen South Koreans were injured.[134]

The reports from the Marines who were involved in the artillery battle on the island are quite compelling. Approximately fourteen hundred civilians live on the island, and a reinforced battalion of South Korean Marines has been deployed on islands in the NLL area to protect them from attack. "First, I saw one or two shells falling. Then immediately, a shower of dozens of shells blanketed the town," recounted Cpl. Park Tae-min. "In an instant, buildings were lifted and flown around, and fires erupted all over." A medic who was on the scene recalled the imagery of the island's emergency room: "The room instantly turned into a sea of blood."[135]

The South Korean Marines returned fire and reportedly hit a North Korean military compound on Mu Island and North Korean positions (around fifteen shells) near Kaemori, where the attack had originated. The Marines apparently had trouble with what proved to be defective anti-artillery radar (AN/TPQ-37) as the North Korean attack commenced. This failure led to less accurate counterfire—at least initially—as they faced the North Koreans. In addition, though South Korean F-15K strike fighters were scrambled in response to the attack, they took no action because the rules of engagement at the time called for strictly an equivalent response.[136] According to a defector group with contacts in North Korea, five North Koreans were killed in the short battle and were officially honored by the North Korean army.[137] One source, who claimed to have received information from a North Korean battalion commander, disclosed in 2012 evidence that as many as ten North Korean soldiers may have been killed and thirty wounded.[138] For a map showing the attack and counterattack areas, see figure 11.

In the weeks following the attack, the official North Korean media outlets "blamed" the attack on the South Koreans, asserting that the lack of a peace treaty was responsible for the deadly provocation that killed four South Koreans.[139] In the wake of a near-complete evacuation of the island's civilian populace, the commander of U.S. Forces, Korea, condemned North Korea for the attack. Meanwhile, in an obvious act of bravado, sources in North Korea revealed that Kim Jong-il and Kim Chong-un had visited the unit that initiated the artillery barrage the day before the attack. Following the attack, propaganda was reportedly promulgated in North Korea that Kim Chong-un had orchestrated the attack. Defectors who had fled the North for the freedom of South Korea said that the younger Kim was touted as an "artillery wizard." The propaganda being spread about the man who is now the leader of North Korea was apparently designed to give him credibility as a man who could lead the military. According to a source inside North Korea, security around Kim Jong-il and Kim Chong-un was intensified in the weeks following the artillery attack.[140] During March 2012, the official newspaper of the Korean Workers' Party, *Rodong Sinmun*, published an article that stated, "When the South prompted the military provocation near the West Sea and Yeonpyeong Island, by the extraordinary strategy and military operations of leader Kim Jong-un, the enemy's provocations were frustrated and Yeonpyeong Island became a sea of fire."[141]

North Korea took several provocative military measures in the weeks and months following the Yeonpyeong Island artillery attack. According to an unidentified South Korean government source, by mid-December 2010, the North Korean military had deployed additional SA-2 missiles on the west coast that could potentially target South Korean aircraft

FIGURE 11: ATTACK AND COUNTERATTACK ON YEONPYEONG ISLAND

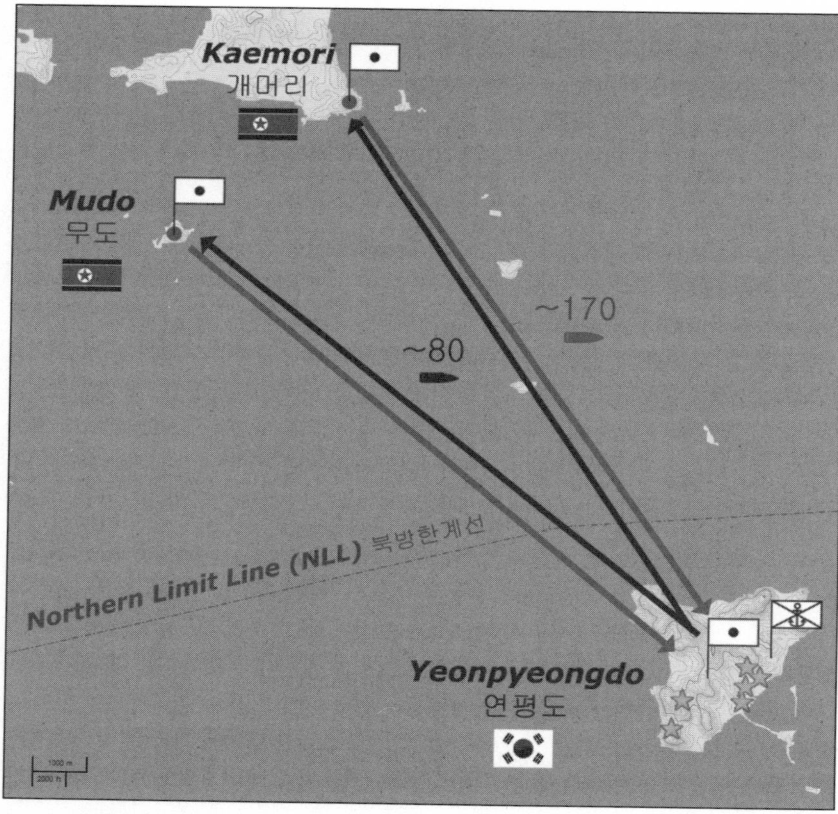

*Source:* Map of the Yeonpyeong shelling of 23 November 2010, courtesy of OpenStreetMap und Mitwirkende, Wikipedia, http://en.wikipedia.org/wiki/File:Yeonpyeong_shelling.png.

engaged in a counterattack against DPRK forces. In addition, the North Koreans set up additional Silkworm antiship missiles near the same area, as well as multiple rocket launchers and coastal artillery.[142] Also that month, North Korean SOF conducted training exercises simulating the taking of the five South Korean islands that sit in the NLL area.[143] During March 2011, the North Korean navy conducted unusual submarine training on the west coast, including the use of new advanced mini subs with increased capabilities.[144]

South Korea took some important initiatives following the North Koreans' artillery attack in November 2010. A key concern for the government in Seoul was that North Korea obviously showed no hesitation in initiating violent provocations that would cause civilian casualties. Rules of engagement were adjusted to shift from a paradigm designed to prevent an escalation to a focus on effectively repulsing attacks.[145] To respond to the asymmetric North Korean threat against the vulnerable islands off the west coast of the Korean Peninsula, South Korea also took several distinct military actions in the weeks following the artillery attack. First, it installed surface-to-air missiles at one of the offshore islands during December 2010. The indigenously produced Cheonma missile has a range of 10 kilometers. President Lee was quoted as saying that he wanted to turn the western border islands into "military fortresses."[146] In January, the South Korean government announced plans to position underwater sensors near its de facto sea border with North Korea along the NLL.[147]

During April 2011, South Korean government officials made pronouncements regarding their response to any new provocations that the North Koreans might initiate in the NLL, and this time they dealt with the extremely important South Korean airpower capability. At a dinner meeting with reporters, South Korean Air Force chief of staff Park Jong-heon stated that the attack on Yeonpyeong Island had led the air force to increase the number of aircraft that could respond quickly to a North Korean attack. General Park remarked that the planes "are on standby, loaded with arms that allow them to precisely bomb long-distance targets." He further commented that the planes are "ready to accurately strike nearby targets mobilized for provocation as well as the origin of provocation."[148] In early May 2011, the South Korean Ministry of National Defense announced that in lieu of building a global defense force, it would focus on building defenses against North Korea and in particular would address the North's capabilities for asymmetric attacks (often used in provocations) and full-scale warfare.[149] Also in May, South Korea was close to completing the reinforcing of its defenses on all five of the islands that sit in the NLL area. The military had deployed more weapons and troops to the islands, and more than a hundred shelters and protected facilities were in the process of being rebuilt with increased protection, including corrugated steel plates to protect them from shell fragments.[150]

A key development in South Korea's reaction to North Korea's violent provocations in the NLL during 2010 was the formation of an area-based defense command, which was able to respond more quickly and efficiently to asymmetric and unexpected provocations and attacks. In December 2010, the Presidential Commission for National Security Review suggested the formation of a Northwestern Islands Defense Command.[151] By June 2011, the commission's recommendation came to fruition. Seven months after the brutal attack on Yeonpyeong Island, the South Korean military had formally established the command. The Northwest Islands Defense Command's initial commander was Lt. Gen. Yoo Nak-jun, the commandant of the ROK Marine Corps. The command structure is a division-size joint unit, with the largest contingent being the ROK Sixth Marine Brigade and the Yeonpyeong Defense Battalion, and includes troops and units from all of the other services. A South Korean Marine Corps major general is the deputy commander of the command and has a staff that includes ninety colonels from all of the military services. The command now oversees the entire area around the five northwest islands. It also works closely with the South Korean Navy because North Korean naval craft pose an obvious threat to the islands. A formal ceremony commencing the new command's establishment was held in June 2011. The command will streamline the ability of South Korean forces to respond to North Korean attacks, enhance command and control, and strengthen rules of engagement.[152]

A year after the North Koreans conducted its artillery attack against Yeonpyeong Island, the South Korean government and military had taken significant measures to safeguard the security of its citizens in the NLL area.

Ground, naval, and antiaircraft forces had been significantly reinforced in terms of both personnel and equipment. The South Korean military tripled the number of self-propelled artillery systems on two key islands and deployed 130mm multiple rocket launchers and Cobra attack helicopters. The rules of engagement were formally revised to allow South Korea to respond with all forces available against North Korean provocations. In addition, during November 2011, the chairman of the ROK Joint Chiefs of Staff and the commander of U.S. Forces, Korea, signed a document to formulate a joint plan to respond to North Korean provocations. Reportedly, the plan will include detailed counterattack options, including equipment and troops.[153]

Perhaps as a result of the actions that the South Korean government and military took, the number of North Korean intrusions across the NLL dropped significantly. Typically in the past, North Korean naval craft and merchant craft—and sometimes aircraft—went across the NLL fairly routinely, only to be chased back across by South Korean forces. According to Song Young-sun of the South Korean National Assembly Defense Committee, through November 2011, North Korea engaged in only sixteen intrusions across the NLL, compared to ninety-five in 2010. Song commented on this significant drop: "It seems that the military authorities have strengthened their military patrols and the government is improving inter-Korean relations, and so the North seems to be controlling tensions in the area."[154] A year after the violent North Korean attack on Yeonpyeong Island, South Korean forces staged a large joint exercise in the area, using their most advanced F-15K aircraft, long-range artillery, multiple rocket launchers, and several naval craft.[155] Predictably, North Korea responded to the military exercise with hostile rhetoric. One of North Korea's propaganda outlets released a statement that said, in part, if the South Koreans decided to "to impair the dignity of (the North) again and fire one bullet or shell toward its inviolable territorial waters, sky and land, the deluge of fire on Yonphyong Island will lead to that in Chongwadae and the sea of fire in Chongwadae to the deluge of fire sweeping away the stronghold of the group of traitors."[156] The term "Chongwadae" refers to what is commonly known as the Blue House in Seoul, or the South Korean equivalent of the White House.

## Conclusions and Implications

An assessment of the South Korean government's actions following the sinking of the *Cheonan* and the shelling of Yeonpyeong Island shows that military and policy officials followed a pragmatic, deliberate, and transparent investigation into the naval tragedy and made clear adjustments to its rules of engagement and forces following the artillery attack. President Lee's decision soon after the first provocation to bring in international teams to investigate was admirable and added to the credibility of the final results, which the representatives of all five participating democratic nations agreed on formally. Following the compelling results of the Joint Civilian-Military Investigative Group's investigation, instead of conducting a retaliatory strike against North Korea—which would have been quite popular with some South Koreans but would have hurt Seoul's credibility in the international arena—Lee took the results to the UN Security Council. Despite the predictably watered-down statement that came out of the UNSC—thanks largely to China—the result has been a clear consensus among nearly every democracy on earth that North Korea conducted the unprovoked attack on the *Cheonan* and that punitive action needed to be taken against Pyongyang. The international reaction to the artillery attack was even more clear-cut. The unprovoked act of aggression did even more to cement the perception globally that North Korea operates as a rogue state while paying little attention to international norms.

Seoul's punitive actions aimed at Pyongyang have been political, economic, and military. The economic measures that South Korea has taken against the North will have an impact on the coffers of the elite in both the short run and the long run. Stepping up its propaganda campaigns aimed at the North and disallowing passage of North Korean ships through South Korean waters, where they had previously been allowed to navigate, are also important moves that send a strong message to the DPRK leadership. And, of course, conducting increased exercises focused on antisubmarine warfare and anti-provocation activities—sometimes conducted with the United States—is equally as important as South Korea's increased participation in the Proliferation Security Initiative. By participating in PSI, South Korea has the potential to hit North Korea where it hurts—that is, in the pocketbook.

Preventing the sales of WMD and illicit and counterfeit goods keeps profits from going directly into the coffers of the North Korea elite.[157]

The United States took important actions following the sinking of the *Cheonan* as well. Of course, American naval experts participated in the JIG investigation. In addition, the actions that the U.S. Congress took were significant because they showed the Americans supported the South Koreans in their resolve. Joint and combined naval exercises with South Korea will also help increase readiness and capabilities against possible future provocations. Washington demonstrated that it took the North Korean actions seriously and intended to take punitive action against Pyongyang for its irresponsible state behavior by increasing sanctions directly aimed at illicit activities—illegal drugs, counterfeit currency, and so on—and WMD proliferation during July and August 2010. The increased sanctions reportedly were aimed at specific bank accounts and front companies that deal in proliferation and illicit activity.[158] Of course, in my view, that the U.S. State Department, to date, has not yet relisted North Korea on the list of nations supporting terrorism is still disappointing. This action would be an important move and may yet still occur, but it has not as of this writing.

And what of North Korea? One can reasonably expect that North Korea can and will initiate more provocations as Kim Chong-un carries on the policies that his father initiated. What strategic and military planners must keep in mind is that, as discussed earlier, one of the four key aspects of nearly all North Korean provocations is that they involve continuously changing tactics and techniques. Thus, while one can expect the North Koreans to conduct more provocations in or near the NLL, one can also expect that the tactics, techniques, and procedures for these operations will likely be quite different from those carried out in the past. This variation makes planning for and, perhaps as important, deterring provocations an extremely challenging undertaking for those in policy and planning circles. During November 2010, the North Koreans once again reasserted that they were not responsible for the *Cheonan* sinking. North Korea's National Defense Commission published a document that said, among other things, it had "decided to disclose before the world what sheer fabrication and conspiratorial farce they orchestrated on the basis of information gathered so far."[159] By "they," the NDC report referred to the South Korean, British,

Australian, American, and Swedish experts who participated in the JIG investigation. North Korea also placed responsibility for the artillery attack on Yeonpyong Island at the feet of the South Koreans, making another accusation that holds no credibility in the international community.

If one thinks North Korea will unilaterally ease tensions in order to get sanctions dropped or to improve relations either with the United States or South Korea, I would say that this possibility is extremely unlikely (except perhaps in the short term from time to time). As long as the DPRK assesses that it can advance its foreign policy through brinkmanship and provocations—and no signs indicate that the leadership in Pyongyang has stopped believing it—we can expect North Korea to take a variety of actions to "push the edge of the envelope." The sinking of the *Cheonan* and the artillery attack months later most certainly set back relations on the Korean Peninsula and in the region by at least a year. But Kim Jong-il and his inner circle knew it would happen when they planned the violent attack. Even as they deployed specially equipped submarines into the waters of the NLL on a violent mission against a South Korean ship, and later moved an artillery battalion to the west coast specifically to shell an island in the NLL, the generals and admirals in North Korea no doubt anticipated—and in fact planned for—much of what has occurred since that tragic day on March 26. Thus, until Pyongyang ends its rogue state behavior, containment of its capabilities and deterrence against its many asymmetric threats are the only practical policies for maintaining security and stability on the Korean Peninsula.

# 4

## PLANNING FOR THE UNTHINKABLE

*Countering a North Korean Nuclear Attack and
Management of Postattack Scenarios*[1]

N orth Korea's nuclear program first came to the forefront as a threat
to world and regional security in 1994, when former American president Jimmy Carter was able to bring Pyongyang back from the brink and
helped to negotiate what would later become known as the Agreed
Framework. Since that time, North Korea has been engaged in on-again,
off-again talks with the United States and other key players in the region;
used numerous acts of brinkmanship with its nuclear program; and conducted its first two underground nuclear tests in 2006 and 2010.[2] The
international community's frustration concerning North Korea's many acts
of brinkmanship with its nuclear program over a period of nearly twenty
years—and the corresponding geopolitical discussions that then ensue—
tends to take away from the reasons that the program is such a concern for
the international community. The unthinkable and seldom-discussed threat
of a nuclear attack is a nightmare scenario not only for the region but also
for all nation-states that have an interest there.

North Korea shows no realistic signs of giving up its nuclear program
any time in the foreseeable future. As Brookings Institution senior scholar
Richard Bush writes, "This is because a DPRK willingness to pursue the
bargain proffered in the 6PT [six party talks] would force the regime to
make fundamental and unpalatable choices about how to ensure its survival
and ensure the security of the state."[3] Following the North Korean attack on
the *Cheonan* on March 26, 2010, the South Korean and U.S. militaries
showed solidarity in deterring Pyongyang's many potential threats.

Washington and Seoul, as discussed in chapter 3, conducted several maritime exercises aimed directly at deterring and containing North Korea's military capabilities and its ability to proliferate WMD. In response to at least one of these exercises, North Korea threatened to continue with a "strong deterrent," a term Pyongyang has often used to refer to its nuclear program.[4] Pyongyang also claimed in the summer of 2010 that it had developed improved nuclear weaponization technology, perhaps giving it the ability to put warheads on ballistic missiles.[5] In its 2009–2010 report assessing nuclear nonproliferation and disarmament, the Arms Control Association gave North Korea the grade of *F*, or the lowest possible rating.[6] All of these developments occurred during increased tensions in the security environment on the Korean Peninsula during 2009–2010, and U.S.-ROK alliance cooperation was as strong and cooperative as it had ever been. The fear of instability in an already unpredictable nation-state armed with nuclear weapons was exacerbated in late December 2011 when Kim Jong-il died. Thus, North Korea's capability to conduct a nuclear attack and the ability of nations with interests in the region—particularly the United States, South Korea, and Japan—to counter this threat have become paramount concerns.

This chapter will outline how the U.S.-ROK alliance should prepare countermeasures in the case of a North Korean nuclear attack on either South Korea or another key location (likely Japan). First, it will first be important to describe North Korea's nuclear capabilities, including the type and number of possible weapons that it could use in a nuclear attack and the ones under development. I then will examine the various types of attack scenarios that the North Koreans could use to implement a nuclear attack. Because a nuclear attack would create such horror and destruction—no matter how or where it occurred—I will address the viability of a preemptive strike by U.S. or South Korean forces, how it would or could occur, how effective it would be, and what the likely reaction from North Korea would be. In considering a possible nuclear attack, understanding what kind of damage it would cause is important. Thus, I will analyze the expected damage from a nuclear attack, the military countermeasures that could be taken, and how consequence management might work. I will also make a judgment on the U.S.-ROK alliance's current military readiness to deter and defend against a North Korean nuclear attack. I will conclude this chapter with some implications for the future.

Many questions about North Korea's nuclear capabilities remain despite the many reports, announcements, negotiations, and the three nuclear tests that Pyongyang has conducted. North Korea has not been transparent about either its intentions or its military capabilities. Thus, the debate over whether North Korea actually has bombs or only "devices" continues today. Policymakers, academics, and intelligence personnel still argue over whether North Korea has—or will have soon—a warhead that could be mounted on a missile as well. Indeed, they have deliberated over North Korea's intentions with its nuclear program ever since the first Korean nuclear crisis of 1994. And, of course, the fears about proliferation were answered definitively in 2007 when Israeli forces destroyed a North Korean–built plutonium reactor in Syria.[7] These many questions and debates are important. They all play a role in planning for countermeasures of an impending or executed North Korean nuclear attack. It will be my goal to answer as many of these questions as possible and conduct analysis that will be useful for a U.S.-ROK response.

## North Korea's Nuclear Capabilities

On October 9, 2006, the North Koreans conducted their first plutonium underground nuclear test, effectively ending any debate about whether they actually had nuclear weapons. Following the test, many analysts assessed it was at least a partially successful detonation of a plutonium nuclear device.[8] According to Siegfried Hecker of Stanford University (and former researcher at Los Alamos National Laboratory), "The DPRK aimed for 4 kilotons and got 1 kiloton. That is not bad for the first test. We call it successful but not perfect."[9] Researcher Hui Zhang of the John F. Kennedy School of Government at Harvard University presented an interesting and practical assessment in his 2007 paper: "If North Korea planned the yield of 4 kt (as reported), the test could be not a failure. It could show that Pyongyang already has confidence to explode a larger nuclear device and is pursuing a much more compact warhead for its missiles."[10] The bottom line is that in 2006 the North Koreans proved to the world that they had the capability to detonate a plutonium nuclear device that was probably a weapon and was at least partially successful.

On May 25, 2009, North Korea conducted its second underground plutonium nuclear test.[11] Preparations for the nuclear test began as early as May 7, 2009.[12] Most analysts agreed that the explosion from this test was significantly larger than the test conducted during 2006 (which was about one kiloton). A variety of estimates by international experts assessed the power of the explosion at two to six kilotons, with around four kilotons as the best guess. Of significance for this chapter, nuclear experts and scientists at the time determined that the explosion from a device that was the same size as the one tested in 2009 could kill tens of thousands of people if detonated over a major city.[13] Official calculations from Washington were also quite compelling. The U.S. Office of the Director of National Intelligence issued the following statement in 2009: "The U.S. Intelligence Community assesses that North Korea probably conducted an underground nuclear explosion in the vicinity of P'unggye on May 25, 2009. The explosion yield was approximately a few kilotons. Analysis of the event continues."[14] The test in 2009 was significantly larger—most estimates place it at around four times larger—than the test of 2006. This development suggests that the North Koreans were able to improve the sequencing process for the detonation of a plutonium nuclear weapon and thus able to get "more bang for their buck."

North Korea conducted its third nuclear test during February 2013. Most estimates placed the explosive power of the test as being significantly higher than either of the first two tests. In fact, the South Korean Ministry of National Defense placed that the estimated yield of the device tested was six to nine kilotons. Intelligence agencies from the United States, South Korea, and Japan had numerous sophisticated collection means deployed during the test but were unable to definitively determine if it was a plutonium or highly enriched uranium (HEU) device. While there was no proof that the test was either plutonium or HEU, many factors suggested it was an HEU test (as I will address next)—though the North Koreans took measures to ensure that it was contained (likely so intelligence agencies could not collect data).[15]

Of interest, and directly related to whether or not North Korea's third nuclear test was plutonium or HEU, Iranians were present at the test. Iran is not known to have a plutonium weaponization program, and thus would likely have no reason to attend the test unless it were to help with their HEU weaponization program. The Iranians reportedly asked Pyongyang if they could send observers to monitor the test in November 2012. The Iranians also reportedly paid the North Koreans tens of millions of dollars to observe the test. The request came from the head of Iran's Atomic Energy Organization and was approved by Iranian president Mahmoud Ahmadinejad. The payment is said to have been made through the Bank of Kunlun in Beijing. Of note, among the Iranians said to have been in attendance at the nuclear test was the man known as the "father of the Iranian nuclear program," Mohsen Fakhrizadeh-Mahabadi. He is said to be the head of Iran's collaboration effort with North Korea to develop a nuclear warhead for a missile. Some analysts believe the weapon tested during February 2013 was a miniaturized warhead for a missile.[16]

More evidence pointing to the February 2013 test being an HEU device comes from the North Koreans. They claimed in public statements that the test was to develop a "smaller and light" warhead. In fact, North Korea's news service announced that they had used a "miniaturized and lighter nuclear device with greater explosive force than previously."[17] The importance of a miniaturized warhead cannot be overstated. The ability to mount an HEU warhead (if in fact that is what was tested in February 2013) on a missile is a true "game changer." North Korea has around a hundred (or more) transporter-erector-launcher mobile ballistic missile platforms. According to an unnamed official in the South Korean government, there are twenty-seven to forty Scud missile launchers, twenty-seven to forty No Dong missile launchers, and fourteen launchers for the Musudan missile.[18] Of course, other launchers also likely exist for developing systems. While sanctions were called for by the UN, there is no doubt that North Korea—a nation-state that has sophisticated tactics and techniques for getting around sanctions—will continue to proliferate its nuclear technology to nations like Iran, as the profits from this endeavor put cash in the pockets of the elite and help to support the military.[19] Based on reports that Iranian experts observed the nuclear test, that the North Koreans announced it was a test of a miniaturized device, and the great care that the North Koreans took not to let particles escape from the test, my assessment is that this test was of an HEU weapon—most likely a warhead that could be mounted on a missile. But as this was never definitively proven, the status of North Korea's HEU nuclear weaponization program remains mired in ambiguity.

While the existence of North Korea's plutonium program is quite linear, a HEU facility is far more difficult to detect because it is much smaller than a plutonium processing facility, can be built underground, and is less vulnerable to technical intelligence collection means than a large, above-ground location such as the North Koreans' facility at Yongbyon would be.[20] But after many years of the North Koreans' denials and the largely anti-Bush (politically motivated) support of these denials from many pundits and scholars both in the United States and South Korea (almost exclusively on the left), the evidence, which had been rather compelling since 2002, became even clearer (publicly) and more difficult to deny as the Bush presidency came to a close.

In a report released to the press in 2009, Pakistani nuclear scientist A. Q. Khan stated that North Korea had already possibly enriched small amounts of uranium by 2002. Khan had toured a plant in North Korea during 2002 that he claims had at least three thousand centrifuges. Khan also stated that Pakistan helped the North Koreans with drawings, vital machinery, and technical advice for at least six years. Khan's travels to North Korea also took him to a plant that made uranium hexafluoride, a gas vital for the uranium enrichment process. North Korean technicians taught the Pakistanis how to make krytons, which are electrical switches used in nuclear detonations, and in turn Pakistan gave Pyongyang essential equipment and software. The biggest part of the trade, though, was a "nukes-for-missiles" deal that gave the Pakistanis No Dong missiles in exchange for HEU technology and assistance. According to Khan's report, top Pakistani political and military officials not only approved of the collaboration but also assisted in carrying it out.[21] Meanwhile, in 2009, South Korean officials confirmed to the press that North Korea had built facilities that can manufacture small amounts of HEU. The underground facilities are said to be located in Sowi-ri, which is in the same administrative district of North Pyongan Province where the Yongbyon nuclear reactor is located.[22]

Perhaps the most compelling aspect of the evidence dealing with Pyongyang's HEU weaponization program came from information that the

North Koreans provided. In June 2009 the state-run Korean Central News Agency released a formal statement that said, "The process of uranium enrichment will be commenced."[23] North Korea's public disclosure did not satisfy some analysts, who continued to politicize this important national security issue. Selig Harrison, a reporter and author who since 2003 has been an outspoken opponent of any evidence regarding North Korea's HEU program, testified before the U.S. Congress on June 17, 2009, "The prospects for capping the arsenal at its present level have improved as a result of Pyongyang's June 13 announcement admitting that it has an R and D program for uranium enrichment. Since this program is in its early stages and it not yet actually enriching uranium, there is time for the United States to negotiate inspection safeguards."[24]

Harrison failed to address evidence regarding North Korea's now widely known nukes-for-missiles deal with Pakistan or the facilities at Sowi-ri (not to mention the DPRK's collaboration with Iran since at least 2003).[25] The North Koreans followed up the June 2009 statement with yet another announcement on September 4, 2009. The DPRK permanent representative to the United Nations said in a letter to the president of the UN Security Council, "Experimental uranium enrichment has successfully been conducted to enter into completion phase."[26] South Korea's minister of unification released a statement to the press in 2009 that North Korea was assessed to have had an HEU program long before the United States publicly raised the accusation in 2002.[27] In fact, in that year, an unclassified point paper from the Central Intelligence Agency that was distributed to Congress says, "We recently learned that the North is constructing a plant that could produce enough weapons grade uranium for two or more nuclear weapons per year when fully operational—which could be by mid-decade."[28]

Yet more evidence regarding North Korea's HEU program came to light during November 2010, when DPRK officials took Stanford University scholar Siegfried S. Hecker on a tour of an HEU facility that he said had more than two thousand centrifuges. In his report he stated, "At the fuel fabrication site, we were taken to a new facility that contained a modern, small industrial-scale uranium enrichment facility with 2,000 centrifuges that was recently completed and said to be producing low enriched uranium (LEU) destined for fuel for the new reactor." Hecker further commented on the facility, writing, "Nevertheless, the uranium enrichment facilities could be readily converted to produce highly-enriched uranium (HEU) bomb fuel (or parallel facilities could exist elsewhere) and the LWR [light water reactor] could be run in a mode to produce plutonium potentially suitable for bombs, but much less suitable than that from their current reactor."[29] Hecker also wrote that he was shown a new light water reactor facility that was under construction. North Koreans also took Jack Pritchard, the president of the Washington-based Korea Economic Institute, for a tour of the facility.[30]

It is unclear if the facilities shown to the Stanford University scholar are the same facilities reported in the South Korean press in February 2009 (at Sowi-ri). Equipment from these facilities possibly could have been moved to the site shown to the Americans in November 2010. Also possible, and perhaps more likely, is the assessment that the North Koreans have more than one facility capable of producing and weaponizing HEU. In fact, according to press reports, American envoy to the International Atomic Energy Agency (IAEA) Glyn Davies told the agency's thirty-five-member governing board that there is a "clear likelihood" Pyongyang has constructed other uranium enrichment facilities. He also reportedly stated that North Korea probably had been pursuing such a capability long before it publicly admitted to it.[31] Of course, the North Koreans denied that they had any uranium enrichment facilities anywhere except Yongbyon. According to sources in the Japanese press, during meetings held with American officials on July 28 and 29, 2011, North Korean vice foreign minister Kim Kye-gwan asserted that Yongbyon was the only uranium enrichment facility in the DPRK.[32] Meanwhile, during that summer, new buildings used for enriching uranium at Yongbyon were revealed in overhead satellite imagery.[33] In 2012, Hecker articulated an important assessment regarding North Korea's HEU capability when he said in an interview with the South Korean press, "It's hard to say exactly how many nuclear weapons the North has because I don't know how many centrifuges it has. What is clear is that the North has more facilities other than those in Yongbyon and will produce highly enriched uranium there. Even if the North invites international inspectors, it will never show them the facilities."[34]

According to a 2011 IAEA report (whose release the Chinese delayed for several months), UN officials confirmed that Pakistan provided the backbone for what is now a well-advanced HEU weaponization program in North Korea. In addition, according to an Institute for Science and International Security assessment, the two thousand centrifuges at the Yongbyon facility are likely part of an overall system of three thousand centrifuges that could make up to fifty kilograms of weapons-grade uranium per year. Moreover, according to the IAEA report, which the Institute for Science and International Security made available on its website, North Korea also provided uranium hexaflouride to Libya in the early 2000s. To do so, Pyongyang had to have a uranium conversion capability prior to 2001.[35] But Libya is not the only country that North Korea has supplied with HEU materials and technology. Proliferation is a key concern as North Korea also has been cited as supplying Iran with software and computer programs for weaponizing uranium. Iran has also given Pyongyang billions of dollars to help it develop centrifuges and obtain raw materials. North Korea is also actively helping Iran build a 500-kilogram HEU warhead for a missile (which will be described in more detail later). But it does not stop there. As noted previously, the United Nations has clearly identified North Korea as "very likely" being the builder of the plutonium nuclear facility in Syria that Israel destroyed in 2007. Further, for several years the DPRK has been suspected of helping Burma with a fledgling HEU weaponization program. Most analysts finally now agree that the HEU program in North Korea originated with its trade deals with Pakistan starting in the late 1990s.[36]

According to experts in South Korea, an HEU facility similar to the one at Sowi-ri could produce one or two nuclear devices per year.[37] Based on the now great deal of evidence, North Korea's HEU program has progressed far beyond the R & D stage. In fact, it appears to be very close—if not already past the completion phase—to producing HEU weapons. As I wrote in my 2010 book *Defiant Failed State: The North Korean Threat to International Security*,

Based on the evidence presented, this program is far beyond the R & D state and may be close to (if not already finished) producing HEU

weapons. In fact, it is my assessment that North Korea is likely to conduct a test of an HEU device when the leadership there feels the
geopolitical situation warrants it. Such a test will put to rest the statements of the many naysayers in the United States and South Korea
who have denied its existence since it was first disclosed publicly in
2002.[38]

Activity consistent with nuclear test preparations was reported at a
facility in North Korea during November 2010.[39] Pyongyang again
appeared ready to conduct a test by the end of May 2012, perhaps only
delaying the test for geopolitical reasons.[40] Thus, based on the evidence
regarding North Korea's highly secretive nuclear program, Pyongyang's
two-track nuclear program is now (or nearly) capable of producing two
types of nuclear weapons—plutonium and HEU-based weapons systems.
Based on this assessment, military officials and policymakers should plan
accordingly.

## Different Scenarios for a North Korean Nuclear Attack

Because the evidence now points to North Korea's development of a two-
track nuclear weaponization program, the various scenarios for a nuclear
attack should be examined based on these capabilities. North Korea could
pursue many possibilities, particularly if one keeps in mind how clever
Pyongyang has been in planning for its asymmetric capabilities.[41] The North
Koreans have developed a skill for planning around allied defenses, using
the element of surprise, and "thinking out of the box" that makes preparing for a Pyongyang-initiated attack so difficult and yet vital. Thus, in this
section I will provide examples of some—but not all—scenarios North
Korea could use for a nuclear attack.

All analysts agree that the North Koreans hold a plutonium nuclear
weapons capability in their arsenal. One must keep several factors about a
plutonium capability in mind. A successful plutonium weapon is generally
going to be larger than an HEU weapon. Because of the amount of explosives
needed and the size of the weapon, a plutonium weapon is also considered
to be far more difficult than an HEU weapon to fit on a missile as a warhead.[42]

North Korea, however, may have developed alternative delivery means, such as bombs. The delivery means for a plutonium bomb are rather diverse. But considering the evaluation that to date any weapon the North Koreans have would be quite primitive, one can reasonably assume that the weapon would have to be quite large, would have an elementary triggering or implosion mechanism to cause the nuclear weapon to detonate, and would have a fission process that would possibly not detonate the weapon to its full capability (as with the assessed production of the underground nuclear test of 2006).

Given the asymmetric thinking that the North Koreans are well known for integrating into their planning process, they could use a number of delivery systems for a plutonium bomb. First, the most obvious method would be to simply drop a plutonium bomb from an aircraft. The North Koreans have H-5 bombers—the Chinese version of the old Soviet IL-28 light bomber—that are capable of conducting such a mission. The Chinese are thought to have given many of these aircraft to the North Koreans during or after the 1960s, and the North Korean air force inventory currently has around eighty H-5s.[43] These aircraft are old (though the air force has likely maintained them well) and vulnerable to air defenses in both South Korea and Japan. In addition, the North Koreans would likely have to limit the weight of the weapon that the H-5 carried so craft could get off the ground. The H-5's weight limit thus is an important consideration. It may have been the reason for the relatively low projected yield of the nuclear weapons the North Koreans tested underground in 2006 and 2009. By limiting the weapon's size, they may have been testing a device that would be small enough to fit on board their aircraft yet large enough to produce an explosion that would kill tens of thousands of people.[44] Despite the sophistication of Japanese and South Korean air defenses, by using asymmetry and even trickery, a North Korean aircraft might be able to find its way into South Korean or Japanese airspace. But it would take intricate planning and a great deal of luck. Thus, if this option is one of the planned delivery systems for a nuclear weapon, it is unlikely to be the primary choice.

Another delivery means for a nuclear weapon that is far more ominous would be using a ship disguised as a merchant cargo vessel or a trawler. This alternative is far more threatening than it sounds. In times of tension

Japanese and South Korean port authorities would likely be looking for North Korean ships transiting their ports. Considering the North Koreans' modus operandi of using surprise as a key aspect of any operation or provocation, what makes the scenario of a ship sailing into a Japanese or South Korean port and then detonating a nuclear weapon even more compelling is that the North Koreans often "re-flag" their ships and sail under the flags of other nations (this method has been largely successful for them in the past).[45] Two key advantages of using a merchant ship or a specially equipped fishing trawler as a delivery means for a nuclear weapon are (1) given the stream of merchant vessel traffic that transits South Korean and Japanese ports, moving this delivery means past defensive measures in South Korea or Japan would be much easier; and (2) the North Koreans would probably not have to limit the size of the primitive weapon as they do when carrying it on an aircraft like the H-5.

The scenarios for using a ship as the delivery means for a nuclear weapon are diverse, and this is perhaps what makes them so ominous. A merchant ship or a fishing trawler could be equipped with a primitive nuclear device and then sailed into a major South Korean port city such as Pusan, Pohang, or Ulsan. Once the weapon was detonated in such a populous area, it would likely kill tens of thousands of people (even if it was a primitive weapon). In a port like Pohang, the home of a ROK Marine division, the possibility exists that a bomb would kill large numbers of military personnel in addition to multitudes of civilians. The Pohang area is also frequently the site of combined training with U.S. and ROK Marines, and if an attack occurred during such exercises, possibly many American personnel would become casualties as well.[46] Detonating a nuclear weapon in Pusan, a key reception and staging portal to the peninsula, would shut down a key shipping and air hub.[47] Pusan is seen as very vulnerable to an attack not only because of its large population but also for its symbolism. It was the only spot not overrun by the DPRK during the Korean War and thus carries with it the shame associated with the notion of a "foreign stronghold" in Korea.[48] The Japanese also have a large presence there.[49] Last, Pusan is located in the province where much of the political power comes from in South Korea. Literally all the presidents, except Kim Dae-Jung, have hailed from Kyong Sang-do (Park Guen-hye was born in Taegu).[50]

Merchant and naval ports would also be susceptible to attack if North Korea chose to use a ship as the delivery means to attack Japan. A merchant ship or fishing trawler could make a port call at the cities of Yokohama or Sasebo (among many others). Yokohama opens into the Tokyo Bay and is a highly populated area, so Japanese casualties would be maximized. Sasebo is also the home of a large U.S. naval base. Detonating a nuclear device there would not only cause thousands of Japanese deaths but also have the potential to kill thousands of Americans, both military and civilians.[51]

If one wonders why North Korea would attack Japan instead of or in addition to South Korea, the answer is rather simple: conducting a nuclear attack on Japan immediately before starting a full-scale war on the Korean Peninsula (or soon thereafter) would create immense problems in both the U.S.-ROK alliance and the U.S.-Japanese alliance. Such an attack would likely cause an outrage among the Japanese populace, and the prime minister would be pressured to act immediately against the North Koreans. This reaction, of course, would generate great angst in Seoul, where any direct Japanese involvement in a war on the Korean Peninsula would be simply unacceptable. As the United States sought to sort out the diplomatic and military minefields that seeking an acceptable solution to both of its key allies in East Asia would cause, North Korean conventional forces could be advancing through the Chorwon Valley and the Kaesong-Munsan Corridor. Indeed, a North Korean nuclear attack on Japan would strike not only a tragic blow to that country but also likely kindle political turmoil that would hamper the military reactions of the United States, South Korea, and Japan.

When considering scenarios that revolve around a North Korean nuclear attack using an HEU weapon, significant differences arise when compared to possible attack instances involving a plutonium weapon. First of all, while it makes sense that North Korea either has completed construction of an HEU weapon or is close to doing so, no definitive proof is available. Evidence remains sketchy, and the North Koreans have not been forthcoming in their disclosure of information regarding the HEU program (except for the two earlier referenced statements to the UN). But the many anecdotal pieces of evidence, when put together like pieces in a puzzle, do form a picture of a program built with the help of the Pakistanis, with years to achieve maturation, and the resources and know-how to build a legitimate weapon.[52] Thus, the following scenarios are based on the assessment that North Korea has completed weaponization of its HEU program or will do so in the near future.

What makes an HEU program particularly threatening when compared to a plutonium program is that HEU weaponization lends itself to building a warhead for a missile. In fact, Pyongyang appears to be going exactly in this direction. An evaluation of evidence uncovered when Libya relinquished its entire nuclear program shows that the Pakistanis had given it the designs for a 500-kilogram HEU warhead for a missile. The plans also had Chinese writing on them, so one must assume (as have most analysts have) that the Pakistanis received the blueprints and designs for an HEU warhead from the Chinese and passed them to the Libyans. This discovery is important regarding North Korea because the Pakistanis also reportedly provided the same blueprints to both the North Koreans and the Iranians.[53] The danger to Northeast Asia is that a 500-kilogram warhead can easily fit on a No Dong missile, which the North Koreans also sold to the Pakistanis and is likely the reason for their pursuing that particular design. The Libyans were reportedly trying to acquire the No Dong missile from the North Koreans before they agreed to dismantle their nuclear program under the eyes of international inspectors.[54] According to numerous sources, the North Koreans and Iranians since at least 2003 have been collaborating on perfecting a design for an HEU warhead that could be mounted on a No Dong, which is known as the Shahab-3 in Iran. Not only is the No Dong the most likely missile that Pyongyang would use in a nuclear attack involving an HEU weapon, but it is also the most likely delivery means that Iran would use should Tehran choose to initiate a nuclear attack (presumably against Israel).[55]

The No Dong missile platform would offer the most stability for a 500-kilogram nuclear warhead. Thus, one needs to consider the range of the No Dong. South Korean and U.S. military officials now assess its range at up to 1,500 kilometers.[56] Thus, a nuclear-armed No Dong missile now has the range to hit Tokyo or other key targets in Japan, including U.S. bases in Okinawa Prefecture, and if fired on a different trajectory, it could hit vital areas in South Korea, such as Pusan, Kunsan, or even Cheju Island. The big question, of course, is whether North Korea has completed the

HEU weaponization program and, perhaps equally as important, has perfected the design for a 500-kilogram HEU warhead that could be mounted on a No Dong missile. Launching a nuclear-capable missile at Japan would create all of the same alliance issues that were discussed earlier with the plutonium weapons. Further, if several missiles, or a "volley," were launched at Japan, Japan would find using ballistic missile defense systems to shoot them down more difficult. The same applies if this tactic were used against South Korea. Of course, similar to the delivery systems for the plutonium program, an HEU weapon could also be launched using the H-5 bomber aircraft or even a ship sailing into an unsuspecting port.

## Preemptive Strikes: A Viable Planning Option?

These scenarios paint a rather ominous picture of the threat that a nuclear-equipped North Korea could present to the region. Even if one adopts the best-case scenario that North Korea has not developed its HEU program to fruition or a capability to mount a nuclear warhead on a missile (perhaps a very dangerous assumption), undoubtedly right now North Korea has the delivery means, such as an H-5 aircraft or a nondescript merchant vessel, for its proven plutonium program. These capabilities lead one to ask, would a preemptive strike be the best methodology for preventing a North Korean nuclear attack? If so, how would it be carried out, and what would be the North Korean government's reaction? In a September 2010 speech given at a seminar cosponsored by the Korea Defense Forum and the Northeast Asia Peace and Security Forum, Chairman of the South Korean Presidential Commission for National Security Review Lee Sang-woo stated, in part, "Only when it possesses the ability to attack targets precisely with non-nuclear weapons and incapacitate North Korea's WMD ability before it is used will South Korea, which maintains a non-nuclear military policy, be able to head off North Korea's military edge."[57] Perhaps in response to this publicly disseminated statement, North Korea's propaganda services stated on September 17, 2010, that their nation was ready for a preemptive strike, saying, "It will get nothing but miserable self-destruction."[58]

The problem of waging a preemptive strike against North Korea is that the locations of its nuclear weapons (bombs or warheads for missiles) are secret. These weapons are probably not located either at Yongbyon (for plutonium and or HEU) or at Sowi-ri (for HEU). In fact, any nuclear weapons are probably dispersed to several places in North Korea.[59] While estimates vary, North Korea may have processed enough plutonium for up to fifteen nuclear weapons, and each bomb may be dispersed at a different location.[60] Based on delivery means, likely one or more bombs are dispersed near airfields where they could be deployed aboard bomber aircraft or near ports where they could be loaded onto merchant vessels. They could also be located at naval bases, where merchant craft could be brought in for loading the nuclear devices. In the case of an HEU weapon—if it exists already—no estimates are available on how many exist. Finally, if the North Koreans have perfected the methodology for mounting a 500-kilogram warhead on a No Dong missile, the obvious place to deploy these weapons would be near No Dong bases. The country has several.[61] Making this issue all the more ominous is that a No Dong can be fired from a transporter-erector-launcher; thus, the missile could be moved to any mobile location in the country and launched. Thus, the option of a preemptive strike would involve much more than simply taking out all of the weapons, even if their locations were known.

Another key factor when evaluating the possibility and results of a preemptive strike is what the reaction of the North Koreans would be. North Korea has deployed hundreds of long-range artillery systems along the DMZ with South Korea that are capable of hitting Seoul.[62] In addition, up to 20 percent of these systems are assessed to be equipped with chemical munitions.[63] An attack could be initiated within a matter of minutes because all of these systems already sit within firing positions. In addition, North Korea would be likely to use all of the tools that were quickly available in its arsenal to strike back at South Korea and the United States. This retaliatory effort would likely include attacks by its Special Operations Forces and the more than eight hundred (up to a thousand) short- and mid-range missiles in its arsenal.[64] Consequently, the U.S.-ROK alliance would have to destroy more than simply the sites where nuclear weapons were believed to be deployed. Any preemptive strike also would have to include a strike on command and control facilities, all airfields where aircraft with nuclear weapons could be deployed and where fighters could be launched in retaliation, long-range artillery sites along the DMZ, naval bases and ports where ships could be carrying nuclear weapons, and key leadership nodes in Pyongyang. In short, the only way to be even modestly sure that the nuclear weapons, the means to control them, and the ability to mount a massive retaliatory strike could be destroyed would be to start an all-out war. Thus, in any planning for a preemptive strike, the assumption that it would start a full-scale war should be an integral part of the process.

## Expected Damages and Consequence Management

As discussed earlier, even a small nuclear detonation of four kilotons or less, such as the North Korean test of 2009, would probably kill tens of thousands of people if it occurred in a densely populated area. According to Rand Corporation analyst Bruce W. Bennett, even a one-kiloton nuclear attack against a city like Pusan could cause up to 72,000 casualties, depending on where the weapon was detonated. An attack on Seoul would likely cause even more casualties.[65] This casualty count is important for North Korea because if Pyongyang did choose to conduct a nuclear attack, the two most likely countries it would target would be Japan or South Korea. This possibility becomes all the more compelling if one considers that some 220,000 foreigners live in Seoul.[66] In my view, Seoul would be a less likely target of a nuclear weapon than another major city in South Korea, not only because of its close proximity to North Korea but also because both North and South Korea regard the city as the historical crown jewel of Korean art, culture, and society. (Besides, North Korea can wreak havoc on Seoul with chemical weapons fired by missiles and long-range artillery.) Meanwhile, a large number of foreigners live and work in other South Korean metropolitan areas as well, and certainly the same applies to Japan. Accordingly, a nuclear attack on South Korea or Japan will also kill a great number of foreigners (many of them Americans) and, if certain key metropolitan areas are targeted, a large number of military personnel as well.

Another important aspect of North Korea's launching a nuclear attack on South Korea or Japan is the terror factor. Both South Korea and Japan have several large, vibrant cities, where world-famous traffic jams are routine.[67] Because many metropolitan areas in both South Korea and Japan are so densely populated, a nuclear attack would likely lead to widespread panic and terror that would extend nationwide. For this reason (and because such a large portion of the civilian populace would be killed), a nuclear detonation in either country would likely be considered an act of terror. Evacuating civilians from South Korea would be particularly tough. The large number of American civilians who live in South Korea would make it literally the largest noncombatant evacuation operation ever conducted in U.S. history.[68] U.S. Forces, Korea, annually conducts such training exercises, but having never experienced such a large evacuation before, the real exodus would present huge challenges for USFK, for U.S. military airlift and sealift, and for the civilian transport services that would undoubtedly be called in to help.[69]

In the cases of consequence management for the governments of South Korea and Japan, the toll of deaths and injuries would be so high that whichever country was attacked with nuclear weapons undoubtedly would have to ask for foreign assistance to handle its dire medical needs. The only case study one can analyze is the aftermath of the atomic bombing of Hiroshima and Nagasaki in 1945. The medical aftermath for the civilian populace that survived the attack in both areas was catastrophic.[70] Today, both South Korea and Japan are modern, cosmopolitan nations, but the required amount of medical personnel after a successful nuclear attack on one of their major cities or ports would still likely be insufficient for treating the sudden influx of badly wounded people. In addition to the overwhelming medical issues that a nuclear attack would generate, consequence management would involve confronting the environmental issues that would probably cause repercussions all over East Asia.[71] As Col. John M. Collins, USA (Ret.), wrote in an article in 2003, "A gigantic crater caused by a nuclear device would instantaneously breach U.S.-ROK forward defenses and release a lethal radioactive cloud that would envelope all forces downwind if just one nuclear weapon erupted anywhere beneath the westernmost third of the DMZ."[72] In short, consequence management for both South Korea and Japan would involve both medical and environmental emergency procedures. While international efforts would likely help to eradicate much of the stress on the medical systems that such an event would cause, the environmental fallout from a nuclear attack would create problems that could take as long as a generation to solve.

## The Military Readiness of ROK and U.S. Forces for a North Korean Nuclear Attack

The ROK and U.S. military forces in Korea train at least twice a year for scenarios that involve fighting a force-on-force conflict with North Korea and other North Korean crisis situations that the U.S.-ROK alliance could potentially encounter in the future. These forces also train and plan for confronting a nuclear scenario as part of their routine military readiness (usually in command post exercises). According to open sources in the press and elsewhere, Operation Plan (OPLAN) 5027 and other corresponding OPLANs include measures for a nuclear scenario and preemptive strike options.[73] Reportedly, some plans include hitting North Korean WMD with a variety of strike packages that could include aircraft and/or submarine platforms—and this would be part of the nuclear umbrella pledged by President Obama to the government of South Korea.[74]

When one addresses how the alliance would respond to a North Korean nuclear strike—either impending or one that has just occurred—of course, political problems arise. Colonel Collins addressed this issue in his writings: "Any of the U.S. options . . . could trigger uncontrollable escalation that would create appalling casualties on both sides of the DMZ and promise a Pyrrhic victory at best. Unilateral actions by the United States without unqualified ROK . . . agreement and willing participation every step of the way would be immoral as well as ill-advised."[75] Colonel Collins gets to the crux of the problem when he addresses agreement between South Korea and the United States. Both nations would have to agree on exactly the type of action to take in response to a North Korean nuclear attack. And this decision would be contingent on where the attack occurred, how many casualties it inflicted, and the political leanings of the governments in both Seoul and Washington.

Of course, being able to plan for and to recognize an impending North Korean nuclear attack is contingent on good intelligence. The United States and South Korea have a huge array of intelligence collection systems that target North Korea. In fact, South Korea is able to rely on its ally for some of the most sophisticated collection systems ever fielded, and they significantly enhance the planning process.[76] But North Korea remains perhaps the most opaque country on earth; thus, the well-guarded secrecy that Pyongyang uses to protect its planning, its weapons systems, and the type of attacks that it will conduct in a nuclear scenario will limit the ability of the U.S.-ROK military alliance to actually verify that a nuclear attack is imminent.[77] That fact takes us back to the dilemma of once again evaluating the level of tensions on the Korean Peninsula, clear-cut evidence that Pyongyang is actually readying a nuclear-equipped delivery means for an attack on South Korea or Japan, and the political leanings of the governments in Seoul and Washington.

To address the dilemma of the DPRK's nuclear weapons, during October 2010, South Korea and the United States set up a joint military committee specifically designed to deter threats from North Korea's nuclear weapons and other WMD capabilities. The Extended Deterrence Policy Committee was formed as a result of the annual Security Consultative Meeting between U.S. defense secretary Gates and South Korean defense minister Kim. It is the first such committee that the United States has created with an ally outside the North Atlantic Treaty Organization (NATO).[78]

In any scenario, Seoul will likely be reluctant to support a nuclear attack on North Korea. The reasons for this stance are obvious. Given that the government's stated policy goal is a reunification of Korea under a liberal democratic government in Seoul,[79] if a full-scale war were to erupt on the Korean Peninsula, the reunified peninsula under Seoul would then have a large area in the north decimated by a nuclear attack. Moreover, if the allied forces' nuclear attack was not a preemptive strike but instead followed a North Korean nuclear attack, the government in Seoul would have the huge and ominous task of having to clean up not one but two nuclear strike sites. As discussed earlier, the environmental and population ramifications would last for at least as long as a generation. Thus if the situation called for a preemptive strike—meaning the level of intelligence available would have to show that this action was absolutely necessary—or for a retaliatory strike, the South Korean government is most likely to push for a response that uses conventional weapons systems.

## Conclusions

Based on the evidence presented in this chapter, even if using the most primitive type of nuclear weapon, North Korea obviously could launch a nuclear strike that would likely kill tens of thousands of people in either South Korea or Japan. Further, North Korea possesses this capability right now. If and when North Korea is able to perfect the technology for fitting an HEU warhead to a missile—that is, if they have brought their HEU weaponization program to fruition, and they may have already done so—North Korea will be able to launch a strike from mobile missiles at either South Korea or Japan. No matter what preparations are made to prepare for such an attack, the immediate casualties would be enormous, as well as the second-order effects for as long as a generation. Intelligence on North Korea's intentions is sketchy at best and thus limits the likelihood of South Korea and/or its allies' launching a preemptive strike. The ramifications also limit launching a preemptive strike. Because of North Korea's ability to retaliate and its unpredictable government, any preemptive strike would have to be so widespread and on such a large scale that undoubtedly it would cause an all-out war on the Korean Peninsula. All of these assessments add up to the premise that avoiding a nuclear war of any kind on the Korean Peninsula can and should remain a high priority. Such a war would have no winner, only varying degrees of great loss.

# 5

# NORTH KOREA AND
# SUPPORT FOR TERRORISM
## An Evolving History

N orth Korea's support for terrorism began at least as early as the 1960s as a story about an ideologically based policy (largely financed by the Soviet Union) and ends with a policy designed to put money into the coffers of the elite in Pyongyang, or in short, a "proliferation for hire" policy.[1] To understand Pyongyang's current policy of supporting non-state actors—most proving to be groups acknowledged as terrorists—first one must understand how this policy evolved. The leaders in Pyongyang did not wake up one morning and simply decide to train and equip terrorist groups at various locations around the globe. Rather, North Korea began actively supporting groups that engage in terrorism—and Pyongyang, in fact, engaged in its own acts of terrorism—as a result of the Cold War. But while global paradigms have radically changed since the Soviet Union collapsed in 1991, North Korea's policy of actively supporting non-state actors engaged in terrorism has not.

This chapter will follow the evolving history of North Korean support for terrorism. In order to understand the early underpinnings of this policy and how it began, it will be important to first address the very beginning of Kim Il-sung's power base—which began with him as the leader of a partisan group fighting against the Japanese. But Kim did not do this alone, nor did he engage in warfare against his neighbor to the south on his own. Thus, this chapter will provide a brief history of the DPRK (because it also is vital to understanding Pyongyang's support for terrorist groups) and of the kind of support that Kim Il-sung received from both the USSR and China. It will also examine briefly how Kim Il-sung consolidated his power, because this had a direct effect on North Korea's foreign policy and the way the communist state worked with its sponsors and allies during the Cold War. Then this chapter will analyze North Korea's role in supporting terrorism during the Cold War years and the specific terrorist groups it supported and why.

As the Cold War ended, the North Koreans had built ties to a variety of state and non-state actors. But while the end of the Cold War meant an end to tyranny around much of the globe, it also presented opportunities—and potential for financial gain—for rogue state regimes like North Korea's. Thus, this chapter will address how North Korea's support for terrorist groups evolved and reinvented itself during the 1990s and then in the regimes of Kim Jong-il and now Kim Chong-un. North Korea is well known for proliferating a variety of weapons to other rogue states. I have examined this important issue in the past,[2] but this chapter will deal specifically with North Korea's support for terrorist groups: the reasons behind it, the goals reached, and the implications for American foreign policy.

## North Korea's Beginnings and Kim Il-sung's Rise to Power

The history of the North Korean regime begins during World War II. During that war, several partisan groups fought with and under the command of both Soviet and Chinese military forces. The Soviets picked Kim Il-sung, a young commander who led one of the partisan groups, to help lead his new nation of North Korea after the war. In the beginning, Soviet "advisers" closely supervised the DPRK, the USSR completely subsidized the new country, and the DPRK military and paramilitary forces utilized Soviet doctrine in their operations and training.[3]

During the Korean War, which North Korea initiated based on a plan drawn up with the advice and supervision of Soviet advisers, Kim Il-sung also developed a relationship with the newly established People's Republic of China. Following a near collapse of DPRK forces after the battle of Inchon and the ensuing northern push of American-led UN forces, China came to Kim's aid. It essentially dedicated large numbers of military forces to the war at the request of Joseph Stalin, who provided funding, logistics, and military equipment to both China and North Korea.[4] Eventually, more

than a million Chinese troops were fighting in the Korean theater of operations by the war's end. This assistance marked the beginning of a relationship that Pyongyang would have with both the USSR and China until
the end of the Cold War.

## Kim Il-sung's Consolidation of Power

The Soviets formally "appointed" Kim the leader of North Korea in 1948
(but he had been the de facto Soviet-appointed leader since 1945), and Kim
was "elected" as the premier of the republic during the same time frame.[5]
Despite Kim's rise to power (with the backing of his Soviet supporters),
from 1945 until the late 1950s, he was unable to gain complete consolidation of power. Of course, the Korean War delayed his taking total control
of the country, but perhaps equally as important, Kim also faced both pro-
Soviet and pro-Chinese factions in his own Supreme People's Assembly
and other key government institutions. Between 1955 and 1958, Kim Il-
sung essentially purged all or most members in both the pro-Chinese and
pro-Soviet factions within the Korea Worker's Party and all other aspects
of government and society. By 1958, all Chinese troops had withdrawn from
North Korea and never returned.[6] These events left Kim in complete control of the country, its economy, its government, its society, and its military
forces. The legacy of totalitarianism continues today.

Kim's rise to power reflects the traditional isolationism of Korean society for hundreds of years and its resistance to outside influence.[7] The end
result by 1958 also reflects a Confucionist tradition of absolute loyalty to
an individual leader. North Korea continued to take massive amounts of
aid from both Moscow, which completely subsidized the country until 1990,
and to a lesser extent from Beijing; but neither the USSR nor China had a
significant impact on how the country was (and is) run.[8]

## North Korea's Foreign Policy Goals and Support
## for Terrorism: 1960–1988

North Korea from 1948 until the end of the Cold War could be described
as a nation-state that fell within the Soviet sphere of influence. But the

nation was far more isolated in every way than even other communist states were, including countries like China and Cuba. This isolationism kept the Stalinist government of Kim Il-sung "pure" and allowed him to completely dominate all aspects of government and society in North Korea. This North Korean philosophy, which Pyongyang formally defined as *juche* (self-reliance), not only kept the DPRK an active communist state but also helped the state avoid being dominated by its larger, more powerful sponsors and neighbors, the Soviet Union and China.[9]

Although Kim Il-sung was free to pursue a policy that suited his perceived needs of building a militarily strong North Korea, maintaining a Stalinist-juche government, and eventually unifying the Korean Peninsula, North Korea simply could not afford to focus on these issues without outsiders completely financing the majority of its resources. These included (and still include) the majority of foodstuffs, oil for its industry and cities, and even the maintenance of the nationwide electrical grid. North Korea is 70 percent mountainous and thus has simply not been capable of agrarian self-sufficiency.[10] In addition, it does not have enough coal or oil to sustain its economy and has never been able to afford to buy the necessary fossil fuels to sustain its economy. This circumstance has led to one of the most profound—and most threatening to U.S. policy—aspects of the Cold War, proxy operations.

During the Cold War, both the United States and the Soviet Union engaged in proxy operations that targeted each other but occurred on the soil of other nation-states, were conducted by the other nation-states, and fairly often involved non-state actors, including terrorist groups. Specifically, some nations supported either insurgent groups or terrorist groups. In the case of such countries as Cuba and North Korea, with the financial backing of the Soviet Union, they supported both. Thus, the reason behind these countries' support for terrorism and terrorist groups during the 1960s, 1970s, and 1980s (largely if not completely financed by the Soviet Union) was that it allowed North Korea and Cuba to maintain their sovereignty and independent policy goals while still "paying back" Moscow for massive subsidies that kept their governments afloat.[11]

As an integral part of fitting into the Soviet sphere of influence and "pulling their weight" among Moscow's allies, the North Koreans actively

supported communist and Marxist movements. Key among these opera-
tions was the long-lasting war in Angola, where by 1984 three thousand
North Korean regular troops and a thousand advisers participated. North
Korea also operated training camps in Angola for guerrillas of the African
National Congress and the South West African People's Organization.
Both organizations were trained in terrorist tactics at these camps. But
North Korea ran far more guerrilla and terrorist training camps within its
own borders. Between 1968 and 1988, North Korea built and administered
at least thirty special training camps within its borders that specialized in
terrorist and guerrilla warfare training. Reports at the time indicated that
more than five thousand recruits from some twenty-five nations visited
these camps to take part in various courses lasting anywhere from three to
eighteen months.[12]

Nation-states engaging in terrorist tactics were not the only partici-
pants that the North Koreans hosted at their camps up until the late 1980s.
In fact, Pyongyang welcomed a number of terrorist groups, particularly
from the Middle East. According to national security analyst Barry Rubin,
"Up until the late 1980s, North Korea trained Palestinian terrorists, both
those belonging to the PLO [Palestine Liberation Organization] and from
Syrian and Libyan-backed groups." Rubin continued:

> In Lebanon during the 1970s and in Libya and Syria from the 1980s
> down to the present, North Korean soldiers have also trained terror-
> ists for many groups including the Basque Spanish ETA [Basque
> Homeland and Freedom], Palestinian Abu Nidal organization, Irish
> Republican Army, Italian Red Brigades, Japanese Red Army, Moro
> National Liberation Front in the Philippines, Turkish radicals, and
> others. While many of these links have lapsed, in the 1990s, North
> Korea added Hezbollah and the anti-Turkish Kurdish PKK
> [Kurdistan Workers' Party] group to its roster of clients.[13]

According to French press reports, several key Hezbollah operatives
spent time in North Korea during the 1980s. They included (but were
probably not limited to) Hassan Nasrallah, the secretary-general; security
and intelligence chief Ibrahim Akil; and Mustapha Badreddine, head of

counterespionage operations. The relationship with Hezbollah began not as an outgrowth of North Korea's partnership with the USSR but because of Pyongyang's ties with Iran.[14] During a special press briefing at the U.S. State Department, Ambassador Philip C. Wilcox, the department's coordinator for counterterrorism, stated on April 30, 1996, "In the 1970s and '80s, North Korea had a very serious record of committing very serious acts of international terrorism."[15]

Another specific case that is particularly interesting—and ties North Korea directly to a terrorist group in the Middle East—is North Korea's relationship with the Japanese Red Army (JRA) and the Popular Front for the Liberation of Palestine (PFLP). In the book titled *The Black Book of Communism: Crimes, Terror, Repression*, Stéphane Courtois and Mark Kramer outline the following scenario:

> Created at the end of the 1960s, when student radicalism in Japan was at its height and Maoism was in the air, the JRA quickly made contact with North Korean agents (the Korean community is quite large throughout the Japanese archipelago). The Korean agents passed instructions to their cadres and brought the arms the JRA was lacking, but they were unable to prevent a split in the group in the early 1970s, which resulted in a bloody conflict between the dissenting and orthodox factions. Accordingly, some of the cadres simply defected to North Korea, taking refuge in Pyongyang, where they remain as businessmen and intermediaries with the West. The other faction decided to internationalize its affairs even further, and joined up with Wadi Hadad. As a result of this alliance, three members of the JRA acted on behalf of the PFLP in killing 28 people at Tel Aviv's Lod airport in May 1972.[16]

The evidence chain connecting the North Korean government to the PFLP (and ultimately the JRA as well) was further cemented when the late leader of the terrorist group, Dr. George Habash, visited North Korea during September 1970. On that trip, he was reportedly able to procure both weapons and funding.[17]

The North Koreans supported state and non-state actors during the Cold War for two reasons. First, it confirmed and strengthened North

Korea's position as a solid ally within the Soviet sphere of influence (and was one of the factors that kept the enormous subsidies coming). Second, it was an active element in North Korea's policy at the time (and now) to actively support state and non-state actors that, like Pyongyang, were hostile to the United States and its allies. One cannot forget that North Korea has always regarded the United States as its primary enemy and its main threat to national survival. The PFLP targeted Israel, one of Washington's key allies and its most important ally in the Middle East. Thus, supporting terrorist groups that targeted Israeli citizens and Jews from other nations was an important element in keeping Washington's efforts focused on these terrorist acts and not on North Korea.[18] North Korea continues to follow this policy, as I will describe in the next section.[19]

## North Korea's Current Policy of Support to Terrorism: It's about the Money

During the Cold War, North Korea was able to build significant ties to groups that engaged in terrorist acts. It sponsored both nation-states that actively engaged in or supported terrorism and actual non-state actors. When the Cold War ended, one would have thought that North Korea also would have stopped supporting terrorism as other nation-states, such as Cuba, did. But this was not the case. North Korea discovered, instead, that it could make money by proliferating weapons to non-state actors that engaged in terrorist acts. This effort has been particularly profitable in the Middle East, where North Korea has been able to get around sanctions using some clever tactics, techniques, and procedures (TTP) for getting its arms distributed.

According to a North Korean defector who was formerly in charge of illicit arms deals, North Korean arms dealers frequently have studied at Pyongyang University of Foreign Studies, where they received training and became fluent in English and Chinese. They then dealt with "traders" in other countries. One method that North Korea uses to get around sanctions is to send containers that are one-third or half filled with weapons across the Yalu River to China. "The forwarder who received this cargo enters a port in a third country, where the containers are filled with freight unrelated to weapons and the paperwork is completed," according to the defector. The containers are then "laundered" in Hong Kong, Singapore, or another major port that has heavy traffic. As the defector reports, "The containers are mixed with other cargo in those transit points. They are searched, but not thoroughly." He continues, "Even if customs or other officials roll their sleeves up and search for weapons, how can they possibly find the arms among the mountains of other containers headed to other countries?"[20] It is important to note that this tactic is one of many.

Another method that the DPRK is well known for using is that of reflagging its ships. North Koreans have been documented in the past as changing the flagging on their merchant ships—in other words, changing the North Korean flag on a ship to one from Cambodia, Mongolia, or some other nation—to make it more difficult for international law enforcement or military personnel to board it.[21] The North Koreans are constantly changing their TTP in order to adjust to the complex international law enforcement environment, and the two examples of combining illicit arms with legitimate cargo in ship containers and the re-flagging of ships point to how the North Koreans skirt sanctions, maritime forces of other nations, and law enforcement agencies around the world that are often very wary of shipments tagged as North Korean. Thus far, it appears these procedures have been largely successful.

One of the key non-state actors that North Korea proliferates arms to is Hezbollah. The North Koreans have also provided training to Hezbollah on several occasions over the years. Hezbollah is interesting, because North Korea provides the group with assistance that neither Iran nor Syria could otherwise easily furnish. Pyongyang deals with Hezbollah through Syria, Iran, and sometimes directly, as the evidence shows. The weapons that the North Koreans have been providing for the longest time (and in the highest volume) are components and improved versions of Katyusha and Grad rockets, which are then fired into Israel.[22] An article written by South Korean scholar Moon Chung-in asserts that Mossad has clear evidence Hezbollah was able to hit the outskirts of Tel Aviv with short-range missiles that contained North Korean–supplied components. According to Moon's report, the missile components first went from North Korea to Iran, where the Iranians assembled the missiles and then transported them to Hezbollah via

Syria.[23] Other reports also indicate that arms shipments originating in North Korea ended up in the hands of Hezbollah. The Reform Party in Syria, an opposition group, reported in 2008 that Hezbollah had acquired the chemical weapons agents of mustard and nerve gas from North Korea, with Syria acting as a conduit. These agents can reportedly be weaponized and mounted on Hezbollah's short-range rockets that target Israel.[24]

Iran and North Korea jointly produce the M600 series rockets, which have a 300-kilometer range, and these rockets are supplied to both Syria and Hezbollah.[25] Syria made a major contribution to the Hezbollah cause—thanks to North Korea—by providing the Islamic militant group reverse-engineered Kornet antitank missiles (originally produced by the USSR) that it used against the Israel Defense Forces during the 2006 war. (Syria now provides the equipment in a joint deal with the North Koreans, who have agreed to mass-produce an advanced version of the weapon.)[26] Ballistic missiles are the latest and perhaps the most compelling weaponry provided to Hezbollah thanks to the North Koreans. While Iran appears to finance this effort, the transit point is Syria.[27] Using a missile factory constructed under the supervision of North Korean advisers, the Syrians are now building Scud missiles. The North Koreans reportedly also continue to help with production processes and quality control.[28] According to British press reports, Hezbollah took delivery of two Scud D missiles (thanks again to the North Koreans) with a range of 700-kilometers in 2010.[29]

According to sources in both the American and Israeli press, North Korea supervised the building of underground facilities for Hezbollah in southern Lebanon. Several reports note that all or most of Hezbollah's underground facilities were built primarily under the supervision of North Korean instructors in 2003–2004. The facilities were quite extensive and included dispensaries for the wounded, food stocks, and arms dumps.[30] It seems likely that North Korean assistance to Hezbollah served as a key factor in the challenges that Israeli military forces faced when they conducted combat operations against Hezbollah during the 2006 conflict. Israeli reporter Lenny Ben-David stated in 2007 that "Hizbullah's military bases, armories, bunkers and communications networks were much more extensive than Israel's intelligence services estimated on the eve of the 2006 war." Ben-David also reported that the group's tunnel-building operations were under the control of the Korea Mining Development Trading Corporation, which the United States has officially sanctioned for its activities.[31] The North Korean tunnel experts reportedly traveled to Lebanon incognito, disguised as servants for Iranian diplomats visiting Lebanon.[32] According to Nicholas Blanford, who wrote the book *Warriors of God: Inside Hezbollah's Thirty-Year Struggle against Israel* in 2011, the bunkers were highly effective, not only for hiding arms caches and other important facilities, but also for placing deadly fire on Israeli forces. Blanford gives an important description of the system when he writes, "After the cease-fire, Israeli soldiers deployed onto the hill and discovered an elaborate bunker and artillery firing system sunk into solid rock some 120-feet deep and spread over an area three-quarters of a square mile."[33]

North Korea's support to Hezbollah did not end after the 2006 war. In fact, these operations are likely to continue as long as the DPRK exists as a nation-state because they are highly profitable endeavors for North Korea and put money into the coffers of the elite and the military. One example of its continued support to Hezbollah is the training that it offered in 2007, immediately following Hezbollah's campaign against Israel. Conspiring with the Iranians, Hezbollah reached an agreement with North Korea and sent around a hundred field commanders to attend training courses in North Korea. The first Hezbollah commanders were on the ground in North Korea by February 2007. Reportedly, the DPRK Special Operations Forces trained the Hezbollah operatives in commando tactics, intelligence, and counterespionage operations.[34]

North Korea's ties to Hezbollah began and continue to be in collaboration with yet another organization that the U.S. State Department has identified as an entity supporting terrorism, namely, the Iranian Revolutionary Guard Corps (IRGC).[35] According to a 2008 Congressional Research Service report, the North Koreans collaborated with IRGC operatives (including active duty military generals) on operations supporting Hezbollah that included everything from shipping short-range missiles and artillery to building underground facilities.[36] The IRGC is the primary element that the Iranian government uses in supporting Hezbollah.[37] The corps is also Iran's main facilitator for acquiring military weapons from North Korea, including WMD—both missiles and components of Iran's

HEU program. The motivations for the unusual relationship between North Korea's arms traders and the IRGC are simple. To quote Jonathan Spyer, a senior researcher at the Global Research in International Affairs Center in Israel: "The factors underpinning North Korean support for Iran and its allies are as simple as they are powerful: common enemies and hard cash."[38] Their common enemy, of course, is the United States. Thus, when it comes to the Middle East, North Korea has ties to both a key insurgent group that uses terrorism as a methodology and the Iranian government–sponsored entity in the region that supports it.

North Korea also has had connections to insurgents and terrorist groups in South Asia. According to Professor Rohan Gunaratna, an international terrorism expert testifying before the Sri Lankan "Lessons Learnt and Reconciliation Commission," North Korea helped the Liberation Tigers of Tamil Eelam (LTTE) procure weapons from 1997 until the conflict on Sri Lanka ended. The professor asserts that LTTE auditor and accountant Ponniah Anandarajah was "operating from outside Thailand and almost all the major weapons were procured from North Korea."[39] In 2000, a video of an LTTE attack on a Sri Lankan Navy ship showed the group used speedboats that were built in North Korea and weapons that were North Korean variants of a Chinese version of the 107mm Katyusha rocket launcher.[40] A *Jane's Intelligence Review* article also provided compelling evidence that the LTTE used armaments of North Korean origin: "In the video, LTTE Sea Tigers can be seen using a variant of the 107mm Katyusha rocket, fired from a lightweight tripod, in pairs. This is believed to be a variant of the Chinese Type 63 107mm launcher. The Chinese produce a single tube version called a Type 85 fired from a man-portable tripod, but the North Koreans produce a double version. This is quite a rare weapon. . . ."[41]

The North Koreans also attempted to provide the LTTE with at least one shipment of 152mm and 130mm artillery shells and 120mm mortars during 2007. The Sri Lankan Navy interdicted the shipment and seized an LTTE boat that was equipped with a 14.5mm machine gun that at the time was also found to have come from the North Koreans.[42] The Sri Lankan Navy intercepted North Korean merchant ships carrying arms to the LTTE in the later years of the Sri Lankans' military war against the LTTE on three different occasions: October 2006, February 2007, and March 2007. The navy reported sinking at least two of the North Korean ships during this period. On several occasions the North Korean merchant ships fired on the Sri Lankan Navy ships patrolling waters near the island's coastline; thus, future counterproliferation efforts should note that the North Korean merchant ships were heavily armed. The Congressional Research Service issued a report in 2008 citing Japan's *Sankei Shimbun*, which states the Sri Lankan government had filed an official protest with the DPRK.[43]

According to the 2010 WikiLeaks releases, which gained much attention in the international press, North Korea also made illicit arms deals with another group active in South Asia, Al Qaeda. The reports released to the press state that Osama bin Laden's financial adviser, "Dr. Amin," and Afghan warlord Gulbuddin Hekmatyar flew to North Korea from Iran on November 19, 2005. The purpose of their visit was to cut a deal to acquire surface-to-air missiles (perhaps shoulder fired). The shipment was to have been sent in 2006. No further details from these reports—nor any other evidence regarding their validity—have surfaced. In fact, to date, no government officials have either officially or unofficially confirmed the reports. But if true, they only add more support to previously confirmed accounts: North Korea will sell anything to anybody who is willing to pay.[44]

Speaking of money, it appears to be the link between North Korea and yet another non-state actor well known for waging acts of terrorism, namely, the Irish Republican Army (IRA). A U.S. court indicted former IRA chief of staff and former Workers' Party president Sean Garland in 2008, but in 2011 an Irish court in Dublin refused an extradition request from American authorities. The judge in the case turned down the request because under Irish law Garland's alleged offenses were considered to have been committed in Ireland. According to the indictment filed by the United States, Garland and several other suspects conspired to distribute millions of counterfeit American hundred-dollar bills. The U.S. Secret Service traced these counterfeit bills to a government-run printing factory in North Korea. The phony currency began turning up in Ireland during the 1990s and at the time led Irish banks to halt exchanging hundred-dollar bills. Reportedly, Garland had traveled to Moscow during the late 1990s. While he was in Russia, surveillance revealed that a sedan with plates registered to North Korea picked him up and then him hustled off to the North Korean

Embassy in Moscow, where he and his wife are said to have had a two-hour visit. He was arrested in Belfast in 2005, after which he fled to the Irish Republic, where he faced indictment by the United States.[45] This episode, of course, is still more evidence that North Korea will sell anything to anybody who pays, even counterfeit currency to a non-state actor like the IRA. North Korea's now infamous counterfeit American hundred-dollar bills are said to be so well made that the Secret Service calls them super notes.[46]

## Containing North Korea's Support for Terrorism: Are Current Methods Effective?

The United States has approached the issue of North Korea's support for terrorism, which in the post–Cold War era is largely through proliferation, using two key methods—the Proliferation Security Initiative and economic sanctions. The Bill Clinton administration had relaxed some sanctions against North Korea by the end of its term, while the succeeding Bush administration chose to initiate more sanctions in its second term largely owing to North Korea's nuclear program.[47] The Obama administration initiated numerous other sanctions following North Korea's rogue state behavior in 2009 and 2010.[48] The other U.S. approach to North Korean proliferation is to initiate and maintain PSI. This effort involves nearly a hundred member states using primarily maritime means but also aircraft to interdict shipments of WMD or other weapons that are proliferated illegally.[49]

The United States initiated PSI in 2003 largely as a result of North Korea's aggressive proliferation to rogue states and non-state actors, but it is also aimed at other states that engaged in similar behavior.[50] As PSI has grown in acceptance with other nation-states, the level of cooperation has increased. Several nations that one would not typically think of as working with the United States to counter proliferation have extended their cooperation. In 2009, the United Arab Emirates confiscated a shipment originating in North Korea that reportedly contained components and detonators for 122mm rockets. Israeli officials have since stated that the shipment was intended for Hezbollah.[51] Another large shipment—this time on a Russian-made cargo plane bound for Iran—was interdicted when it stopped in Thailand. The aircraft had on board more than thirty-five tons of military equipment, including rockets and rocket-propelled grenades. Officials believe the shipment was also bound for Hezbollah through Iran.[52] The same year, Greece confiscated the North Korean cargo of a French-owned and German-flagged ship carrying chemical weapons suits to Syria, some of which may have also been bound for Hezbollah.[53] In 2011, forces for the North Atlantic Treaty Organization intercepted a ship carrying a North Korean cargo of fifteen tons of rockets, surface-to-air missiles, and explosives to Eritrea. The United Nations has Eritrea under an arms embargo because of allegations that its government is involved in training and supplying weapons to Al Qaeda and has connections with Somali Islamic rebels.[54] While the examples previously stated are important (and are only a few of many examples), it is also important to consider that because of the skill the North Korean traders use, evidence indicates that the vast majority of shipments continue to get through. Nevertheless, the pressure put on North Korea makes it more difficult to conduct illicit proliferation activities.

As discussed earlier, during both the Clinton and Bush administrations, the United States had imposed at various levels economic sanctions on North Korea that included measures taken by both economic and military entities. But after North Korea's nuclear and ballistic missile tests of 2009, the United Nations Security Council initiated Resolution 1874 and adopted it on June 12, 2009. This resolution not only extended the arms embargo on North Korea but also allowed member states to inspect North Korean vessels or any vessel carrying North Korean illicit cargo on land, sea, and air. UNSC Resolution 1874 led nation-states around the globe to carry out sanctions that, at least in the short term, may have forced a change in the TTP for North Korea's proliferation system.[55]

Following North Korea's violent attack on the ROK Navy corvette *Cheonan* in 2010, the United States looked to impose still more detailed sanctions on North Korea. Washington publicly identified two hundred known North Korea–linked bank accounts, and analysts at the time assessed about a hundred of them would be targeted. Banking officials in important places where North Korea has traditionally hidden its accounts, such as Luxembourg, Switzerland, and Hong Kong, agreed to help the United States in tracking down the accounts.[56] In early August 2010, Washington reported that President Obama intended to initiate an executive order expanding the sanctions on North Korea. Robert Einhorn of the State Department announced at a press conference that "the United States will soon adopt and begin implementing new country-specific measures . . . that will target entities engaged in the export or procurement of conventional arms by or for North Korea, the procurement of luxury goods for North Korea, and other illicit activities, which are often conducted by or for North Korean officials."[57] Also during August 2010, a UNSC report surfaced that revealed seventeen key North Korean officials who had violated UNSC Resolution 1874 and earlier resolutions. Among the individuals were Chang Sung-taek, Gen. O Kuk-ryol, Kim Young-chun, Chu Kyu-chang, and Hyun Cheol-hae. All of these people held very high positions in the North Korean government, were quite close to Kim Jong-il, and were considered mentors or key advisers to his son Kim Chong-un.[58]

On August 30, 2010, President Obama signed Executive Order 13551, which "expanded the scope of the national emergency declared in Executive Order 13466 to deal with the unusual and extraordinary threat to the national security, foreign policy, and economy of the United States posed by the continued actions and policies of the Government of North Korea."[59] As predicted and announced days before, these sanctions against North Korea froze assets of individuals, organizations, and companies (many of them "front companies") linked to North Korea's proliferation efforts and its nuclear programs. They also took aim at two key institutions in North Korea that enable and engage in proliferation—Office Number 39, which handles the money and "makes the deals," and the Reconnaissance Bureau, which often engages in the illicit distribution.[60]

On April 18, 2011, President Obama issued another executive order that augmented the previous executive orders issued by both the Obama and Bush administrations. To quote the president, in part, "On April 18, 2011, I signed Executive Order 13570 to take additional steps to address the national emergency declared in Executive Order 13466, and expanded in Executive Order 13551, to ensure the implementation of the import restrictions contained in United Nations Security Council Resolutions 1718 and 1874 and complement the import restrictions provided for in the Arms Export Control Act."[61] Executive Order 13570 imposed sanctions on fifteen more firms, including both North Korean firms and those who traded with them.[62] By September 2011, a total of twenty-seven North Korean entities—banks, front companies, and so on—and five individuals had been successfully targeted. Among the key entities listed were the Korea Taesong Trading Company (and bank) and the Bank of East Land, and some of the key individuals were Kim Tong-myong, reportedly the caretaker of the Kim family's secret funds overseas, and Kim Yong-chol, director of the Reconnaissance General Bureau.[63] While these targeted sanctions have been robust and detailed, the difficulties rise with North Korea's continued skill at moving money from front company to front company and shutting down one firm only to open another.

According to defectors and press sources, the offspring of North Korea's most senior leaders hold much of the real power in North Korea's international proliferation network, including those operations with non-state actors.[64] This observation makes sense, because as the privileged members of the regime, they would be considered the most trustworthy delegates to engage in international activity that would bring money into Pyongyang's coffers. While using an often-changing array of front companies and banks, Office Number 39 leads and conducts overseas operations and answers directly to the highest leadership in Pyongyang. Beginning in 2010, a high school classmate of Kim Jong-il's, Jon Il-chun, ran this organization.[65] A spin-off of Office Number 39 is Office Number 38. Headed by Kim Tong-un, this office reportedly focuses specifically on the slush fund that supports Pyongyang's elite. Thus, it is no wonder that both entities and their associated key, trusted individuals who report to the top brass in Pyongyang and control both the money and the proliferation operations are the targets of American sanctions.

According to press reports attributed to unnamed South Korean government officials, by December 2010 North Korea was experiencing problems in using at least some of its accounts overseas (individuals who were blacklisted in the American sanctions were probably part of this group).[66] How much this effort slowed down proliferation to state and non-state actors is not clear, but North Korea, often through Office Number 39, has in the past been able to adjust quickly. Based on anecdotal evidence, the sanctions that the international community has imposed on North Korea and the actions that member states of the U.S.-led PSI have taken at least have created difficulties for the DPRK. How much difficulty—or how much cash has been lost—is impossible to estimate. What is certain is that North Korea's proliferation networks are constantly adjusting, evolving, and re-inventing themselves in order to survive and provide money for the Kim family, the elite, and the military. Thus, international sanctions and actions taken under PSI must also continue to evolve and adjust accordingly.

## Conclusions

North Korea has shown throughout its history that it is intent on engaging in rogue behavior and providing support for terrorism. The reasons for this behavior are twofold. First, the North Korean leadership both fears and resents the governments of the United States and its allies. Pyongyang perceives the proliferation of training, weapons, and technology to non-state actors that engage in terrorist acts against America's allies in the Middle East, particularly Israel, as an effective way of ratcheting up contentious issues for Washington. Second, economics has played an important role in Pyongyang's motivations for supporting terrorism, largely because North Korea's stability originally depended on subsidies from the Soviet Union and because support for terrorism now provides some of the badly needed hard currency for Pyongyang's elite.

Given the large amount of available evidence, one wonders why the United States (at least as of this writing) has not restored North Korea to its State Department list of state sponsors of terrorism.[67] This inaction appears to be based on politics, not on definitive evidence. If and when Washington decides to relist North Korea as a state sponsor of terrorism, the proof will certainly silence any naysayers. But whether or not Washington takes this important symbolic action, which some analysts feel should have been done several years ago, containing and combating North Korea's support for terrorism will continue to be a foreign policy dilemma for the United States as long as the current regime is in place.

# 6

## CONCLUSION

*The Impact of the Last Years of the Kim Jong-il Regime on the Future of North Korea*

---

The premise of this book is that the final days of Kim Jong-il had a profound impact on what was to come later. Ultimately, Kim Jong-il apparently did not feel compelled to begin a succession process in any kind of focused way until after he had suffered a stroke in 2008.[1] The reasons for this are still quite puzzling. In Confucian societies, the oldest son is the traditional heir, yet both the first and second sons proved not to be "up to the task," at least in the eyes of Kim Jong-il and the North Korean elite.[2] Kim Jong-il's father had started the succession process for him in 1974, or twenty years before he actually assumed power.[3] Perhaps because Kim Jong-il's two older sons were considered unfit, the succession process with the third son, Kim Chong-un, was only rushed into motion after— and likely because of—Kim Jong-il's stroke (probably beginning early in 2009).[4] The rushed succession process, Kim Jong-il's bad health, and the unstable security situation on the Korean Peninsula (based on a variety of factors) led to many actions—some of which were already under way but pursued with increased intensity from 2008 forward—that would continue to affect the DPRK's key institutions and its primary foreign policy goals.

North Korea is a country and a system that have been in existence since the end of World War II. While the means for the regime to survive and to maintain a credible threat to its neighbor to the south largely changed after the end of the Cold War, the institutions and basic philosophy for leading the country did not.[5] Thus, it is important to analyze and assess the key factors involving North Korea's actions at the end of the Kim Jong-il era that affected the North Korean government, its military, and its foreign policy once he was gone. This analysis will provide the capability to make realistic predictions regarding the status of the regime, which (at least for now) continues to function and maintains the status quo of distrust and fear on the Korean Peninsula; its foreign policy of providing support to fellow rogue states and non-state actors engaging in terrorism, which poses a threat to the United States and its allies; and its nuclear program, which Pyongyang shows no transparent signs of dismantling. Thus, I will make some final assessments regarding the issues highlighted throughout this book. As we look to a regime that is now on its third leader in what can only be called a dynastic government, the evidence that has mounted since Kim Jong-il's stroke in the summer of 2008 (and other illnesses) has proven to be important. Indeed, immediately following the death of the Dear Leader, a poll conducted in the United States showed that 77 percent of the respondents believed North Korea remained a threat to America.[6]

Because North Korea's military is not only a threat to the region but also a major power-brokering institution in the country, I will evaluate its importance and what its capabilities mean for the future of the DPRK. In addition, based on the evidence of what occurred in the Northern Limit Line during 2010—and the tensions that remain—I will assess the strategy that precedent shows North Korea is likely to use in the NLL as we enter the new Kim Chong-un era. For a variety of reasons, North Korea's nuclear program remains perhaps the most compelling threat in the eyes of most in the international community; thus, I will consider the actions that the regime is likely to take in this area in both the near and long term. I will also address why the DPRK will be unwilling to abandon or even decrease its support for non-state actors that engage in terrorism and for the rogue states that support them.

While on the surface North Korea has been diplomatically isolated since the final years of the Kim Jong-il regime, in fact Pyongyang has often engaged in successful statecraft methods and domestic policies and is likely to continue them. I will examine how its processes are apt to evolve based on evidence from the recent past. This chapter also addresses how a country that does not even allow open Internet access or cell phone usage for the majority of its citizens can effectively use information as a tool to advance its national interests in an era when the leadership of the country exists in a potentially very unstable environment. Finally, before moving on to final thoughts, I will evaluate how Kim Jong-il laid a baseline for his successor and the system that he left behind. In what ways could this system be adjusted for the new leadership?

## North Korea's Military: Why Is It Still Important?

I have devoted an entire chapter of this book to North Korea's military (and its relationship to Kim Chong-un)—and with good reason. North Korea has one of the largest conventional militaries in the world.[7] Indeed, the North Korean military also plays a major role in policymaking and the brokering of power in the DPRK.[8] It is because of these reasons—both internal power and the external threat posed to the region—that the North Korean military will remain a formidable threat and primary international security concern as long as the regime in Pyongyang remains in power. There is a great deal of debate about the intentions of North Korea's military. In fact, there are those (more than a few) who have stated that the North Korean military is purely a defensive force—used to deter the United States and South Korea from invading (reflected in this analysis as perhaps paranoia by the regime in Pyongyang).[9] The fact remains however, that North Korea has a huge military and has continued to evolve it in order to maintain a capability to inflict catastrophic damage to the south. Thus, it is important to consider what in my view is an appropriate definition of a "military threat": capability + intent = threat.[10] Since chapter 2 outlined and analyzed the capabilities of the North Korean military, it is important to discuss the intent that the power brokers in Pyongyang have for this very large, very potent, asymmetrically equipped force.

According to a study published in 2012 by Kongdan Oh and Ralph Hassig,

> The role of DPRK forces would be to open a front inside South Korea, bypassing the conventional defense lines. Taking these forces into consideration, it becomes even more difficult to predict the short-term outcome of battle, although in the long term, South Korean-U.S.

forces would almost surely prevail because special forces can disrupt but not defeat the South Korean forces. Even if they expect that their forces will be bested by South Korean forces, the North Korean generals may believe they hold a short-term advantage if they use their special forces to strike quickly and then negotiate for a cease-fire before being hit by the superior South Korean-U.S. conventional forces.

Oh and Hassig also correctly assert that South Korea has far more high-value targets than the north does; thus, the potential wartime situation is exacerbated. Perhaps as important, they point to a significant difference in the decision-making capability between North and South Korea:

> The two Koreas have different approaches to *military decisionmaking*. In the South, the civilian leadership would make the final decisions about warfighting (in conjunction with decisions by American civilian and military authorities). In North Korea, the top members of the Kim regime would make the initial decisions without being held accountable to anyone. However, after the first days of the war, by which time the North's communications links might be cut, combat would probably be directed by low-level military officers, who would be unlikely to take a strategic view of war or be concerned about North Korea's international reputation.[11]

Thus, in discussing the threat, clearly the leadership in Pyongyang remains intent on building and planning for an offensive threat to its South Korean neighbor.

Most analysts agree that North Korea probably could not defeat a combined U.S.–South Korean military force in a military conflict.[12] But, as Oh and Hassig point out, the problem is that the North Korean military actually does have a chance of advancing as far as Seoul (or perhaps even beyond) and then of attempting to broker a deal with Seoul, all before sufficient American reinforcements could arrive on the peninsula. Is this scenario realistic? Perhaps not, but the issue is whether the North Korean leadership actually believes it is or not. Indications are that they do. In 2010, South

Korean military officials revealed to the press that North Korea had revised its war plans in response to upgraded ROK and U.S. weapons systems, and during an invasion, the DPRK expects to focus on taking the Seoul metropolitan area and then to negotiate a cease-fire.[13] This strategy points to the necessity of sustaining a strong U.S.-ROK military alliance, because as long as it endures, the alliance will be able to deter even an unstable North Korean government, which probably believes it can defeat a South Korean force that does not have swift U.S. support. In the short term, this means that as long as the North Korean regime in its present form survives, the DPRK is likely to maintain an asymmetrically equipped, offensive-minded military. It also means that eventually more provocations along the lines of those described in chapter 3 are not only possible but also likely to occur.

## The North Korean Northern Limit Line Strategy: Why Pyongyang Uses It

The primary goal of the North Korean leadership—both before Kim Jong-il's death and afterward—is regime survival.[14] But one must look further to understand North Korea's other motivations for the actions it takes on the international and regional stage. In addition to regime survival, Pyongyang also has the eventual goal of unifying or dominating the Korean Peninsula.[15] Because the U.S.-ROK military alliance has deterred large-scale aggression from North Korea since 1953, the leadership in Pyongyang has had to find a way to incite fear, to create tension, and to attempt to undermine the government in South Korea—and this helps to bring North Korea closer to the goal of dominating the Korean Peninsula. From the end of the Korean War until the end of the 1980s, the method North Korea often used was to conduct acts of terrorism against the South.[16] But in recent years, North Korea has chosen to carry out small-scale acts of violent aggression against its neighbor to the south in the disputed NLL area.

If one examines the provocations that North Korea has executed in the NLL since 1999, one rather easily questions its motives behind the numerous violent actions. As analyzed in chapter 3, North Korea's provocations in the NLL during 2010 seem to show a remarkable brazenness to either escalation because of reactions by the South Koreans or because of expected international reactions. In fact, the North Koreans correctly judged that the Chinese would rationalize Pyongyang's actions and call for "restraint on all sides."[17] But still the ultimate question of why North Korea would conduct such violent acts that that the government knew would set back North-South relations, put multilateral talks on hold with regional powers about their nuclear program, and further isolate the regime from the international community remains unanswered.

The answer is actually rather simple. The government and the military in North Korea have found that the NLL is the perfect area to conduct asymmetric warfare. Because of the relative vulnerability of the area's five ROK-controlled islands—each with a sizable civilian population—the North Korean People's Army can attack naval craft patrolling the area or targets on the islands. Further, the North Koreans have cleverly conducted deceptive and hidden operations, which they did with the submarine attack on the *Cheonan*, and have shown an ability to mass key forces in order to launch attacks that involve both overwhelming weapons systems and surprise, as they did with the attack on Yeonpyeong Island. This also gives the North Koreans the opportunity to do exactly what I discussed earlier—to incite fear, create tension, and attempt to undermine the government in South Korea—thus, moving the government in Pyongyang steps closer to its goal to dominate the geopolitical environment on the Korean Peninsula. In judging how effectual North Korea was in inciting fear and creating tension in South Korea, my assessment would be that Pyongyang was quite successful. Meanwhile, the conservative government of Lee Myung-bak also planned for future provocations, and the South Korean populace decried China's failure to condemn the NLL provocations in 2010.[18] Nevertheless, North Korea succeeded in gaining attention for its military's prowess on the regional stage and, once again, in causing confusion, finger pointing, and a sense of emergency among the South Korean populace, military, and government officials.[19]

The timing of the violent military attacks in the NLL area also may have been directly related to the succession process. As Jin-ha Kim of the Korean Institute for National Unification states, the attacks "may have been planned to consolidate the power elites of the military-first ruling coalition and to lay a foundation for Kim's succession by empowering relatively young hardliners of Kim Jong-un's guardian cadres."[20] Because provocations in the NLL are part of North Korea's asymmetric strategy to intimidate its neighbor to the south and because the succession process in North Korea remains at the top of Pyongyang's agenda, future attacks are not only possible but also likely. How these attacks will be conducted, what types of forces will conduct them, and the possible escalation effects from the attacks are all factors that are unknown. But the North Koreans have proven that they can be successful at carrying out these military operations, and thus are likely to continue them unless and until South Korea is able to conduct deterrence that is effective.

## North Korea's Nuclear Program: A Change with New Leadership?

There have been the questions one would expect from those who are interested in international security issues, about the possibility of changes to North Korea's nuclear weaponization policy following the death of Kim Jong-il and the rise of his third son to power.[21] Under Kim Jong-il, North Korea engaged in a policy of nuclear weaponization, proliferated key technology to other rogue nation-states, and used Pyongyang's nuclear weapons programs as a diplomatic tool to gain concessions from the DPRK's neighbor to the south and other nations with interests in the region, particularly the United States.[22] Thus, with the succession from father to son being forced into place following the death of the "Dear Leader" at the end of 2011, the question regarding any changes to a policy that allowed North Korea to not only build nuclear weapons, but also to proliferate the technology, is a legitimate one to ask.

From the actions that the North Korean regime took during the Kim Jong-il era, the leadership obviously was willing to face international isolation in order to build and maintain a nuclear weapons capability. But this international isolation also put pressure on the regime and will do the same for Pyongyang's new leadership. As a team of scholars at the East Asia Institute in South Korea wrote, "So long as Kim Jong-un sticks to 'rule by his deceased father's will,' then North Korea will face the inevitable dilemma it has faced for the last seventeen years. Pursuing regime security by huddling onto nuclear weapons will only continue to ensure Pyongyang's international isolation. This isolation in turn brings about economic hardship, which consequently has a negative effect on the stability of the Kim Jong-un regime as its legitimacy is still rather weak."[23] Thus, continued isolation could have a negative impact on the stability of a ruler who already rules under extremely tenuous conditions. But as Korean analyst John Feffer points out,

> The North Korean system, more so than Western political systems or even rigidly hierarchical systems like China, enforces institutional roles for its public figures. It does not matter if Kim Jong-un took a fancy to Swiss fondue, Western sports idols, or democratic processes. He will not have the political opportunity to shape North Korean institutions to his individual predilections. He is bound by the conventions established by his grandfather Kim Il-sung and maintained by his father Kim Jong-il. He must operate within a narrow ideological space circumscribed by the nationalism that has replaced communism as the touchstone of governance.[24]

Thus, in order to remain in power, the new regime in Pyongyang will need to maintain the policies of the previous leadership, including a nuclear weapons capability (though, as the Kim Jong-il regime did, the current regime may use rhetoric to the contrary).

This point leads to another question: what are the chances that North Korea will actually use a nuclear weapon? Because the North Koreans have seen the well-publicized announcements that South Korea is now under the American nuclear umbrella, Pyongyang likely would only use a nuclear weapon against the United States or one of its key allies if the situation is desperate and if it sees no other alternative.[25] The government of Kim Jong-il surely understood (as the new government does ) that a nuclear attack on the United States or one of its allies would mean an all-out war—a war that would end in the ultimate destruction of North Korea as a nation-state.[26] While the government in North Korea (which in my estimate is a rational state actor) is therefore expected only to use a nuclear weapon as a last-ditch, desperate measure, they still proliferate nuclear weaponization technology to nation-states that would bring harm to America's allies. As noted in chapter 4, North Korea's proliferation of a plutonium nuclear reactor to Syria is now well known.[27] Pyongyang has actively disseminated technology, advice, and raw materials to the Iranians' HEU program as well.[28] Because the primary motivation behind North Korea's nuclear proliferation is money—not ideology—and because the regime's isolation is inclined to make incoming funds an ongoing issue, this highly dangerous proliferation policy is probably going to continue under the new regime. As U.S. director of National Intelligence James Clapper stated in Senate testimony on January 31, 2012, "We don't expect Kim Jung-un, North Korea's new young leader, to change Pyongyang's policy of attempting to export most of its weapon systems."[29]

## North Korea's Support for Terrorism: How Likely Will It Continue?

I devoted chapter 5 of this work entirely to North Korea's involvement in terrorist activities. Understanding how this process has evolved is important. North Korea began its campaign by conducting acts of terror against South Korea in the 1950s and 1960s.[30] This effort evolved into extending support for third world insurgent and terrorist groups in the 1970s and 1980s. To quote a study by the Library of Congress,

> By 1990 North Korea had provided military training to groups in sixty-two countries—twenty-five in Africa, nineteen in Central and South America, nine in Asia, seven in the Middle East, and two in Europe. A cumulative total of more than 5,000 foreign personnel have been trained in North Korea, and over 7,000 military advisers, primarily from the Reconnaissance Bureau, have been dispatched to some forty-seven countries. As of mid-1993, military advisers from North Korea were in approximately twelve African countries.[31]

Of course, the Soviets subsidized all of these operations until 1990, and North Korea served as a willing proxy for implementing the USSR's foreign policy until that year.[32]

Following the end of the Cold War and Kim Il-sung's death, North Korea continued its support for terrorist groups. But this time it had nothing to do with being a proxy state of the Soviet Union or with communist ideology. Instead, it became a cash-and-carry effort. Since the end of the Cold War, North Korea has shown that it is willing and able to support any non-state actor that chooses to engage in terrorism—that is, as long as it can pay. For example, until Sri Lankan military forces defeated them, the Tamil Tigers received financial support from many ethnic Tamils around the world.[33] Of course, much of the funds funneled to the rebel group ended up in the North Koreans' coffers because the North Koreans provided various arms for several years to the Tamil Tigers and undoubtedly profited from the endeavor. But I would assess that the North Koreans' most profitable endeavor with non-state actors that engage in terrorism likely has been their long-standing relationship with Hezbollah. While the group does not benefit from a diaspora around the world in the way the Tamil Tigers did, Hezbollah does have two important benefactors—Iran and Syria.[34] Thus, North Korea has been able to provide support to Hezbollah—primarily arms shipments and military training—with funds provided by Syria and Iran.

North Korea has also supported other groups that engage in terrorist activities (largely through governments who sponsor them), though any shipments to these groups are probably smaller and less frequent. It is a safe bet that if a country supports terrorist groups—for example, Eritrea—and is on a UN or other embargo list, that country will have to turn to arms producers who will sell anything to anybody. North Korea fits the bill perfectly. North Korea actually has been caught attempting to export arms to Eritrea, and assessments indicate that much of this shipment was bound for the terrorist group al-Shabaab.[35] Given that few of the shipments that North Korea makes are successfully interdicted, in all probability many of Pyongyang's shipments to Eritrea have actually made it through and the arms have been provided to al-Shabaab.

Pyongyang is an isolated state that is desperate for hard currency to provide for the elite and the military and lacks many natural resources to keep the country running. In fact, Kim Jong-il himself stepped up his country's efforts to support non-state actors that engage in terrorism because he likely saw them as an important way to raise funds for his regime. Now that he has died, if his son wishes to stay in power, keep the elite happy, and continue to build a slush fund overseas that benefits the Kim family's coffers, he will need to continue this relationship with non-state actors and the rogue nations that support them. Thus, these activities—actions that disrupt stability in both the Middle East and Africa—are likely to continue as long as the regime in the DPRK exists.

## Did Kim Jong-il Lay the Proper Baseline for Successful Succession?

As addressed earlier, Kim Jong-il's late start to the succession process remains quite puzzling. Perhaps he waited because of the obvious faults attributed to his two older sons. Perhaps he was reluctant to give up any of his power to his eventual heir (though his father had done so in detail for him). The fact remains, however, that the system Kim Il-sung had set up and that Kim Jong-il perpetuated was in place for Kim Chong-un when his father died. Nevertheless, specific tasks still needed to be done and institutional adjustments needed to be made.

A variety of issues can contribute to instability in North Korea, but they are largely institutional, exacerbated by corruption, and complicated by the lack of legitimacy for a young leader who is the third son in line for the Kim family dynasty.[36] One issue that the new leadership will not likely encounter is a popular revolt because the elaborate and detailed security system that Kim Jong-il maintained while he was in power now exists for his son. As David S. Maxwell, the associate director of the Center for Peace and Security Studies at Georgetown University, states,

> Kim Il-sung established a security and control system that would have made Joseph Stalin blush. From the "rule of threes" (anyone found to be disloyal in word or deed will have three generations "expunged"— at best all three generations go to the gulag and at worst all three are totally expunged, as in execution) to the establishment of a personal loyalty system—i.e., you get promoted or get ahead or are simply allowed to exist by demonstrating personal loyalty to the regime and

not by merit—means that there is a system of control that is totally focused on protecting the regime from rebellion.[37]

This security system, which Kim Il-sung put into place and Kim Jong-il ruthlessly and efficiently maintained, is likely to ensure that a popular rebellion will not occur.

Another way that Kim Jong-il took steps to guarantee the dynastic succession process would proceed smoothly was by handing out promotions to the children of high-ranking power brokers in the party, the military, and the security services. Thus, he placed a new and younger generation in positions to support Kim Chong-un. For example, International Secretary Kim Young-il is the son-in-law of Jeon Moon Seob (former State Inspection Committee chairman), and General Affairs Secretary Tae Jong-su is the son-in-law of former deputy prime minister Jeong Il-ryong. Oh Il-jung, the vice director of the Workers' Party, is the son of the late general O Chin-u, a longtime confidant of both Kim Il-sung and Kim Jong-il. Choi Yong-hae, recently promoted to the Central Military Commission, is the son of former high-ranking general Choi Hyun. The head of the Chosun Central Bank, Baek Yong-chun, is the son of former foreign minister Baek Nam-sun. And in an important move, Trade Minister Lee Yong-nam is the nephew of Lee Myung-soo, a power broker who runs one of North Korea's key security services.[38] These changes to the institutional leadership were made to support Kim Chong-un and point to the dynastic nature of the regime—not only for the top leader but also for all those in the elite who hold powerful positions beneath him. By promoting members of the younger generation to key positions, Kim Jong-il was attempting to surround his son with peers who would be loyal along with a small cadre of older people who could mentor him and help influence policy. It was done much the same way when Kim Il-sung was preparing his son's place in the regime but on a much longer timeline.

Because Kim Chong-un is so young and because the succession process was rushed following his father's stroke, he almost undoubtedly did not hold the same power in the beginning of 2012 that his father had when he assumed the leadership role in 1994. While the process ensured that Kim Chong-un had a power base in the key institutions and a group of individuals in the key institutions that had loyalty to him, the simple fact is that he did not have a great deal of time to build these important relationships for holding power in North Korea. Thus, as 2012 began, in reality, the primary institutions in the country (the military, security services, the party, and the inner family elite) were largely being run by power brokers who did exactly what Kim Chong-un told them to do, and what he told them to do was exactly what they told him he should tell them to do. While for appearance's sake in 2012 he was the new ruler of the country, in reality, he was likely being guided by a small cadre of individuals who themselves had power bases (each of them) in one of the key institutions—yet none of these individuals had power (real power) over more than one institution. This completely unique situation in North Korea has never happened before in its history. Kim Chong-un's oldest brother, Kim Chong-nam (now apparently in self-exile), commented on this very tenuous process: "I expect the existing ruling elite to follow in the footsteps of my father while keeping the young successor as a symbolic figure. . . . It's difficult to accept a third-generation succession with normal reasoning." Kim Chong-nam also said that he had doubts that Kim Chong-un "with some two years of training can retain the absolute power."[39]

As Kim Chong-un assumed power, he needed to resolve two key issues—consolidating his base, and his real power, in all of the country's institutions (as his father and grandfather did), and gaining the knowledge, which takes time, to actually guide these institutions effectively. Meanwhile, a variety of dangers can arise as Kim Chong-un attempts to consolidate his power. As Korea Institute for National Unification scholar Hyeong Jung Park states, "There are four main structural factors which can influence the future trajectories of political succession and North Korean politics: regime survival and hereditary succession; ruler-state relations; ruler-society relations; relations between foreign powers and domestic actors."[40]

The issue of decision making when the decision maker has neither the knowledge nor the background to lead a nation-state also presents a very frightening scenario. While North Korea is and always has been a rational state actor, many of Pyongyang's decisions in the past have seemed unpredictable (which they were intended to be) but often advanced the regime's policy goals. Further, the two previous leaders were both experienced and held absolute power in the country. This situation has changed. A leader who does not have an in-depth understanding of either foreign policy or domestic policy could potentially be misled.

As David S. Maxwell points out,

> The regime is not suicidal at all and everything that it does and will do is focused on protecting its vital national interest. However, as irrational as it may seem to us that could include launching a war (particularly if the regime believes it is threatened and has no other alternative). And what is really dangerous to the region is that by the nature of the system no one is going to tell Kim Jong-un that his military is not capable of winning and the information that he receives from people around him (who have to act like sycophants in order to survive) can make a very irrational decision to us seem very rational to him.[41]

Kim Jong-il did make two "adjustments" to the system during his seventeen-year reign over North Korea. First, because of the horrible famine conditions that existed in the country during the mid- to late 1990s, he opened up markets in several cities and rural areas of North Korea. In these markets, sellers were actually able to make a profit. While some have hailed this development from time to time as a move toward a more open, capitalistic society, the government often shut the markets down if and when it felt they were becoming too much of a nuisance. Moreover, they were and are only allowed to function in North Korea because the leadership in Pyongyang feels it has no choice.[42] The other "adjustment to the system" that was made during the Kim Jong-il era was the building of a mobile phone system, including the complete cell tower infrastructure. The mobile phone system—a compelling modernization measure completed under a contract with Egyptian Orascom Telecom—reportedly had 535,000 phone users by the end of 2011.[43] While this move too may seem designed to "open up" the country, the North Korean leaders likely allowed it because they realized the country's infrastructure simply could not operate without modernizing its phone system. Nevertheless, the North Korea security services closely monitor communications on the network (used almost exclusively by those in the elite) and from time to time even jam signals on a separate set of cell phones that is used by those who do business with China (this is a separate Chinese cell phone system, and the North Koreans have had more trouble controlling it—though its illicit use has grown widely since 2008).[44]

Though Kim Jong-il waited until he was quite ill to start the regime succession process in any kind of focused way, the evidence has shown that during his final years in power, he laid the groundwork for what was to follow after his death. Nevertheless, because Kim Jong-il waited so long to set the actual foundation for a specific successor, his successor now must attempt to operate the government and the infrastructure of the country exactly as he did (or very close to it). Kim Chong-un's failure to do so will likely mean collapse of the DPRK as a nation-state and its probable absorption by the south. Thus, as David S. Maxwell says,

> There will be no change in the behavior of the regime. It is the ultimate catch 22—there are no options for survival except to continue to muddle through by conducting provocations to gain economic and political concessions, make deals that provide near term benefits and then later renege on the deal (and blame the South or United States for the deals being broken). Anything the regime could do to improve its economic system or become a responsible member of the international community will cause regime legitimacy to be undercut and lead to its downfall.[45]

## Conclusions

My assessment is that Kim Jong-il made a number of policy moves during the last years of his rule that will have a profound effect on how North Korea evolves in coming years. A defiant foreign and military policy, a track record of proliferation, and the development of a nuclear weaponization program, among other key issues, point to the conclusion that his plan was for North Korea to continue operating as an aggressive, authoritarian state. There were no indications that his plans included making any concessions or real confidence-building measures with other nation-states in the region that would ease tensions or put the Korean Peninsula on the road to security and stability. Indeed, one of the decisive moves that he made in the final years of his rule was to begin the succession process to his son, Kim Chong-un. But Kim Jong-il's late start and the rushed process made the situation following his death very tenuous. Thus, for those who analyze North Korean affairs and consider the many questions about the solidity of Kim Chong-un's power base and his knowledge to actually rule North Korea, about the DPRK's continuing economic and political instability, and about the legitimacy of Kim Chong-un as a hereditary ruler in North Korea, a logical conclusion would allow at least a fifty-fifty chance that the government could collapse.[46]

A variety of scenarios could occur in North Korea that could lead to collapse. While there are many "branches and sequels" that could occur, three very basic scenarios could ensue. The first is a palace coup in which those who overthrow the current government attempt to sue for peace with the South and perhaps seek reunification. While this may seem unlikely (and probably is), there are those (though closely watched) in the North Korean regime who do not see a long-term means for North Korea as a viable nation-state. The second basic scenario is a complete breakdown of the government. Without a viable leader to control the key institutions (as Kim Il-sung and Kim Jong-il were), there would be a complete breakdown in both the infrastructure and society, and anarchy would ensue. The third basic scenario is even worse. This would involve an overthrow of the regime, but with no one man to lead the government (which is literally the situation that would exist), competing factions would be fighting for control. This scenario would involve civil war and would result in even more of a breakdown in the infrastructure and society of North Korea.[47]

All of these scenarios would almost certainly mean that South Korea would have to intervene. In addition, it is likely (and planned for) that the United States would support Seoul in this effort.[48] In any collapse or stabilization scenario, several key missions will need to be accomplished to address the ensuing problems. Bruce W. Bennett of the Rand Corporation and Jennifer Lind of Dartmouth College list five: "(1) stability operations, including direct humanitarian relief and policing of major cities and roads; (2) border control; (3) elimination of WMD; (4) disarmament of conventional weapons; and (5) deterrence or defeat of any military resistance."[49]

Such daunting operations will be very expensive and likely require hundreds of thousands of troops, the majority of which would likely be South Korean. There is simply no way of getting around the fact that if North Korea collapsed, it would have a profound effect on the region for several years and on the Korean Peninsula for at least a generation.[50]

And what of the Chinese? Clearly Beijing considers the status quo the optimum situation for its national security. The existence of a state—and an ally—that gives China a strategic and operational depth from American forces on the mainland of Asia is likely a goal that has not ceased to exist.[51] Reportedly, in December 2011, Hu Jintao told military officials that they must not let their guard down should armed conflict break out in North Korea. Also accounts at the end of 2011 showed that Chinese troops had been mobilized near the border with North Korea. Chinese officials denied these reports and others that said that they would send troops into North Korea in the event of a crisis. But as one unnamed Chinese military source told the Japanese press, "We will be able to enter Pyongyang in a little more than two hours if necessary."[52] The ambiguous way that China has dealt with the United States and South Korea regarding any future possible collapse scenarios in the DPRK means that planning for these scenarios will always have to include the wild card of the China factor.

It is my assessment that China does not wish to send actual troops into North Korea should collapse (or other catastrophic scenarios) occur. Nevertheless, China will insist on being a key player in any process that involves reunifying the Korean Peninsula under a liberal democratic government in Seoul. The exact concessions that the Chinese will want and the agreements that they will insist be placed into effect remain unclear—at least in unclassified channels.[53] But if and when North Korea collapses, Beijing clearly will be involved. One hopes that talks between the United States, South Korea, and China will occur before any crisis arises and that they will address issues to alleviate any confusion, to allow Korea to once again become a unified nation, and to prevent any clashes between China and the U.S.–South Korea alliance.

Of course, as I stated earlier, in my view, a fifty-fifty chance exists that North Korea will eventually be unable to function as a nation-state under its new leader, and that consequence could lead to one of the several collapse scenarios. If it does not happen, the region and the Korean Peninsula are faced with what I believe is actually the worst scenario: the government will manage to muddle on, the misery will continue for the North Korean people, and the instability on the Korean Peninsula that has prevailed in one form or another since 1953 will persist. In that case, we can expect to see more provocations, greater advances and growth of the nuclear weaponization program, increased proliferation of WMD and other military materials to rogue states and non-state actors, and massive internal purges and suffering that will reach even the elite in North Korea. The South Korea–U.S. military alliance—and the world—needs to remain vigilant because of a North Korea that is both defiant and unstable.

# NOTES

## 1. Introduction

1. For an example of analysis that reflects criticism of Washington's recent North Korea policy, see Gregory J. Moore, "America's Failed North Korea Nuclear Policy: A New Approach," *Asian Perspective* 32, no. 4 (2008), http://www.asianperspective.org/articles/v32n4-b.pdf.

2. For an example of analysis that reflects a pro-engagement policy and that addresses North Korea's economic woes, see Esther Pan, "North Korea's Capitalist Experiment," Council on Foreign Relations, Backgrounder, June 8, 2006, http://www.cfr.org/publication/10858/.

3. For an important analysis that "compares and contrasts" the policy of several American presidents regarding North Korean, see Cheon Seongwhun, "Changing Dynamics of U.S. Extended Nuclear Deterrence on the Korean Peninsula," Special Report (Berkeley, CA: Nautilus Institute for Security and Sustainability, November 10, 2010), http://www.nautilus.org/publications/essays/napsnet/reports/changing-dynamics-of-u.s.-extended-nuclear-deterrence-on-the-korean-peninsula.

4. For details on the challenges of the North Korean succession process and what it means for Pyongyang's survival, see Scott A. Snyder, "Kim's Survivability Scorecard," *The Diplomat*, December 28, 2011, http://the-diplomat.com/2011/12/28/kims-survivability-scorecard/.

5. For examples of works that address North Korea's nuclear programs and the challenges they present to American policy, see Victor D. Cha and David C. Kang, *Nuclear North Korea: A Debate on Engagement Strategies* (New York: Columbia University Press, 2003); Gordon C. Chang, *Nuclear Showdown: North Korea Takes on the World* (New York: Random House, 2006); Michael O'Hanlon and Mike Mochizuki, *Crisis on the Korean Peninsula: How to Deal with a Nuclear North Korea* (Washington, DC: Brookings Institution Press, 2003); and James M. Minnich, *The Denuclearization of North Korea: The Agreed Framework and Alternative Options Analyzed* (Milton Keynes, UK: Lightning Source, 2003). For excellent examples of works that give insight into North Korean internal politics, see Young Whan Kihl and Hong Nack Kim, eds., *North Korea: The Politics of*

*Regime Survival* (Armonk, NY: M. E. Sharp, 2006); and Sung-chol Choi, ed., *Understanding Human Rights in North Korea* (Seoul, Korea: Center for the Advancement of North Korean Human Rights, 1997). Examples of works that address North Korean foreign policy include: Tae-hwan Kwak and Seung-ho Joo, eds., *The United States and the Korean Peninsula in the 21st Century* (Aldershot Hampshire, UK: Ashgate, 2006); Chuck Downs, *Over the Line: North Korea's Negotiating Strategy* (Washington, DC: AEI Press, 1999); and Ted Galen Carpenter and Doug Bandow, *The Korean Conundrum: America's Troubled Relationship with North and South Korea* (New York: Palgrave MacMillan, 2004). Works that include studies of North Korea's unique economic challenges include Robert Daniel Wallace, *Sustaining the Regime: North Korea's Quest for Financial Support* (Lanham, MD: University Press of America, 2007); and Nicholas Eberstadt, *The North Korean Economy: Between Crisis and Catastrophe* (New Brunswick, NJ: Transaction Publishers, 2009). Works that contain studies addressing the ROK-U.S. alliance include: David I. Steinberg, ed., *Korean Attitudes toward the United States: Changing Dynamics* (Armonk, NY: M. E. Sharpe, 2005); Donald W. Boose, Jr., Balbina Y. Hwang, Patrick Morgan, and Andrew Scobell, eds., *Recalibrating the U.S.–Republic of Korea Alliance* (Carlisle, PA: Strategic Studies Institute, 2003); and Lee Suk Bok, *The Impact of U.S. Forces in Korea* (Washington, DC: National Defense University Press, 1987). Works that examine the long-standing and unusual North Korea–South Korea relationship include: Don Oberdorfer, *The Two Koreas: A Contemporary History* (New York: Basic Books, 2001); Ho-Youn Kwon, ed., *Divided Korea: Longing for Reunification* (Chicago: North Park University Press, 2004); Edward A. Olsen, *Korea, the Divided Nation* (Westport, CT: Praeger Publishers, 2005); and Roland Bleiker, *Divided Korea: Toward a Culture of Reconciliation* (Minneapolis: University of Minnesota Press, 2005).

6. For an example of the debate about North Korea's delisting from the State Department's list of nations that support terrorism, see Laura Rozen, "Ackerman: Put North Korea Back on Terrorism List," *Politico*, May 19, 2010, http://www.politico.com/blogs/laurarozen/0510/Ackerman_Put_North_Korea_back_on_terrorism_list.html.

7. See Bernard Gwertzman, "North Korea's Uncertain Succession," interview with Scott Snyder, Washington, DC: Council on Foreign Relations, December 19, 2011, http://www.cfr.org/north-korea/north-koreas-uncertain-succession/p26858.

8. See Tetsuya Hakoda and Yusuke Murayama, "Lee's Visit Highlights S. Korea's Status as Key U.S. Ally," *Asahi Shimbun*, October 15, 2011, http://ajw.asahi.com/article/asia/korean_peninsula/AJ2011101514652.

9. One notable exception to this is a very good study published in 2001, though there are almost no books published since then in the United States or in the West that address the North Korean People's Army. See Joseph S. Bermudez, Jr., *The Armed Forces of North Korea* (London: I. B. Tauris, 2001). One other notable exception to this, which is also a useful work, is: Andrew Scobell and John M. Sanford, *North Korea's Military Threat: Pyongyang's Conventional Forces, Weapons of Mass Destruction, and Ballistic Missiles*, Strategic Studies Institute Monograph (Carlisle, PA: U.S. Army War College, April 2007), http://www.strategicstudiesinstitute.army.mil/pdffiles/PUB771.pdf.

10. For a discussion on the viability of preemptive strikes against North Korean nuclear weapons and the legalities under international law, see Kelly J. Malone, "Preemptive Strikes and the Korean Nuclear Crisis: Legal and Political Limitations on the Use of

Force," *Pacific Rim Law & Policy Journal* 12, no. 3 (2003), http://digital.law.washington.edu
/dspace-law/bitstream/handle/1773.1/744/12PacRimLPolyJ807.pdf?sequence=1.

11. For an excellent example of the types of activities carried out by Kim Il-sung's partisan
anti-Japanese group during World War II, see Ah Xiang, "Communists and the Japanese
Invasion of Manchuria," *Republican China*, September 20, 2011, http://republicanchina.org
/COMMUNISTS-AND-JAPAN-INVASION-MANCHURIA.v0.pdf.

## 2. Maintaining a Rogue Military

1. For more details on the size of North Korea's military, see "North Korea: Suspicious
Minds," *Frontline*, January 2003, http://www.pbs.org/frontlineworld/stories
/northkorea/facts.html#03.

2. For an example of analysis that claims resource constraints impact negatively on
North Korean military readiness and capabilities, see "North Korea Downsizes to
Remain Competitive," *Strategy Page*, December 30, 2010, http://www.strategypage.com
/htmw/htlead/articles/20101230.aspx.

3. See Stephan Haggard and Marcus Noland, "Hunger and Human Rights: The Politics of
Famine in North Korea" (Washington, DC: U.S. Committee for Human Rights in North
Korea, 2005), http://www.hrnk.org/uploads/Hunger_and_Human_Rights.pdf.

4. "N. Korea's Morale 'Weakening,'" *Chosun Ilbo*, July 6, 2011, http://english.chosun.com
/site/data/html_dir/2011/07/05/2011070500529.html.

5. See Lee Seok Young, "AWOL and Hungry Soldiers Making Trouble," *DailyNK*,
September 21, 2011, http://www.dailynk.com/english/read.php?catId
=nk01500&num=8197; and Mark Willacy, "N. Korean Children Begging, Army
Starving," *ABC News*, July 15, 2011, http://www.abc.net.au/news/2011-06-27/n-korean
-children-begging-army-starving/2772472.

6. "Former N.K. Soldiers Testify about Worsening Food and Rights Conditions,"
Yonhap, February 21, 2011, http://english.yonhapnews.co.kr/northkorea/2011/02
/21/35/0401000000AEN20110221009500315F.HTML.

7. Im Jeong Jin, "Military-First, but Still No Heating on Bases," *DailyNK*, January 24,
2011, http://www.dailynk.com/english/read.php?catId=nk01500&num=7290.

8. For a discussion of how economic woes affected the North Korean military during
the 1990s, see Daniel A. Pinkston, "North Korea's Foreign Policy towards the United
States," *Strategic Insights* 5, no. 7 (September 2006), http://cns.miis.edu/other/pinkston
_strategic_insights_sep06.pdf.

9. Howard LaFranchi, "Al Qaeda? North Korea? Who Americans See as the Greatest
Security Threat," *Christian Science Monitor*, December 8, 2010, http://www.csmonitor.com
/USA/Foreign-Policy/2010/1208/Al-Qaeda-North-Korea-Who-Americans-see-as
-greatest-security-threat.

10. "'N. K. Overwhelmingly Superior to S. Korea in Asymmetrical Forces': Gov't Data,"
Yonhap, December 5, 2010, http://english.yonhapnews.co.kr/national/2010/12
/05/26/0301000000AEN20101205000200315F.HTML.

11. Wallace "Chip" Gregson, "Statement for the Record by Wallace 'Chip' Gregson,
Assistant Secretary of Defense for Asian & Pacific Security Affairs, Department of
Defense," submitted to the Senate Armed Services Committee, September 16, 2010,

http://armed-services.senate.gov/statemnt/2010/09%20September/Gregson%2009 -16-10.pdf.

12. Jim Garamone, "Thurman Wants to Bolster Ties with South Korea," *Armed Forces Press Service*, June 30, 2011, http://8tharmy.korea.army.mil/20110630thurman -garamone.asp.

13. Joseph S. Bermudez, Jr., "North Korea's Long Reach in Profile," *Jane's Intelligence Review*, November 11, 2003, http://www.janes.com/defence/land_forces/news/idr /idro31111_1_n.shtml.

14. "N. Korea Capable of Producing up to 1.25 Million Chemical Bombs: Expert," Yonhap, October 13, 2010, http://english.yonhapnews.co.kr/news/2010/10/13 /0200000000AEN20101013007600315.HTML.

15. For details regarding DPRK deployment of new artillery systems, their capabilities, and measures taken to improve survivability, see Yonhap, "N. Korea Deploys More Multiple Rocket Launchers: Source," *Free Republic*, December 3, 2010, http://www.freerepublic.com/focus/news/2636508/posts; Kim Min-seok, "North Repositions Artillery: Sources," *Joongang Ilbo*, August 3, 2010, http://joongangdaily .joins.com/article/view.asp?aid=2924081; Yonhap, "N. Korea Adds More Multi-Rocket Launchers along Border with S. Korea: Source," *OANA News*, September 19, 2010, http://www.oananews.org/view.php?id=135119&ch=AST; Associated Press, "Report: North Korea Boosts Multiple-Launch Rockets," Fox News, December 2, 2010, http://www.foxnews.com/world/2010/12/02/report-north -korea-boosts-multiple-launch-rockets/; and Kwon Hyuck-chul, "Military Responds to Tokyo Shimbun's Prediction of Strike on Gyeonggi Province," *Hankyoreh*, December 4, 2010, http://english.hani.co.kr/arti/english_edition/e_northkorea/452167.html.

16. See Joseph S. Bermudez, Jr., "A History of Ballistic Missile Development in the DPRK: CNS Occasional Paper #2" (Monterey, CA: Center for Non-Proliferation Studies, Monterey Institute, 1999), http://cns.miis.edu/pubs/opapers/op2/index.htm.

17. "Syria Improves Its SCUD D Missile with Help from North Korea," *Geostrategy-Direct*, February 22, 2006, http://www.geostrategy-direct.com/geostrategy%2Ddirect/.

18. Kim Min-seok and Brian Lee, "Pyongyang Reportedly Tests New Scud," *Joongang Ilbo*, July 19, 2006, http://joongangdaily.joins.com/200607/18 /2006071821383514799000090309031.html.

19. Wisconsin Project on Nuclear Arms Control, "North Korea's Nuclear-Capable Missiles," *The Risk Report* 2, no. 6 (November–December 1996), http://www .wisconsinproject.org/countries/nkorea/nukemiss.html.

20. James Dunnigan, "North Korea's SS-21 Missiles," *Strategy Page*, May 12, 2005, http://www.strategypage.com/dls/articles2005/512213718.asp.

21. Paul Kerr, "North Korea Increasing Weapons Capabilities," *Arms Control Today*, December 2005, http://www.armscontrol.org/act/2005_12/Dec-NKweapons.asp.

22. "NK Fired Russian Missile: Official," *Korea Times*, May 4, 2005, http://times.hankooki.com /lpage/nation/200505/kt2005050422050611990.htm.

23. Alon Ben-David, "Iran Acquires Ballistic Missiles from DPRK," *Jane's Defence Weekly*, December 29, 2005, http://www.janes.com/security/international_security/news/jdw /jdwo51229_1_n.shtml.

24. "Press Gets 1st Look at N. Korean Mid-Range Missile," *Chosun Ilbo*, October 11, 2010, http://english.chosun.com/site/data/html_dir/2010/10/11/2010101101060.html.

25. "N. Korea's Latest IRBM Believed to Be Able to Carry Nuclear Warhead: Expert," Yonhap, December 23, 2010, http://english.yonhapnews.co.kr/national/2010/12/23/46 /0301000000AEN20101223004200315F.HTML.

26. See "N. Korea Sets up Special Missile Division: Source," Yonhap, March 9, 2010, http://english.yonhapnews.co.kr/national/2010/03/09/8 /0301000000AEN20100309001600315F.HTML; Jung Sung-ki, "NK Creates Mid-Range Ballistic Missile Unit," *Korea Times*, March 9, 2010, http://www.koreatimes .co.kr/www/news/nation/2010/03/205_62096.html; and Bruce Klingner, "New North Korean Missile Unit Reflects Growing Missile Threat," Web Memo 2831 (Washington, DC: Heritage Foundation, March 11, 2010), http://www.heritage.org /Research/Reports/2010/03/New-North-Korean-Missile-Unit-Reflects-Growing -Missile-Threat.

27. Jack Kim, "North Korea Has 1,000 Missiles, South Says," Reuters, March 17, 2010, http://www.nytimes.com/reuters/2010/03/17/world/international-us-korea-north -missiles.html.

28. Bill Gertz, "North Korea Making Missile Able to Hit U.S.," *Washington Times*, December 5, 2011, http://www.washingtontimes.com/news/2011/dec/5/north-korea -making-missile-able-to-hit-us/?utm_source=RSS_Feed&utm_medium=RSS.

29. See Anthony H. Cordesman, *Iran's Military Forces and Warfighting Capability: The Threat in the Northern Gulf* (Westport, CT: Praeger, 2007), 152–153; William J. Broad, James Glanz, and David E. Sanger, "Iran Fortifies Its Arsenal with the Aid of North Korea," *New York Times*, September 28, 2010, http://www.nytimes.com/2010/11/29/world /middleeast/29missiles.html?_r=0; Richard Spencer, "N Korea 'Tests New Missile in Iran,'" *The Telegraph*, May 17, 2007, http://www.telegraph.co.uk/news/worldnews /1551868/N-Korea-tests-new-missile-in-Iran.html; Anthony H. Cordesman, "Iranian Weapons of Mass Destruction: Capabilities, Developments, and Strategic Uncertainties," *Center for Strategic and International Studies*, October 14, 2008, http://csis.org /files/media/csis/pubs/081015_iran.wmd.pdf; "Iran Develops Missile with 4,000-KM Range," *Middle East Newsline*, March 2, 2006, http://www.menewsline.com/stories /2006/march/03_02_1.html, also available on http://regimechangeiran.blogspot.com /2006/03/iran-develops-missile-with-4000-km.html; and Charles P. Vick, "Has the No-Dong B/Shahab-4 Finally Been Tested in Iran for North Korea?," Global Security.org, May 2, 2006, http://www.globalsecurity.org/wmd/library/report/2006 /cpvick-no-dong-b_2006.htm.

30. The Taepo Dong 1 failed to successfully enter its third stage in 1998, while the Taepo Dong 2 blew apart and fell into the sea while attempting to go from its first stage to its second stage in 2006. For more details of these two launches, see "U.S. Officials: North Korea Tests Long-Range Missile," CNN.com, July 5, 2006, http://www.cnn.com /2006/WORLD/asiapcf/07/04/korea.missile/. For analysis of the 2009 Taepo Dong launch, see "North Korea's Missile Flew 500 Miles Farther Than It Was Expected," *Pravda*, April 13, 2009, http://english.pravda.ru/world/asia/13-04-2009/107390 -North_Korea_missile-0; "N. Korea Rocket 'Flew Farther Than Previously Thought,'" *Chosun Ilbo*, April 13, 2009, http://english.chosun.com/w21data/html/news/200904

/200904130006.html; and Julian E. Barnes and Greg Miller, "North Korea Shows Progress in Mastering Missile Technology," *Los Angeles Times*, April 6, 2009, http://www.latimes.com/news/nationworld/world/la-fg-north-korea-missile6 -2009apr06,0,4471509.story.

31. See "New N. Korean Space Launch Site Appears Completed," *Chosun Ilbo*, February 17, 2011, http://english.chosun.com/site/data/html_dir/2011/02/17/2011021700080.html; "N. Korea Finishes New Missile Facility: Reports," *Korea Herald*, February 20, 2011, http://www.asiaone.com/News/Latest+News/Asia/Story/A1Story20110220 -264443.html; and "N. Korea Lays Tracks to New Missile Site," *Chosun Ilbo*, July 25, 2011, http://english.chosun.com/site/data/html_dir/2011/07/25/2011072500862 .html.

32. See "N. Korea Tells Int'l Agency of Rocket Launch Plan," *Chosun Ilbo*, March 19, 2012, http://english.chosun.com/site/data/html_dir/2012/03/19/2012031900617.html; Song Sang-ho, "N. K. Says Will Launch 'Satellite' in Mid-April," *Korea Herald*, March 16, 2012, http://www.koreaherald.com/national/Detail.jsp?newsMLId =20120316001167; and "DPRK Announces Another 'Satellite' Launch," *NK News*, March 16, 2012, http://www.nknews.org/2012/03/dprk-announces-another-satellite -launch/.

33. "Exclusive: North Korea's Expected Rocket Trajectory," *North Korea Tech*, March 21, 2012, http://www.northkoreatech.org/2012/03/21/exclusive-north-koreas-expected -rocket-trajectory/.

34. For details regarding the launch site and similarities to Iran's facilities, see Kim Hee-jin and Lee Hyun-taek, "North's Rocket Launch Site Said to Be Similar to Iran's," *Joongang Ilbo*, March 20, 2012, http://koreajoongangdaily.joinsmsn.com/news/article /article.aspx?aid=2950149.

35. "S. Korea, US to Recover Debris of NK Rocket," KBS World, March 19, 2012, http://rki.kbs.co.kr/english/news/news_Po_detail.htm?No=89001&id=Po.

36. For details regarding North Korea's missile launch plans and the puzzling agreement with the United States that was broken only days later, see "N. Korean Rocket Launch 'Long and Carefully Planned,'" *Chosun Ilbo*, March 22, 2012, http://english.chosun.com /site/data/html_dir/2012/03/22/2012032201436.html; and Kim Yoon-mi, "N. K. Told U.S. about Satellite Plan Last Year," *Korea Herald*, March 21, 2012, http://www.koreaherald.com/national/Detail.jsp?newsMLId=20120321000992.

37. See "Air Traffic Warned of Rocket Drop Zone," *North Korea Tech*, March 21, 2012, http://www.northkoreatech.org/2012/03/22/air-traffic-warned-of-rocket-drop -zone/; and "Seoul Diverts Flight Paths Due to N. Korea's Rocket Plan," *Chosun Ilbo*, March 21, 2012, http://english.chosun.com/site/data/html_dir/2012/03/21 /2012032100648.html.

38. "Exclusive: DPRK Satellite to Send Data, Video," *North Korea Tech*, March 20, 2012, http://www.northkoreatech.org/2012/03/20/itu-confirms-dprk-satellite-launch -plans/.

39. "S. Korea to Refer NK Missile Launch to UN Security Council," *Donga Ilbo*, March 21, 2012, http://english.donga.com/srv/service.php3?biid=2012032160438.

40. "Japan to Deploy 3 Aegis Ships to Intercept Falling N. Korean Rocket," *Kyodo News*, March 24, 2012, http://english.kyodonews.jp/news/2012/03/148631.html.

41. Choe Sang-hun, "North Korea Moves Rocket to Launching Pad," *New York Times*, March 25, 2012, http://www.nytimes.com/2012/03/26/world/asia/north-korea -moves-rocket-to-launching-pad.html.

42. Matthew Pennington, "US: Debris from N Korea Rocket Risks Casualties," *Inquirer Global Nation* (Philippines), March 29, 2012, http://globalnation.inquirer.net/30911 /us-debris-from-north-korea-rocket-risks-casualties.

43. "North Korea Begins Launch Pad Preparations for April Rocket Launch: A 38 North Exclusive," 38 North, March 29, 2012, http://38north.org/2012/03/tongchang0329/.

44. Park Byung-soo, "North Korea's Rocket Launch Plans Moving Forward," *Hankyoreh Ilbo*, March 30, 2012, http://english.hani.co.kr/arti/english_edition/e_northkorea /526036.html.

45. See Paul Richter, "No Free Launch, Obama Tells North Korea," *Los Angeles Times*, March 30, 2012, http://latimesblogs.latimes.com/world_now/2012/03/obama-to -.html; and "N. Korea: US Breaking Deal over Rocket," Voice of America, March 31, 2012, http://voznews.com/edition/n-korea-us-breaking-nuclear-deal-over-rocket -general-news.

46. "US Dispatches Advanced Radar ahead of NK Rocket Launch," KBS World, March 31, 2012, http://rki.kbs.co.kr/english/news/news_In_detail.htm?No=89291&id=In.

47. "Destroyers, Missiles Leave for Okinawa ahead of N. Korean Launch," *Asahi Shimbun*, March 31, 2012, http://ajw.asahi.com/article/behind_news/politics/AJ201203310027.

48. For details regarding the progress made on the North Korean missile launch preparations by April 1, 2012, see "New Evidence on Advanced Preparations for DPRK Rocket Launch: 38 North Exclusive," 38 North, April 1, 2012, http://38north.org/2012/04/tongchang0401/.

49. For details and analysis regarding the three stages of the Taepo Dong 2, its "genesis," and the technology associated with it, see Mike Wall, "North Korea's Rocket Technology Explained: An Observer's Guide," SPACE.com, April 2, 2012, http://www.space.com/15130-north-korea-rocket-missile-technology.html; Larry Shaughnessy, "North Korea's Rocket Began Life Underwater," CNN, April 4, 2012, http://security.blogs.cnn.com/2012/04/04/north-koreas-rocket-began-life -underwater/; and Greg Thielmann, "Long-Range Ballistic Missile Development: A Tale of Two Tests," *Arms Control Association Threat Assessment Brief* (Washington, DC: Arms Control Association, May 10, 2012), http://www.armscontrol.org/files/TAB _Long-Range-Ballistic-Missile-Development-A-Tale-of-Two-Tests.pdf.

50. Bill Gertz, "Red Alert: Pentagon Activates Missile Defenses for North Korean Launch," *Free Beacon*, April 2, 2012, http://freebeacon.com/red-alert/.

51. For details regarding the deployments of Aegis-equipped ships to waters where they could monitor the North Korean Taepo Dong 2 launch of 2012, see Jeong Yong-soo and Kim Hee-jin, "Aegis Destroyers to Keep Eye on Sky for North Korean Rocket," *Joongang Ilbo*, April 4, 2012, http://koreajoongangdaily.joinsmsn.com/news/article /article.aspx?aid=2950948.

52. "Foreign Journalists Arrive in N. Korea to Cover Rocket Launch," Yonhap, April 8, 2012, http://english.yonhapnews.co.kr/national/2012/04/08/65 /0301000000AEN20120408000500315F.HTML.

53. Associated Press, "North Korea Moves Rocket into Position for Launch," *The Guardian*, April 8, 2012, http://www.guardian.co.uk/world/2012/apr/08/north-korea-rocket -positioned-launch.

54. "North Korea's Rocket Plans Prompt Asian Airlines to Change Flight Paths," CBS News, April 9, 2012, http://www.cbsnews.com/8301-202_162-57411313/north -koreas-rocket-plans-prompt-asian-airlines-to-change-flight-paths/.

55. Agence France-Presse (hereafter AFP), "North Korea Set to Install Satellite on Rocket, Official," *Vancouver Desi*, April 10, 2012, http://vancouverdesi.com/news /n-korea-set-to-install-satellite-on-rocket-official/.

56. Jean H. Lee, "Live Feed at Command Centre Shows N Korea Rocket Covered as Engineers Pump Fuel into Carrier," Associated Press, April 11, 2012, http://news.yahoo.com/live-feed-command-centre-shows-nkorea-rocket-covered -043720189.html.

57. Details about the American delegation's trip to North Korea days before the missile launch remain unconfirmed and murky, though rumors regarding the trip have been widely reported in the press. See Steve Herman, "North Korea Warned of Deeper Isolation Should Provocations Continue," Voice of America, May 21, 2012, http://www.voanews.com/articleprintview/781384.html.

58. See "U.S. Officials in Secret Visit to N. Korea before Rocket Launch," *Chosun Ilbo*, May 24, 2012, http://english.chosun.com/site/data/html_dir/2012/05/24/2012052400631 .html; and AFP, "US Officials 'Flew to N Korea' before Rocket Launch," *Daily Times*, May 25, 2012, http://www.dailytimes.com.pk/default.asp?page=2012%5C05%5C25%5Cstory _25-5-2012_pg4-4.

59. For details about the failed North Korean Taepo Dong 2 launch of April 13, 2012, and the context surrounding what occurred, see "North Korean Rocket Launch Fails," British Broadcasting Corporation (BBC), April 13, 2012, http://www.bbc.co.uk/news /world-asia-17698438; "N. Korea Rocket Could Fly 10,000 KM," *Chosun Ilbo*, April 16, 2012, http://english.chosun.com/site/data/html_dir/2012/04/16 /2012041601302.html; Kim Young-jin, "North Korea May Have Aborted Launch," *Korea Times*, May 7, 2012, http://www.koreatimes.co.kr/www/news/nation/2012/05/113 _110490.html; Park Bang-ju, "North Rocket Didn't Separate: Expert," *Joongang Ilbo*, April 24, 2012, http://koreajoongangdaily.joinsmsn.com/news/article/article.aspx ?aid=2951910; Park Bang-ju, "North Likely to Launch Another Rocket, Says Expert," *Joongang Ilbo*, April 16, 2012, http://koreajoongangdaily.joinsmsn.com/news/article /Article.aspx?aid=2951497; "North Korean Rocket Boosters Fail to Separate," KBS World, April 16, 2012, http://rki.kbs.co.kr/english/news/news_Po_detail.htm?No =89653&id=Po; and "Navy Set to End Search for Debris from N. Korean Rocket," *Korea Times*, April 17, 2012, http://www.koreatimes.co.kr/www/news/nation/2012 /04/205_109121.html.

60. Margaret Basheer, "UN Security Council Condemns North Korea Rocket Launch," Voice of America, April 13, 2012, http://www.voanews.com/content/un-security -council-condemns-north-korea-rocket-launch-147343395/179340.html.

61. See Lee Chi-dong, "U.S. Cancels Food Aid for N. Korea: White House," Yonhap, April 14, 2012, http://english.yonhapnews.co.kr/national/2012/04/14/52 /0301000000AEN20120414000400315F.HTML.

62. For context and more details on the statement the North Korean Foreign Ministry made in response to UN and U.S. actions, see: "N. Korea Denounces UNSC Move, Declares End to Feb 29 Deal," *Korea Times*, April 17, 2012, http://www.koreatimes.co.kr/www/news/nation/2012/05/120_109189.html.

63. For details regarding the American list of proposed sanctions presented to the UNSC, see Michinobu Yanagisawa, "U.S. Seeks Asset Freeze," *Yomiuri Shimbun*, April 19, 2012, http://www.yomiuri.co.jp/dy/world/T120418005891.htm.

64. For details on the sanctions that the UNSC imposed on North Korea in May 2012, see Louis Charbonneau, "U.N. Committee Sanctions 3 North Korea Companies: Rice," Reuters, May 2, 2012, http://www.newsdaily.com/stories/bre84116z-us-korea-north-un/.

65. For the technical aspects detailing exactly how the technology for a three-stage missile and a "satellite platform" that the North Koreans claimed their Taepo Dong 2 test launches were designed to carry was exactly the same except for the payload, see Charles P. Vick, "Taep'o-dong 2 (TD-2), NKSL-X-2," Global Security.org, March 20, 2007, http://www.globalsecurity.org/wmd/world/dprk/td-2.htm.

66. To read an in-depth interview that Evans Revere gave to the Japanese press regarding contacts he had with the North Koreans before the long-range ballistic missile test launch of 2012, see Takashi Oshima, "INTERVIEW/Evans Revere: North Korea's Launch Plan Started Last Summer," *Asahi Shimbun*, April 9, 2012, http://ajw.asahi.com/article/asia/korean_peninsula/AJ201204090045.

67. Bruce E. Bechtol, Jr., "Ramifications of N. Korean Satellite Launch," *Korea Times*, March 26, 2012, http://110.45.173.105/www/news/opinon/2012/04/198_107731.html.

68. See Donald Kirk, "Why Iranian Engineers Attended North Korea's Failed Rocket Launch," *Christian Science Monitor*, April 18, 2012, http://www.csmonitor.com/World/Asia-Pacific/2012/0418/Why-Iranian-engineers-attended-North-Korea-s-failed-rocket-launch; "Iran Sent Delegation to Observe Launch," *Sankei Shimbun* (in Japanese), April 14, 2012, http://sankei.jp.msn.com/; and John McCreary, "Nightwatch: 20120417," *Nightwatch*, April 16, 2012, http://www.kforcegov.com/NightWatch/NightWatch_12000074.aspx.

69. See "Countdown to Pyongyang's Missile Launch: Unha Rocket Stages at Assembly Building," 38 North, November 29, 2012, http://38north.org/2012/11/sohae112912/; Bill Gertz, "Inside the Ring: North Korean Missile Launch Set," *Washington Times*, November 28, 2012, http://www.washingtontimes.com/news/2012/nov/28/inside-the-ring-north-korean-missile-launch-set/?page=all.

70. See Foster Klug, "NKorea Says it Will launch Long-Range Rocket Soon," Associated Press, December 1, 2012, http://www.washingtontimes.com/news/2012/dec/1/nkorea-says-it-will-launch-long-range-rocket-soon/?page=all; "N. Korea to Launch 'Satellite' Between Dec 10 and 22," Yonhap, December 1, 2012, http://english.yonhapnews.co.kr/northkorea/2012/12/01/0401000000AEN20121201002600320.HTML.

71. For more details regarding North Korea's use of technology from former Soviet Republics, see "N. KoreaTried to Import Foreign Missile Technology," *Chosun Ilbo*, December 3, 2012, http://english.chosun.com/site/data/html_dir/2012/12/03/2012120300676.html.

72. For details regarding the announced splash-down areas for sections of the Taepo Dong 2 missile and the reactions to the launch preparations by the United States and South Korea, see "First Stage Rocket in Position at N. Korea's Launch Pad," Yonhap, December 3, 2012, http://english.yonhapnews.co.kr/northkorea/2012/12/03 /0401000000AEN20121203009351315.HTML; Kim Eun-jung, "S. Korea, U.S. Step up Monitoring ahead of N Korean Launch," Yonhap, December 3, 2012, http://english.yonhapnews.co.kr/national/2012/12/03/8 /0301000000AEN20121203001600315F.HTML; "North Korea Notifies U.N. Maritime Agency of Maritime Coordinates," Yonhap, December 4, 2012, http://english.yonhapnews.co.kr/northkorea/2012/12/04 /0401000000AEN20121204003600315.HTML; David Wright, "North Korea Gives Locatin of Splashdown Zones, Begins Assembling Rocket," *All Things Nuclear*, December 4, 2012, http://allthingsnuclear.org/north-korea-gives-location-of -splashdown-zones-begins-assembling-rocket/; Lee Sang Yong, "North Informs IMO of Launch Plan," *DailyNK*, December 4, 2012, http://www.dailynk.com /english/read.php?cataId=nk00100&num=10099.

73. For details regarding the placement of the missile stages on the launch pad, and the deployment of the American "X-Band" radar, see "North Korea Installing all Three Stages of Rocket into Position: Source," Yonhap, December 4, 2012, http://english .yonhapnews.co.kr/national/2012/12/04/61/0301000000AEN20121204009700315 F.HTML; "N. Korea Completes Installation of Long-Range Rocket on Launch Pad," Yonhap, December 5, 2012, http://english.yonhapnews.co.kr/national/2012 /12/05/54/0301000000AEN20121205005852315F.HTML; "High-Spec U.S. Radar to Monitor N. Korean Rocket," *Chosun Ilbo*, December 6, 2012, http://english.chosun .com/site/data/html_dir/2012/12/06/2012120601027.html.

74. See Jack Kim and Ju-min Park, "North Korea Replacing Rocket Stage, Likely to Launch as Planned: Report," Reuters, December 10, 2012, http://in.reuters.com /article/2012/12/10/korea-north-rocket-idINDEE8B900420121210; Kim Eun-jung, "N. Korea's Rocket Defect Related to Direction Control System: Source," Yonhap, December 11, 2012, http://english.yonhapnews.co.kr/national/2012/12/11/85 /0301000000AEN20121211004500315F.HTML.

75. For information regarding misleading analysis by pundits following the December 12, 2012 test launch of the Taepo Dong 2, the reports confirming the successful launch of a three-stage ballistic missile platform, and the stated reaction from a White House spokesman, see "North Korea Rocket has '10,000 km Range,'" BBC News, December 23, 2012, http://www.bbc.co.uk/news/world-asia-20830605; Jack Kim and Mayumi Negishi, "North Korea Rocket Launch Raises Nuclear Stakes," Reuters, December 12, 2012, http://www.reuters.com/article/2012/12/12/us-korea-north -rocket-idUSBRE8BB02K20121212; Foster Klug and Matthew Pennington, "North Korea Still Years Away from Reliable Missiles," Associated Press, December 14, 2012, http://www.bostonglobe.com/news/world/2012/12/14/nkorea-still-years-away-from -reliable-missiles/umbpW4AgepD4YwOi6IkCaI/story.html; Park Hyun, "White House Says NK Missiles Still Can't Reach Continental US," *The Hankyoreh*, December 15, 2012, http://english.hani.co.kr/arti/english_edition/e_northkorea/565535.html.

76. For more details regarding the Iranian delegation "visit" to North Korea before and during the test launch on December 12, 2012, See: Yaakov Lappin, "Iran Stations Defense Staff at North Korean Site," Reuters, December 2, 2012, http://www.jpost.com /IranianThreat/News/Article.aspx?id=294244; "Iranian Experts at N. Korea's Rocket Site: Report," *Bangkok Post*, December 11, 2012, http://www.bangkokpost.com/news/asia /325432/iranian-experts-at-n-korea-rocket-site-report; "NHK: N. Korea Informed Iran of Rocket Launch Plan in October," *KBS News*, December 19, 2012, http://world.kbs.co.kr/english/news/news_In_detail.htm?lang=e&id=In&No =95442&current_page=.

77. For detailed results of the analysis conducted on the Taepo Dong 2 first-stage components recovered by South Korean technicians during December of 2012, see Kim Eun-jung, "Rocket Debris Reveals N. Korea's Intention to Test ICBM Technology," Yonhap, December 23, 2012, http://english.yonhapnews.co.kr/national /2012/12/22/99/0301000000AEN20121222002300315F.HTML.

78. See Choe Sang-hun, "Evidence Shows Military Purpose in North Korean Rocket, Seoul Says," *New York Times*, December 23, 2012, http://www.newsits.com/news/world /evidence-shows-military-purpose-in-north-korean-rocket-seoul-says/.

79. See Gertz, "North Korea Making Missile."

80. For details regarding the sketchy capabilities of the new missile, its TEL, and the questions regarding Chinese proliferation, see Associated Press, "North Korea Shows off New Missile at Military Parade," Yahoo! News, April 15, 2012, http://news.yahoo .com/nkorea-shows-off-missile-military-parade-054632037.html; Shaun Waterman, "Analysts: China Broke Sanctions if N. Korea Using Its Missile Launcher," *Washington Times*, April 16, 2012, http://www.washingtontimes.com/news/2012/apr/16/experts -china-likely-gave-n-korea-illegal-missile-/; Simon Martin, "North Korea Seeks Leverage with New Missile," *Montreal Gazette*, April 16, 2012, http://www.montrealgazette.com /technology/North+Korea+seeks+leverage+with+missile+analysts/6464669/story .html; Hao Zhou, "China Denies Selling Launcher to N. Korea," *Global Times*, April 19, 2012, http://www.globaltimes.cn/NEWS/tabid/99/ID/705780/China-denies -selling-launcher-to-NKorea.aspx; "UN Probes Claim China Broke N Korea Sanctions: Report," AFP, April 19, 2012, http://www.google.com/hostednews /afp/article/ALeqM5issdHPy5iiVrNeEv1ezO6WehnlWw?docId=CNG.c48edd1d1de a9c6d92f8c17aefcd2f24.4a1; AFP, "US Raises China's Alleged Aid for N. Korean Missile," Channel News Asia, April 21, 2012, http://www.channelnewsasia.com /stories/afp_asiapacific/view/1196592/1/.html; Matt Spetalnick, "Chinese Firm Suspected in Missile-Linked Sale to N Korea: US Official," Reuters, April 22, 2012, http://www.reuters.com/article/2012/04/21/us-korea-north-china-usa -idUSBRE83K0GP20120421; and Song Sang-ho, "Chinese Firm Sold 8 Military Vehicles to N. Korea: Report," *Korea Herald*, April 27, 2012, http://view.koreaherald .com/kh/view.php?ud=20120427000923&cpv=0.

81. See Missy Ryan, "China Assisting North Korean Missile Program: U.S. Defense Secretary," Reuters, April 19, 2012, http://www.reuters.com/article/2012/04/19/us -usa-northkorea-china-idUSBRE83I1JQ20120419.

82. See Harry P. Dies, Jr., "North Korean Special Operations Forces: 1996 Kangnung Submarine Infiltration," *Military Intelligence Professional Bulletin*, October–December,

2004, http://findarticles.com/p/articles/mi_m0IBS/is_4_30/ai_n13822276; and Ministry of National Defense, Republic of Korea, "Defense White Paper," 2010, http://www.mnd.go.kr/.

83. "North Korean Special Operations Forces and the Second Front," Special Operations.com, 2000, http://www.specialoperations.com/Foreign/North _Korea/Second_Front.htm.

84. See "North Korea's Underground Bunkers," Radio Free Asia, November 16, 2009, http://www.rfa.org/english/news/korea/bunkers-11162009134509.html; and "N. Korea Planned to Invade South Despite Sunshine Policy," *Chosun Ilbo*, November 18, 2009, http://english.chosun.com/site/data/html_dir/2009/11/18/2009111800451.html.

85. "N. Korean Special Forces Dressed in S. Korean Uniforms," Yonhap, December 28, 2010, http://english.yonhapnews.co.kr/national/2010/12/28/90 /0301000000AEN20101228003000315F.HTML.

86. "N. Korea's Special Forces Capable of Striking Most Targets in S. Korea," Yonhap, June 7, 2011, http://english.yonhapnews.co.kr/national/2011/06/07/76 /0301000000AEN20110607005200315F.HTML.

87. Hwang Jang-yop, "Testimonies of North Korean Defectors," Republic of Korea, National Intelligence Service, January, 1999, http://www.fas.org/irp/world/rok/nis -docs/index.html.

88. "N. Korean Special Force Trains Shooting on High-Speed Train," *Korea Times*, February 14, 2011, http://www.koreatimes.co.kr/www/news/nation/2011 /02/113_81352.html.

89. Park Sung-kook, "Tasks of the General Bureau of Reconnaissance," *DailyNK*, May 7, 2010, http://www.dailynk.com/english/read.php?cataId=nk02900&num=6341.

90. "N. Korea Commands 195,000 Troops for Terror Attacks on S. Korea: Defector," Yonhap, July 27, 2011, http://english.yonhapnews.co.kr/northkorea/2011 /07/27/39/0401000000AEN20110727010300315F.HTML.

91. Jin Dae-woong, "N. Korea Augments Special Warfare Units," *Korea Herald*, January 1, 2008, http://www.koreaherald.com/national/Detail.jsp?newsMLId =2008010100011.

92. Capt. Duk-Ki Kim, Republic of Korea Navy, "The Republic of Korea's Counter-Asymmetric Strategy: Lesson from ROKS Cheonan and Yeonpyeong Island," *Naval War College Review* 65, no. 1 (Winter 2012): 58.

93. Kim Deok-hyun, "N. Korea Deploys New Battle Tanks, Boosts Special Forces," Yonhap, December 30, 2010, http://english.yonhapnews.co.kr/national/2010 /12/30/89/0301000000AEN20101230005300315F.HTML.

94. See "N. Korean Infrared Missiles Threaten S. Korean Fighters," *Chosun Ilbo*, April 7, 2011, http://english.chosun.com/site/data/html_dir/2011/04/07/2011040701179 .html; and "F-15K's Vulnerable to N. Korean Infrared Missiles," *Korea Times*, July 19, 2011, http://www.koreatimes.co.kr/www/news/nation/2011/07/113_91160.html.

95. See "N. Korea Successfully Test Fired Short-Range Missile," *Chosun Ilbo*, June 14, 2011, http://english.chosun.com/site/data/html_dir/2011/06/14/2011061400518.html; and Jeong Yong-soo and Christine Kim, "North Test-Fires Missiles off Coast," *Joongang Ilbo*, June 8, 2011, http://joongangdaily.joins.com/article/view.asp?aid=2937286.

96. For details on confirmed new North Korean submarine capabilities, see "N. Korea Builds up Submarine Force," *Chosun Ilbo*, March 21, 2011, http://english.chosun.com/site /data/html_dir/2011/03/21/2011032100584.html; "N. Korea Tests New Submarine in Naval Drills," Yonhap, April 6, 2011, http://english.yonhapnews.co.kr/national /2011/04/06/29/0301000000AEN20110406003300315F.HTML; and Lee Young-jong and Christine Kim, "North's New Midget Subs Are Torpedo Equipped," *Joongang Ilbo*, December 7, 2010, http://joongangdaily.joins.com/article/view.asp?aid=2929318.

97. For details about the hovercraft naval base in Koampo, North Korea, see "N. Korean Hovercrafts Can Launch Surprise Attack on South," *Korea Times*, April 3, 2011, http://www.koreatimes.co.kr/www/news/nation/2011/04/117_84366.html; and AFP, "New N. Korean Base Near Frontline Islands, Say Media Reports," *Channel News Asia*, February 1, 2011, http://www.channelnewsasia.com/stories/afp_asiapacific/view /1108206/1/.html.

98. For details regarding the 2011 deployment of North Korean elite naval infantry to Pipagot and the military drills they conducted, see "North Korean Troops May Raid S. Korean Islands in West Sea," *Korea Times*, September 20, 2011, http://www.koreatimes .co.kr/www/news/nation/2011/09/113_95113.html; and "North Korea Deploys Sniper Brigade of 3,000 Personnel at Pip'agot," *Donga Ilbo* (in Korean), September 21, 2011, http://www.donga.com/.

99. Tony Capaccio, "North Korea Improves Cyber Warfare Capacity, U.S. Says," Bloomberg, October 22, 2012, http://www.businessweek.com/news/2012-10 -22/north-korea-improves-cyber-warfare-capacity-u-dot-s-dot-says.

100. For details on North Korean cyber attacks since 2009, see "March DDoS Attack Was N. Korean Cyber War Drill," *Donga Ilbo*, July 9, 2011, http://english.donga.com /srv/service.php3?biid=2011070995138; "N. Korea Masterminded March Cyber Attacks: Police," Yonhap, April 6, 2011, http://english.yonhapnews.co.kr/techscience /2011/04/06/94/0601000000AEN20110406003800315F.HTML; and Lee Youkyung, "S. Korea Charts out National Cyber Security Strategy," Yonhap, August 8, 2011, http://www.usnewslasvegas.com/foreign/s-korea-charts-out-national-cyber -security-strategy/.

101. See "South Korean Defense Chief Confirms North Korea behind GPS Jamming Last Week," *Katakami*, March 9, 2011, http://indonesiakatakami.wordpress.com/2011/03/09 /south-korean-defense-chief-confirms-north-korea-behind-gps-jamming-last-week/; "N. Korea Still Jamming GPS Signals," *Chosun Ilbo*, March 10, 2011, http://english .chosun.com/site/data/html_dir/2011/03/10/2011031000575.html; and "GPS Jammers in Action," *Strategy Page*, September 13, 2011, http://www.strategypage.com/htmw /htecm/20110913.aspx.

102. See "DPRK Jamming GPS Signals, Says Seoul," *North Korea Tech*, May 3, 2012, http://www.northkoreatech.org/2012/05/03/dprk-jamming-gps-signals-says-seoul/; Daniel Piper, "North Korea Accused of Jamming Signals of Hundreds of Civilian Flights," *Fox News*, May 2, 2012, http://www.foxnews.com/world/2012/05/02/north -korea-accused-jamming-signals-hundreds-commercial-jets/; and AFP, "North Korea Jamming Affects Flights—Seoul Official," *Straits Times,* May 2, 2012, http://www.straitstimes.com/BreakingNews/Asia/Story/STIStory_794633.html.

103. See Shin Hyon-hee, "GPS Jamming Highlights N. K. Cyber War Threat," *Korea Herald*, May 8, 2012, http://view.koreaherald.com/kh/view.php?ud=20120508001326&cpv=0; and "122 Ships Affected by Suspected N. Korean GPS Jamming," Yonhap, May 4, 2012, http://english.yonhapnews.co.kr/national/2012/05/04/50/0302000000AEN20120504005000315F.HTML.

104. See Mok Yong-jae, "No Sign of End to GPS Jam," *Daily NK*, May 14, 2012, http://www.dailynk.com/english/read.php?catId=nk00100&num=9225; "N. Korea's Jamming Is Terrorism Pure and Simple," *Chosun Ilbo*, May 11, 2012, http://english.chosun.com/site/data/html_dir/2012/05/11/2012051101175.html; and "N. Korean GPS Jamming Threatens Passenger Planes," *Chosun Ilbo*, May 10, 2012, http://english.chosun.com/site/data/html_dir/2012/05/10/2012051000917.html.

105. See Chung Hee-hyung, "Seoul Defenseless against N. Korea's GPS Jamming," *Korea Times*, May 15, 2012, http://www.koreatimes.co.kr/www/news/nation/2012/05/116_111042.html; "N Korea Stops Sending out GPS Jamming Signals against S. Korea: Source," Italicize Yonhap, May 15, 2012, http://english.yonhapnews.co.kr/northkorea/2012/05/15/90/0401000000AEN20120515003000315F.HTML; and "S. Korea to Protest against N. Korea's Electronic Jamming Signals," Yonhap, May 9, 2012, http://english.yonhapnews.co.kr/national/2012/05/09/76/0301000000AEN2012050 9005200315F.HTML.

106. See Chris Pocock, "UAV Crash in Korea Linked to GPS Jamming," *Aviation International News Online*, June 1, 2012, http://www.ainonline.com/aviation-news/ain-defense-perspective/2012-06-01/uav-crash-korea-linked-gps-jamming.

107. Kim, "The Republic of Korea's Counter-Asymmetric Strategy," 58.

108. "NK Politics/Regime: National Defense Commission," KBS World, October 31, 2008, http://world.kbs.co.kr/english/event/nkorea_nuclear/general_03f.htm.

109. Kim Sung Chull, *North Korea under Kim Jong Il: From Consolidation to Systemic Dissonance* (Albany: State University of New York Press, 2006), 89–91.

110. "N. Korean Leader Dies at 69 after Decades of Iron-Fist Rule," Yonhap, December 19, 2011, http://english.yonhapnews.co.kr/national/2011/12/19/41/0301000000AEN20111219005700315F.HTML.

111. "NK Military, People, Pledge to Follow Kim Jong-un's Leadership: KCNA," *Korea Times*, December 19, 2011, http://www.koreatimes.co.kr/www/news/nation/2011/12/120_101112.html.

112. "North Korea: Kim Jong-un 'Issued First Military Order before Father's Death Was Announced,'" *Telegraph* (UK), December 21, 2011, http://www.telegraph.co.uk/news/worldnews/asia/northkorea/8970079/North-Korea-Kim-Jong-un-issued-first-military-order-before-fathers-death-was-announced.html.

113. AFP, "Kim Jong-un Assumes 'Supreme Commandership' of North Korea's Army: State Media," *National Post (Canada)*, December 30, 2011, http://news.nationalpost.com/2011/12/30/kim-jong-un-assumes-supreme-commandership-of-north-koreas-army-state-media/.

114. Kim Se-jeong, "N. Korea Creating Personality Cult around Next Leader Kim Jong-un," *Korea Times*, October 20, 2010, http://www.koreatimes.co.kr/www/news/nation/2010/10/116_74912.html.

115. Chong Song-chang, "The Third Conference of North Korea's Workers Party of Korea Representatives and the Establishment of a Succession System for Kim Jong-eun," *Sejong Commentary* no. 196 (in Korean) (Seongnam, South Korea: Sejong Institute, September 30, 2010).

116. Brent Choi, "[Viewpoint] Pondering the New Political Option," *Joongang Ilbo*, October 11, 2010, http://joongangdaily.joins.com/article/view.asp?aid=2926964.

117. Im Jeong Jin, "People's Army Starts Kim Jong Eun Campaign," *DailyNK*, October 6, 2010, http://www.dailynk.com/english/read.php?cataId=nk01500&num=6876.

118. Lee Young-jong, "Path of Succession in North Growing Clearer by the Day," *Joongang Ilbo*, October 6, 2009, http://joongangdaily.joins.com/article/view.asp?aid=2910930.

119. "What Group Photo Says about New N. Korean Power Elite," *Chosun Ilbo*, October 1, 2010, http://english.chosun.com/site/data/html_dir/2010/10/01/2010100101010.html.

120. "Promotions Reveal Lineup of Kim Jong-un Regime," *Chosun Ilbo*, October 4, 2010, http://english.chosun.com/site/data/html_dir/2010/10/04/2010100400528.html.

121. "Kim Jong-un 'Masterminded Attacks on South Korea,'" *Chosun Ilbo*, August 3, 2011, http://english.chosun.com/site/data/html_dir/2011/08/03/2011080300499.html.

122. See Christine Kim and Lee Young-jong, "Kim Jong-un in Charge of Intelligence: Source," *Joongang Ilbo*, April 21, 2011, http://joongangdaily.joins.com/article/view.asp?aid=2935144; and "Kim Jong-il's Son 'Effectively Control Security Forces,'" *Chosun Ilbo*, April 13, 2011, http://english.chosun.com/site/data/html_dir/2011/04/13/2011041300546.html.

123. Kim Seung-hyun and Kim Mi-ju, "Jong-un's Allies Getting Positions, Says Spy Chief," *Joongang Ilbo*, April 20, 2011, http://joongangdaily.joins.com/article/view.asp?aid=2935088.

124. Mok Yong-jae, "North Korea's 'Princelings' Unveiled," *DailyNK*, April 18, 2011, http://www.dailynk.com/english/read.php?cataId=nk00400&num=7587.

125. "N. Korea Promotes Power Elite ahead of Anniversary," *Chosun Ilbo*, April 14, 2011, http://english.chosun.com/site/data/html_dir/2011/04/14/2011041400679.html.

126. Kim Yong-hun, "Lee Myung-su Covers Many Security Bases," *DailyNK*, April 8, 2011, http://dailynk.com/english/read.php?cataId=nk00400&num=7548.

127. "N. Korea's Defense Minister Sidelined in Hereditary Succession Process: Official," Yonhap, August 11, 2011, http://english.yonhapnews.co.kr/northkorea/2011/08/11/0401000000AEN20110811005000315.HTML.

128. See Kiyohito Kokita, "North Korean 'New Military' Led by Hard-Line General," *Asahi Shimbun*, December 8, 2010, http://www.asahi.com/english/TKY201012070215.html; and Yoshihiro Makino, "'New Military' Close to Jong un Rises in North Korea," *Asahi Shimbun*, October 30, 2010, http://www.asahi.com/english/TKY201010290317.html.

129. Yonhap, "N. Korean Heir-Apparent Wields Command."

130. See Joseph Bermudez, Jr., "SIGINT, EW, and EIW in the Korean People's Army: An Overview of Development and Organization," in *Bytes and Bullets: Information Technology, Revolution, and National Security on the Korean Peninsula*, ed. Alexandre Y. Monsourov (Honolulu: Asia Pacific Center for Security Studies, 2005), http://www.apcss.org/Publications/Edited%20Volumes/BytesAndBullets/CH13.pdf.

131. Toshimitsu Shigemura, "Will Chance Come for [Japan's] Diplomacy to Resolve Abduction Issue? Forecast of Future of North Korea, Shaken over Who Will Succeed Kim Jong-il," *Seiron* (in Japanese), November 30, 2008, 138–43.

132. Kim Ji-hyun, "[Interview] Views Mixed on Post-Kim North," *Korea Herald*, January 1, 2008, http://www.koreaherald.co.kr/NEWKHSITE/data/html_dir/2009/01/01/200901010037.asp.

133. See Ministry of National Defense, Republic of Korea, "Defense White Paper."

134. See "N. Korean Regime Intensifies 'Reign of Terror,'" *Chosun Ilbo*, January 13, 2011, http://english.chosun.com/site/data/html_dir/2011/01/13/2011011300997.html; and "N. Korea Holds Public Execution over S. Korean Propaganda," *Chosun Ilbo*, January 24, 2011, http://english.chosun.com/site/data/html_dir/2011/01/24/2011012401103.html.

135. Kim So-yeol, "Cloak and Dagger on the Pyongyang Streets?," *DailyNK*, January 24, 2011, http://www.dailynk.com/english/read.php?cataId=nk00400&num=7288.

136. For detailed information about purges, executions, and "mysterious" deaths in 2010 and 2011, see "2 Senior N. Korean Apparatchiks Executed," *Chosun Ilbo*, April 4, 2011, http://english.chosun.com/site/data/html_dir/2011/04/04/2011040400443.html; "N. Korea Purges Deputy Spy Chief," *Chosun Ilbo*, May 20, 2011, http://english.chosun.com/site/data/html_dir/2011/05/20/2011052000884.html; and "N. Korea Purges 30 Officials Involved in Inter-Korean Talks," *Donga Ilbo*, July 15, 2011, http://english.donga.com/srv/service.php3?biid=2011071598898.

137. For details on how younger individuals were being granted key posts within the security services in 2011, see Lee Beom-ki and Lee Seok-young, "Younger Men Taking over Security World," *DailyNK*, June 21, 2011, http://www.dailynk.com/english/read.php?cataId=nk01500&num=7853.

138. "Kim Jong-un's Barbaric Purge of 'Unsound' Military Brass," *Chosun Ilbo*, March 22, 2012, http://english.chosun.com/site/data/html_dir/2012/03/22/2012032200933.html.

139. Associated Press, "N Korea Names New Defense Minister amid Rocket Row," Fox News, April 10, 2012, http://www.foxnews.com/world/2012/04/10/north-korea-names-new-defense-minister-amid-rocket-row/.

140. For a synopsis of the key positions that Kim Chong-un was appointed to during April 2012, see Choe Sang-hun, "As Rocket Launching Nears, North Korea Continues Shift to New 'Supreme Leader,'" *New York Times*, April 11, 2012, http://www.nytimes.com/2012/04/12/world/asia/young-north-korean-leader-kim-jong-un-chosen-as-head-of-ruling-party.html; "Kim Jong-un Named First Chairman of National Defense Commission," Yonhap, April 13, 2012, http://english.yonhapnews.co.kr/northkorea/2012/04/13/0401000000AEN20120413007700315.HTML; and Associated Press, "Kim Jong-un Named as Top Political Official," *Tulsa (Oklahoma) World*, April 12, 2012, http://www.tulsaworld.com/news/article.aspx?subjectid=13&articleid=20120412_13_A6_CUTLIN494889.

141. See Kim So-yeol, "The Rise and Rise of Choi Hyong-rae," *Daily NK*, April 11, 2012, http://www.dailynk.com/english/read.php?cataId=nk00100&num=9095.

142. See Yonhap, "N. Korea Appoints New Members."

143. See "Jang Song-taek Gains Control of Kim Jong-un's Guards," *Chosun Ilbo*, April 30, 2012, http://english.chosun.com/site/data/html_dir/2012/04/30/2012043001371.html.

144. Kosuke Takahashi, "What's Going on in North Korea?" *The Diplomat*, July 19, 2012, http://thediplomat.com/2012/07/19/whats-going-on-in-north-korea/.

145. N.Korean Army Chief Refused to go Quietly," *Chosun Ilbo*, July 20, 2012, http://english.chosun.com/site/data/html_dir/2012/07/20/2012072000583.html.

146. For an example of reporting that reflects concern over Yi's purging in July of 2012, See: "North Korea's Kim Jong-un Named Marshal," *BBC News*, July 18, 2012, http://www.bbc.co.uk/news/world-asia-18881524.

147. See: "N. Korean Army Chief Demoted After Defections," *Chosun Ilbo*, October 11, 2012, http://english.chosun.com/site/data/html_dir/2012/10/11/2012101100931 .html; "Allegation of Collective Escape of 10-Odd DPRK High-Ranking Elites 'Including Kim Jong-Gak's Son: Raised . . . Government Unable to Confirm," *Chosun Ilbo* (in Korean), December 13, 2012, http://www.accessmylibrary.com/article-1G1- 311352794/south-korean-report-says.html.

148. For more details regarding the changing defense minister in North Korea during 2012, see Choe Sang-hun, "Top North Korean Defense Official Replaced, South Korea Says," *New York Times*, November 29, 2012, http://www.nytimes.com/2012/11 /30/world/asia/top-north-korean-defense-official-replaced-seoul-says.html?_r=0.

149. For more analysis on the purges and shuffling of positions in the North Korean military during 2012, see Kim Hee-jin, "In First Year, Taming the Army Was Kim's Goal," *Joongang Ilbo*, December 17, 2012, http://koreajoongangdaily.joinsmsn.com /news/article/article.aspx?aid=2964066&cloc=rss%7Cnews%7Cjoongangdaily; "Top 4 N. Korean Military Officials Fall Victim to Shakeup," *Chosun Ilbo*, November 30, 2012, http://english.chosun.com/site/data/html_dir/2012/11/30/2012113001209.html.

150. For more background on the history of purges in North Korea, see Kim Hyun-a, "Purges Keep Regime Alive," *Radio Free Asia*, November 8, 2012, http://www.rfa.org /english/commentaries/purge-11082012131640.html.

151. See "Kim Jong-un Still Trying to Get Control of Military," *Chosun Ilbo*, November 19, 2012, http://english.chosun.com/site/data/html_dir/2012/11/19/2012111901287.html; "Kim Jong-un Checks Loyalty of Top N. Korean Officials," *Chosun Ilbo*, November 21, 2012, http://english.chosun.com/site/data/html_dir/2012/11/21/2012112100848.html.

152. "Kim Jong-un Beefs up Security Amid Fear of Unrest," *Chosun Ilbo*, December 6, 2012, http://english.chosun.com/site/data/html_dir/2012/12/06/2012120601143.html.

153. "Kim Far behind in Succession Stakes," *DailyNK*, June 29, 2011, http://dailynk.com /english/read.php?cataId=nk00100&num=7891.

154. Yoo Ho-yeol, "Kim Jong-il Succession Could Mean Crisis or Opportunity," *Chosun Ilbo*, October 4, 2010, http://english.chosun.com/site/data/html_dir/2010/10/04 /2010100401232.html.

155. Kim Yong-hun, "There Is Still a Possibility of Uprising in North Korean Society," *DailyNK*, July 21, 2011, http://www.dailynk.com/english/read.php?num =7967&cataId=nk00300.

156. For in-depth analysis about the disruptions in elite elements of North Korean society during the transition period that began in earnest during 2010, see Kim Yong-hun, "Kim Jong-nam Standing on the Highway," *DailyNK*, September 22, 2011, http://www.dailynk.com/english/read.php?cataId=nk00100&num=8203.

157. "Doctors Identify Kim Jong-il's 3 Main Health Problems," *Chosun Ilbo*, February 14, 2011, http://english.chosun.com/site/data/html_dir/2011/02/14 /2011021401098.html.

158. See Song Sang-ho, "N. K. Succession Appears Smoother than Expected," *Korea Herald*, September 28, 2011, http://www.koreaherald.com/national/Detail.jsp?newsMLId =20110928000820.

159. See "How N. Korea's Fate Hangs on Kim Jong-il's Health," *Chosun Ilbo*, February 19, 2011, http://english.chosun.com/site/data/html_dir/2011/02/19 /2011021900214.html; and Associated Press, "Committee of Advisers May Help Kim Jong Un," *The (Macon, Georgia) Telegraph*, December 21, 2011, http://www.macon.com /2011/12/21/1833330/committee-of-advisers-may-help.html#storylink%3dcpy.

160. For more analysis on the differences in the succession process between Kim Jong-il and Kim Chong-un, see Kongdan Oh, "The Death of Kim Jong-il," *Analysis* (Washington, DC: Brookings Institution, December 22, 2011), http://www.brookings .edu/opinions/2011/1219_north_korea_oh.aspx.

161. Some portions of the first part of this chapter were previously published in Bruce E. Bechtol, Jr., "Maintaining a Rogue Military: North Korea's Military Capabilities and Strategy at the End of the Kim Jong-il Era," *International Journal of Korean Studies* 16, no. 1 (Spring/Summer 2012): 160–91. Other excerpts in this chapter were previously published in Bruce E. Bechtol, Jr., "Developments in the North Korean Asymmetric Threat: Missiles and Electronic Warfare Missiles and Electronic Warfare," *International Journal of Korean Studies* 16, no. 2 (Fall/Winter 2012): 107–29. The author would like to thank Dr. Hugo Kim, the editor. Some of the analysis reflected in this chapter was also done with the sponsorship of the Air Force Research Institute for a study on the role of airpower in Asia out to the year 2020. The author would like to thank the Air Force Research Institute.

162. For details on South Korean efforts to reverse national defense mistakes that the Roh administration made, and the budget adjustments that ensued as a result, see "Military Reform 2020 Seeing Gradual Elimination," *Donga Ilbo*, October 4, 2010, http://english.donga.com/srv/service.php3?biid=2010100466248; Lee Chi-dong, "S. Korea Unveils Vision for Defense Industry," Yonhap, October 19, 2010, http://english.yonhapnews.co.kr/national/2010/10/19/46/0301000000AEN201010 19004200315F.HTML; and "Defense Industry Requests Budget Increase for Better Combat Readiness," Yonhap, July 7, 2011, http://english.yonhapnews.co.kr /national/2011/07/07/52/0301000000AEN20110707000400315F.HTML.

163. For more details of planned and ongoing ROK acquisitions of command and control systems and intelligence collection aircraft, see "Three Firms Chosen to Develop Advanced Military Communications Network," Yonhap, October 20, 2010, http://english .yonhapnews.co.kr/national/2010/10/20/63/0301000000AEN20101020005100315F .HTML; Jung Sung-ki, "Korean Air to Develop UAV for Division Operations," *Korea Times*, September 13, 2010, http://www.koreatimes.co.kr/www/news/nation/2011 /08/205_72981.html; and "ROK TV Shows First Spy Plane E-737 AEW&C Arriving for Deployment," KBS TV (in Korean), August 1, 2011, http://www.kbs.co.kr/tv/1tv.html.

164. See "Air Force Gets Two More F-15K Jets," Yonhap, March 14, 2011, http://english .yonhapnews.co.kr/national/2011/03/14/44/0301000000AEN20110314008800315F

.HTML; Jung Sung-ki, "US Approves Sale of Stealthy F-15 to South Korea," *Korea Times*, September 12, 2010, http://www.koreatimes.co.kr/www/news/nation/2010/09/205 _72945.html; and Song Sang-ho, "S. Korea Accelerates Stealth Fighter Acquisition Efforts," *Korea Herald*, March 3, 2011, http://www.asianewsnet.net/home /news.php?id=17714&sec=1 .

165. Evan Ramstead, "U.S., Seoul, Make Plans to Respond to Attacks," *Wall Street Journal*, July 8, 2011, http://online.wsj.com/article/SB10001424052702303544604576431470481160628 .html.

166. For more information about measures that ROK military forces have taken to counter North Korean Special Operations Forces, see "Frontline Defenses to Be Beefed Up," *Chosun Ilbo*, April 6, 2011, http://english.chosun.com/site/data/html _dir/2011/04/06/2011040601083.html.

167. See Yonhap, "S. Korean, U.S. Militaries Sign Pact to Bolster Joint Drills," *Korea Times*, April 27, 2012, http://www.koreatimes.co.kr/www/news/nation/2012/05/113 _109824.html.

168. "Korea Confirms Delay of U.S. Base Relocation," *Korea Herald*, March 29, 2011, http://media.daum.net/foreign/englishnews/view.html?cateid=1047&newsid =20110329183307759&p=koreaherald.

169. For details on ROK-U.S. missile defense cooperation and ongoing Japanese-U.S. BMD efforts, see Hwang Doo-hyong, "U.S., S. Korea Sign Agreement on Missile Defense System Development: Pentagon," Yonhap, April 16, 2011, http://english .yonhapnews.co.kr/national/2011/04/16/13/0301000000AEN20110416000100315 F.HTML; "S. Korea, U.S. Conduct Joint Study on Missile Defense System," Yonhap, April 15, 2011, http://english.yonhapnews.co.kr/national/2011/04/15 /0301000000AEN20110415007500320.HTML; "Japan to Deploy Missile Interceptors Nationwide on North Korea Threat," *Kyodo News*, December 9, 2010, http://www.freerepublic.com/focus/f-news/2641150/posts; and "U.S. Tells Japan of 2-Yr Delay in Development of Missile Interceptor," *Mainichi News*, September 17, 2011, http://mdn.mainichi.jp/mdnnews/news/20110917p2g00m0dm011000c.html.

170. See John Power, "Should S. Korea Increase Its Missile Range?," *Asia One*, April 24, 2012, http://www.asiaone.com/News/AsiaOne+News/Asia/Story/A1Story20120424 -341667.html.

171. During the spring of 2012, South Korean president Lee Myung-bak made public statements that the 300-kilometer limit for the South Korean missile's range is not sufficient. See Christian Oliver, "South Korea Out to Extend Missile Range," *Financial Times*, March 21, 2012, http://www.ft.com/cms/s/0/ad35d806-7333-11e1-9014 -00144feab49a.html#axzz1w8iX13PF.

172. For more information on the numbers and locations of U.S. Patriot batteries deployed on the Korean Peninsula to protect U.S. bases, see "U.S. to Withdraw Patriot Missiles from Gwangju," *Chosun Ilbo*, August 24, 2006, http://english.chosun.com/site/data /html_dir/2006/08/24/2006082461011.html.

173. For details regarding the 2012 agreement between Seoul and Washington on the range of South Korea's missiles targeting the North, see Chico Harlan, "South Korea Extends Missile Range Under New Deal With U.S.," *Washington Post*, October 7, 2012, http://articles.washingtonpost.com/2012-10-07/world/35502039_1_missile-guideline

-unha-3-missile-technology-control-regime; Sung-won Shin, "U.S., South Korea Agree on Longer Range Ballistic Missiles," Reuters, October 7, 2012, http://www.reuters .com/article/2012/10/07/us-korea-usa-missile-idUSBRE89602J20121007; and Mok Yong Jae, "South Overjoyed with Missile Victory," *Daily NK*, October 8, 2012, http://www.dailynk.com/english/read.php?catId=nk00100&num=9890.

174. For details regarding the 2012 agreement between Seoul and Washington to cooperate on BMD, and the capabilities of the PAC-2 BMD system, see Kim Hee-jin and Jeong Yong-soo, "Korea, U.S. Agree on More Missile Defense," *Joongang Ilbo*, October 26, 2012, http://koreajoongangdaily.joinsmsn.com/news/article/article.aspx ?aid=2961367; "S. Korea Moves to Upgrade Patriot Missile Defense System," Yonhap, October 28, 2012, http://english.yonhapnews.co.kr/national/2012/10/28/4 /0301000000AEN20121028000800315F.HTML; "ROK-US Security Consultive Meeting Fails to Clarify Suspicions on Korea's Participation in Missile Defense," *Kyunghyang Shinmun*, October 26, 2012, http://english.khan.co.kr/khan_art_view.html ?artid=201210261432017&code=790101; "Joint Communique': The 44th U.S.-ROK Security Consultative Meeting," *United States Department of Defense*, October 24, 2012, http://www.defense.gov/news/44thSCMJointCommunique.pdf.

175. See Hyung-Jin Kim, "N Korea Says South, US are Within Its Missile Range," Associated Press, October 9, 2012, http://news.yahoo.com/nkorea-says-south-us -within-missile-range-035424765.html.

176. Kim Min-seok and Brian Lee, "Key Defense Mission to Go to Korean Military," *Joongang Ilbo*, April 11, 2005, http://www.worldsecuritynetwork.com/showArticle3.cfm ?article_id=11239.

177. For details about North Korea's long-range artillery capabilities and the weaknesses in South Korea's ability to counter them, see "S. Korea Lacks Radar to Detect N. Korean Artillery," *Chosun Ilbo*, August 22, 2011, http://english.chosun.com/site/data /html_dir/2011/08/22/2011082201021.html; and "S. Korea Must Bolster Its Defense against N. Korean Artillery," *Chosun Ilbo*, August 22, 2011, http://english.chosun.com /site/data/html_dir/2011/08/22/2011082201024.html.

178. Kim Min-seok, "War Plan by U.S. and Seoul Needs Updating, Upgrade," *Joongang Ilbo*, October 5, 2010, http://joongangdaily.joins.com/article/view.asp?aid=2926768.

179. See "Joint Communiqué: The 42nd U.S.-ROK Security Consultative Meeting," *U.S. Defense News*, October 8, 2010, http://www.defense.gov/news/d20101008usrok.pdf.

180. "S. Korea–U.S. Drill to Prepare for Regime Collapse in N. Korea," *Chosun Ilbo*, February 15, 2011, http://english.chosun.com/site/data/html_dir/2011/02/15 /2011021500290.html.

181. "S. Korea, U.S. to Practice Destroying N. Korean WMDs," *Chosun Ilbo*, August 8, 2011, http://english.chosun.com/site/data/html_dir/2011/08/08/2011080800747.html.

182. See "S. Korea, U.S. Practice Stabilizing N. Korea in Civil War," *Chosun Ilbo*, April 8, 2012, http://english.chosun.com/site/data/html_dir/2012/04/06 /2012040600891.html.

183. "CONPLAN 5029 Cedes Control to U.S. and China in N. Korean Emergency," *Hankyoreh*, July 30, 2011, http://english.hani.co.kr/arti/english_edition /e_northkorea/489727.html.

184. Kim Yoon-mi, "Powers Rushing to Ensure Stability in Korea," *Korea Herald*, December 30, 2011, http://www.koreaherald.com/national/Detail.jsp?newsMLId =20111230000424.

## 3. THE SINKING OF THE *CHEONAN* AND THE SHELLING OF YEONPYEONG ISLAND

1. See Joint Civilian-Military Investigative Group, Republic of Korea, Ministry of National Defense, "Investigation Result on the Sinking of the ROKS Cheonan," Global Security.org, May 20, 2010, http://www.globalsecurity.org/military /library/report/2010/100520_jcmig-roks-cheonan/100520_jcmig-roks-cheonan.pdf.

2. Bruce E. Bechtol, Jr., "The Cheonan Incident and North Korea's Northern Limit Line Strategy" (Washington, DC: American Enterprise Institute [AEI] Center for Defense Studies, May 25, 2010), http://www.defensestudies.org/?p=2575.

3. Reid G. Miller, "S. Korea Sinks N. Korea Ship—about 30 N. Korean Sailors Believed Killed," *Seattle Times*, June 15, 1999, http://www.thefreelibrary.com/S.+KOREA +SINKS+N.+KOREAN+SHIP+—+ABOUT+30+NORTH+KOREAN+SAILORS .-a064245394.

4. Ministry of National Defense, Republic of Korea, "The Naval Clash on the Yellow Sea on 29 June 2002 between South Korea and North Korea: The Situation and ROK's Position," Global Security.org, July 1, 2002, http://www.globalsecurity.org /wmd/library/news/rok/2002/0020704-naval.htm.

5. Ser Myo-ja and Kim Min-seok, "Seoul Goes on Alert after Sharp Attack by Pyongyang," *Joongang Ilbo*, January 19, 2009, http://joongangdaily.joins.com /article/view.asp?aid=2900020.

6. Kim Hyun and Sam Kim, "Tensions Rise over N. Korea's Renewed Sea Border Claim," Yonhap, January 17, 2009. http://english.yonhapnews.co.kr/news/2009 /01/17/0200000000AEN20090117002600315.HTML.

7. Sam Kim, "Chinese Boats Vanish as Tension Rises in Waters between Koreas," Yonhap, February 10, 2009, http://english.yonhapnews.co.kr/national/2009 /02/10/97/0301000000AEN20090210006900315F.HTML.

8. John McCreary, "Nightwatch: 11 February 2009," *AFCEA Intelligence*, February 11, 2009, http://nightwatch.afcea.org/NightWatch_20090211.htm.

9. For more about Kim Kyok-sik's background and reassignment, see "A Provocation by General Kim Kyok-sik Plotting Comeback in Pyongyang?," *Joongang Ilbo*, March 16, 2009, http://nk.joins.com/news/view.asp?aid=3335047&cont=news_polit.

10. AFP, "N Korea's Kim Picks Hawk for Top Military Post," Yahoo!News, February 20, 2009, http://asia.news.yahoo.com/090220/afp/090220064136asiapacificnews.html.

11. See Jeong Yong-soo, "North Korea's Military Strengthens Its Grip," *Joongang Ilbo*, April 21, 2009, http://joongangdaily.joins.com/article/view.asp?aid=2903832.

12. For more detailed information about the short skirmish that occurred on November 10, 2009, and Kim Jong-il's reported vow of revenge, see "N. Korean Officer Says North Sank Cheonan," *Chosun Ilbo*, April 20, 2010, http://english.chosun.com/site /data/html_dir/2010/04/20/2010042000972.html; and "Rumors Link Cheonan

Sinking to Revenge for Naval Skirmish," *Chosun Ilbo*, April 19, 2010, http://english
.chosun.com/site/data/html_dir/2010/04/19/2010041901395.html.

13.  For more details of the live-fire artillery drills that North Korea conducted near the
     NLL during January 2010, see "DPRK Fires Artillery Again near Disputed Sea
     Border: Gov't," *Xinhua*, January 28, 2010, http://english.cctv.com/20100129/102716
     .shtml; "N. Korea Fires Artillery near Sea Border for Third Day," AFP, January 29,
     2010, http://www.france24.com/en/20100129-nkorea-fires-artillery-near-border-
     third-day; "N. Korean Artillery Fire Was Time-on-Target Drill," *Chosun Ilbo*, January
     29, 2010, http://english.chosun.com/site/data/html_dir/2010/01/29
     /2010012900402.html; "N. Korea Resumes Shooting, Agrees to Help Recover U.S.
     War Remains," Yonhap, January 28, 2010, http://english.yonhapnews.co.kr/national
     /2010/01/28/59/0301000000AEN20100128004300315F.HTML; and Yoo Jee-ho
     and Lee Min-yong, "North's Action Called Measured Message," *Joongang Ilbo*, January
     29, 2010, http://joongangdaily.joins.com/article/view.asp?aid=2915953.

14.  See "S. Korean Ship Sinking in Yellow Sea," Yonhap, March 26, 2010,
     http://english.yonhapnews.co.kr/national/2010/03/27/13/0301000000AEN201003
     27000100315F.HTML; and Shin Hae-in, "S. Korea Continues Rescue Operations on
     Sunken Ship," Yonhap, March 27, 2010, http://english.yonhapnews.co.kr/national
     /2010/03/27/77/0301000000AEN20100327002900315F.HTML.

15.  "DPRK's Scout Planes Reportedly Come down near NLL 26 Mar," KBS TV (in
     Korean), March 28, 2010, http://www.kbs.co.kr/plan_table/channel/1tv/index.html.

16.  Lee Tae-hoon, "More Questions Raised Than Answered over Sunken Ship," *Korea
     Times*, March 28, 2010, http://www.koreatimes.co.kr/www/news/nation/2010
     /03/113_63157.html.

17.  Oh Kyu-wook, "Testimonies from Survivors," *Korea Herald*, March 28, 2010,
     http://www.koreaherald.co.kr/NEWKHSITE/data/html_dir/2010/03/29
     /201003290037.asp.

18.  Lee Chi-dong, "Navy Rules out Internal Explosion as Cause of Ship Sinking,"
     Yonhap, March 30, 2010, http://english.yonhapnews.co.kr/national/2010/03/30
     /0301000000AEN20100330009200315.HTML.

19.  "New Clues to Sinking of the Cheonan Emerge," *Chosun Ilbo*, March 31, 2010,
     http://english.chosun.com/site/data/html_dir/2010/03/31/2010033100669.html.

20.  "N. Korean Submarine 'Left Base before the Cheonan Sank,'" *Chosun Ilbo*, March 31,
     2010, http://english.chosun.com/site/data/html_dir/2010/03/31
     /2010033101024.html.

21.  "No North Korean Submarine Detected on Night Navy Ship Sank," Yonhap, April 1,
     2010, http://english.yonhapnews.co.kr/news/2010/04/01/0200000000AEN20100
     401010300315.HTML.

22.  "Suspicion of N. Korean Hand in Sinking Mounts," *Chosun Ilbo*, April 2, 2010,
     http://english.chosun.com/site/data/html_dir/2010/04/02/2010040200382.html.

23.  Christine Kim, "South Korea Says Torpedo May Have Sunk Navy Ship," Reuters,
     April 2, 2010, http://news.yahoo.com/s/nm/20100402/wl_nm/us_korea_ship_1.

24.  Kang Min-Seok and Lee Min-yong, "Torpedo Likely Cause of Sinking," *Joongang Ilbo*,
     April 3, 2010, http://joongangdaily.joins.com/article/view.asp?aid=2918721.

25. "Seoul Requests Washington's Help in Finding Cause of Warship Explosion," Yonhap, April 5, 1010, http://english.yonhapnews.co.kr/national/2010/04/05/98 /0301000000AEN20100405004600315F.HTML.

26. "Coast Guard Finds Two Bodies from Ship Wreck in Yellow Sea," Yonhap, April 3, 2010, http://english.yonhapnews.co.kr/national/2010/04/03/3 /0302000000AEN20100403003100315F.HTML.

27. "Navy Gearing up to Salvage Sunken Warship," Yonhap, April 4, 2010, http://english .yonhapnews.co.kr/national/2010/04/04/17/0301000000AEN20100404000900315F .HTML.

28. "Rescue Divers Believe the Cheonan Was Hit from Below," *Chosun Ilbo*, April 5, 2010, http://english.chosun.com/site/data/html_dir/2010/04/05/2010040500841.html.

29. "Torpedo Attack Likeliest Cause of Shipwreck," *Chosun Ilbo*, April 5, 2010, http://english.chosun.com/site/data/html_dir/2010/04/05/2010040500926.html.

30. "NIS Says N. Korean Attack on Cheonan Impossible sans Kim Jong-il Approval," *Hankyoreh Daily*, April 7, 2010, http://english.hani.co.kr/arti/english_edition /e_national/414775.html.

31. "N. Korean Military 'Put on Alert after Shipwreck,'" *Chosun Ilbo*, April 8, 2010, http://english.chosun.com/site/data/html_dir/2010/04/08/2010040800537.html.

32. "Seoul to Invite More Foreign Experts to Probe Naval Disaster: PM," Yonhap, April 7, 2010, http://english.yonhapnews.co.kr/news/2010/04/07/0200000000AEN 20100407004200315.HTML.

33. Shin Hae-in, "Overseas Experts to Assist Probe of Sunken S. Korean Ship: Official," Yonhap, April 8, 2010, http://english.yonhapnews.co.kr/news/2010/04/08 /0200000000AEN20100408007000315.HTML.

34. Jung Sung-ki, "Multinational Joint Investigation Team to Examine Wreckage to Uncover Cause of Ship Sinking," *Korea Times*, April 15, 2010, http://www.koreatimes .co.kr/www/news/nation/2010/04/205_64257.html.

35. "S. Korea to Move Part of Sunken Ship amid Bad Weather," Yonhap, April 12, 2010, http://english.yonhapnews.co.kr/national/2010/04/12/40/0301000000AEN 20100412008000315F.HTML.

36. Jung Sung-ki, "More Weight Put on Outside Impact for Ship Sinking," *Korea Times*, April 13, 2010, http://www.koreatimes.co.kr/www/news/nation/2010/04/205_64153.html.

37. Lee Tae-hoon, "External Impact Likely Cause of Ship Sinking," *Korea Times*, April 15, 2010, http://www.koreatimes.co.kr/www/news/nation/2010/04/113_64242.html.

38. "External Explosion Likely Caused Sinking," *Donga Ilbo*, April 16, 2010, http://english.donga.com/srv/service.php3?biid=2010041748108.

39. "S. Korea Steps Up Investigation into Ship Sinking," Yonhap, April 20, 2010, http://english.yonhapnews.co.kr/national/2010/04/20/57/0301000000AEN 20100420008900315F.HTML.

40. "U.S. Gets More Active in Cheonan Investigation," *Chosun Ilbo*, April 20, 2010, http://english.chosun.com/site/data/html_dir/2010/04/20/2010042000432.html.

41. Ser Myon-ja, "Foreign Experts to Sign Off on Cheonan Probe: Lee," *Joongang Ilbo*, April 21, 2010, http://joongangdaily.joins.com/article/view.asp?aid=2919464.

42. Yoo Jee-ho, "North's Denial on Cheonan Is Very Familiar," *Joongang Ilbo*, April 20, 2010, http://joongangdaily.joins.com/article/view.asp?aid=2919418.

43. Pak Pyong-chin and Na Ki-chon, "Sinking of ROK's Cheonan Attributed to General Reconnaissance Bureau of North," *Segye Ilbo* (in Korean), April 10, 2010, http://www.segye.com/Articles/Main.asp.

44. "Lawmaker Points to Signs Linking N. Korean Sub to Shipwreck," *Chosun Ilbo*, April 6, 2010, http://english.chosun.com/site/data/html_dir/2010/04/06 /2010040600350.html.

45. "N. Korean Leadership 'Closely Involved in Cheonan Sinking,'" *Chosun Ilbo*, May 27, 2010, http://english.chosun.com/site/data/html_dir/2010/05/27 /2010052701465.html.

46. Kim So-hyun, "Reconnaissance Bureau Is Heart of N. K. Terrorism," *Korea Herald*, May 26, 2010, http://www.koreaherald.com/national/Detail.jsp?newsMLId =20100526000675.

47. "N. Korea Sharply Increased Underwater Military Training in 2009: Sources," *Kyodo News*, May 16, 2010, http://www.breitbart.com/article.php?id=D9FNSBB00&show _article=1.

48. Shin Joo-hyun, "North Korean Submarine Helmsman Breaks 14-Year Silence," *Daily NK*, June 1, 2010, http://www.dailynk.com/english/read.php?cataId=nk02500 &num=6445.

49. Yoshiro Makino, "US, ROK Confirm North Korean Sub Exported to Iran," *Asahi Shimbun* (in Japanese), June 9, 2010, http://www.asahi.com.

50. Kim Tae-hong, "Google Earth Torpedoes North Korean Lie," *Daily NK*, June 1, 2010, http://www.dailynk.com/english/read.php?cataId=nk00100&num=6444.

51. "Cheonan Sinking Likely Caused by Bubble Jet from Explosion," *Hankyoreh Daily*, April 17, 2010, http://english.hani.co.kr/arti/english_edition/e_national/416519.html.

52. "Military Intelligence Immediately Suspected N. Korea in Ship Sinking: Source," Yonhap, April 22, 2010, http://english.yonhapnews.co.kr/national/2010/04/22/10 /0301000000AEN20100422007000315F.HTML.

53. Lee Sung-jin, "Cheonan Sinking Rumor Proudly Circulating in North Korea," *Daily NK*, April 27, 2010, http://www.dailynk.com/english/read.php?cataId=nk01500 &num=6286.

54. Kim So-hyun, "Kim Visits Army Unit Spying on S. Korea," *Korea Herald*, April 27, 2010, http://www.koreaherald.com/national/Detail.jsp?newsMLId =20100427000663.

55. Evan Ramstead, "Standoff over Ship Escalates," *Wall Street Journal*, April 25, 2010, http://online.wsj.com/article/SB10001424052748704446704575205400833858626.html? KEYWORDS=EVAN+RAMSTAD.

56. "'Non-Contact Explosion' the Most Likely Cause of Sinking: Official," Yonhap, April 25, 2010, http://english.yonhapnews.co.kr/national/2010/04/25/60 /0301000000AEN20100425002000315F.HTML.

57. "S. Korean Mine Ruled Out as Cause of Ship Sinking," Yonhap, April 28, 2010, http://english.yonhapnews.co.kr/news/2010/04/28/0200000000AEN201004 28004100315.HTML.

58. Byun Duk-kun, "Seoul Seeks Support of China, Russia to Refer Warship Sinking to U.N.," Yonhap, April 28, 2010, http://english.yonhapnews.co.kr/national/2010/04/28/40 /0301000000AEN20100428008000315F.HTML.

59. "Scientists Say Direct Heavy Torpedo Sank Cheonan," *Chosun Ilbo*, April 30, 2010, http://english.chosun.com/site/data/html_dir/2010/04/30/2010043000459.html.

60. "Torpedo Attack 'Could Be Proved from State of Wreck Alone,'" *Chosun Ilbo*, April 30, 2010, http://english.chosun.com/site/data/html_dir/2010/04/30/2010043000421.html.

61. Lee Chi-dong, "S. Korea, China Hold Talks as Seoul Seeks Cooperation on Sunken Ship," Yonhap, April 30, 2010, http://english.yonhapnews.co.kr/northkorea/2010/04/30/0401000000AEN20100430007700315.HTML.

62. Jonathan Thatcher, "South Korea Stops Just Short of Blaming North for Sinking," Reuters, May 4, 2010, http://www.reuters.com/article/idUSTRE6430HT20100504.

63. Lee Myung-bak, "Opening Remarks by President Lee Myung-bak at a Meeting with Top Commanders of the ROK Armed Forces, May 04, 2010," Office of the President, Republic of Korea, May 4, 2010, http://english.president.go.kr/pre_activity/speeches/speeches_view.php?uno=3119&board_no=E03.

64. Jung Sung-ki, "Military to Boost Surveillance, Anti-Sub Capability," *Korea Times*, May 4, 2010, http://www.koreatimes.co.kr/www/news/nation/2010/05/205_65361.html.

65. See Kim Min-seok and Ser Myo-ja, "Cheonan Probe Detects TNT Type," *Joongang Ilbo*, May 14, 2010, http://joongangdaily.joins.com/article/view.asp?aid=2920461.

66. "U.S. Senators Call for Thorough Probe of Cheonan Sinking," Yonhap, May 13, 2010, http://english.yonhapnews.co.kr/national/2010/05/14/4/0301000000AEN20100514000800315F.HTML.

67. "N. Korea Denied Role in S. Korean Ship Sinking: Chinese Envoy," Yonhap, May 17, 2010, http://english.yonhapnews.co.kr/national/2010/05/17/0301000000AEN20100517006500315.HTML.

68. "Cheonan Investigators Find Pieces of Torpedo Propeller," *Chosun Ilbo*, May 18, 2010, http://english.chosun.com/site/data/html_dir/2010/05/18/2010051800420.html.

69. Song Sang-ho, "Explosive Traces Identical to Those of N. K. Torpedo," *Korea Herald*, May 18, 2010, http://www.koreaherald.com/national/Detail.jsp?newsMLId=20100518000726.

70. "Cheonan Probe Results to Go to 30 Major Nations," *Donga Ilbo*, May 19, 2010, http://english.donga.com/srv/service.php3?bicode=050000&biid=2010051961128.

71. Sam Kim, "S. Korea Briefs Envoys of China, Russia, Japan on Warship Sinking," Yonhap, May 19, 2010, http://english.yonhapnews.co.kr/northkorea/2010/05/19/33/0401000000AEN20100519004100315F.HTML.

72. Jung Sung-ki and Kang Shin-who, "NK Lettering Discovered on Torpedo Fragments," *Korea Times*, May 19, 2010, http://www.koreatimes.co.kr/www/news/nation/2010/05/205_66153.html.

73. Joint Civilian-Military Investigative Group, "Investigation Result on the Sinking of ROKS Cheonan," *Republic of Korea, Ministry of National Defense*," May 20, 2010, http://www.globalsecurity.org/military/library/report/2010/100520_jcmig-roks-cheonan/100520_jcmig-roks-cheonan.pdf.

74. Chris Green, "Q&A Reveals Cheonan Disaster Details," *Daily NK*, May 20, 2010, http://www.dailynk.com/english/read.php?cataId=nk00100&num=6395.

75. Hwang Doo-Hyong, "U.S. Denounces N. Korea for Torpedoing S. Korean Warship," Yonhap, May 19, 2010, http://english.yonhapnews.co.kr/news/2010/05/20 /0200000000AEN20100520004600315.HTML.

76. Kim Deok-hyun, "S. Korea Confirms North's Torpedo Sank Warship," Yonhap, May 20, 2010, http://english.yonhapnews.co.kr/national/2010/05/20/50 /0301000000AEN20100520005000315F.HTML.

77. "US Bill Urges Return of NK to Terrorism List," *Donga Ilbo*, May 20, 2010, http://english.donga.com/srv/service.php3?bicode=060000&biid=2010052084218.

78. Lee Chi-dong, "Lee Convenes NSC Meeting for Countermeasures against N. Korea," Yonhap, May 21, 2010, http://english.yonhapnews.co.kr/national/2010/05/21/73 /0301000000AEN20100521002100315.HTML.

79. "S. Korea to Seek U.N. Resolution on N. Korea over Ship Attack," Yonhap, May 23, 2010, http://english.yonhapnews.co.kr/national/2010/05/23/52 /0301000000AEN20100523000400315F.HTML.

80. "72 Pct. Say NK Caused Cheonan Sinking," *Donga Ilbo*, May 22, 2010, http://english.donga.com/srv/service.php3?bicode=050000&biid=2010052219238.

81. Kim Deok-hyun, "U.N. Command to Probe Whether N. Korea Violated Armistice," Yonhap, May 21, 2010, http://english.yonhapnews.co.kr/national/2010/05/21/12 /0301000000AEN20100521002400315F.HTML.

82. "Full Text of President Lee's National Address," Yonhap, May 24, 2010, http://english.yonhapnews.co.kr/national/2010/05/24/42 /0301000000AEN20100524003400315F.HTML.

83. "South Korea Govt Introduces Ban on Citizens' Travel to North Korea," *Itar-Tass*, May 24, 2010, http://www.itar-tass.com/eng/level2.html?NewsID=15157163&PageNum=0.

84. Kim So-hyun, "Gaesong Industrial Park a Hot Potato," *Korea Herald*, May 24, 2010, http://www.koreaherald.com/national/Detail.jsp?newsMLId=20100524000751.

85. "N. Korea Says Will Sever All Inter-Korean Relations," Yonhap, May 25, 2010, http://english.yonhapnews.co.kr/northkorea/2010/05/25/0401000000AEN201005 25009000315.HTML.

86. "What Will Be the Impact of S. Korean Sanctions on N. Korea?," *Chosun Ilbo*, May 25, 2010, http://english.chosun.com/site/data/html_dir/2010/05/25/2010052501417 .html.

87. "'Psychological Warfare' against N. Korea Resumes," *Chosun Ilbo*, May 25, 2010, http://english.chosun.com/site/data/html_dir/2010/05/25/2010052501410.html.

88. Song Sang-ho, "N. K. Merchant Ship Deterred from Border," *Korea Herald*, Mary 26, 2010, http://www.koreaherald.com/national/Detail.jsp?newsMLId =20100526000768.

89. Hwang Doo-hyong, "House Approves Resolution Condemning N. Korea for Ship Sinking," Yonhap, May 25, 2010, http://english.yonhapnews.co.kr/national/2010/05/26 /17/0301000000AEN20100526000900315F.HTML.

90. "60% Approve of Sanctions against N. Korea," *Chosun Ilbo*, May 27, 2010, http://english.chosun.com/site/data/html_dir/2010/05/27/2010052700524.html.

91. Park In-ho, "South Korea Refutes North Korean Refutations of Investigation Results," *Daily NK*, May 31, 2010, http://www.dailynk.com/english/read.php?cataId =nk00100&num=6439.

92. Lee Chi-dong, "S. Korea Refers N. Korea's Naval Attack to U.N. Security Council: President Lee," Yonhap, June 4, 2010, http://english.yonhapnews.co.kr/northkorea/2010/06/04/0401000000AEN20100604008400315.HTML.

93. Hwang Doo-hyong, "U.S. Expects UNSC to Take Appropriate Response to N. Korea for Ship Sinking: State Dept.," Yonhap, June 4, 2010, http://english.yonhapnews.co.kr/national/2010/06/05/39/0301000000AEN20100605000300315F.HTML.

94. "Mandate of U.N. Panel on N. Korea Sanctions Extended for 1 Yr+," Breitbart, June 7, 2010, http://www.breitbart.com/article.php?id=D9G6GRD01&show_article=1.

95. "Experts to Explain Cheonan Findings to UN Security Council," *Chosun Ilbo*, June 10, 2010, http://english.chosun.com/site/data/html_dir/2010/06/10/2010061000862.html.

96. Chang Jae-soon, "No Objections from U.N. Security Council Members on Sunken Ship Probe: Official," Yonhap, June 15, 2010, http://english.yonhapnews.co.kr/national/2010/06/15/46/0301000000AEN20100615004200315F.HTML.

97. Hwang Doo-hyong, "U.N. Condemns Attack of S. Korean Warship without Naming N. Korea," Yonhap, July 8, 2010, http://english.yonhapnews.co.kr/national/2010/07/10/17/0301000000AEN20100710000900315F.HTML.

98. "[Editorial] After UNSC Statement," *Korea Herald*, July 9, 2010, http://media.daum.net/cplist/view.html?cateid=100000&cpid=22&newsid=20100709165836216&p=koreaherald.

99. See Donald Kirk, "Why North Korea Cheonan Sinking Gets Wrist Slap from UN," *Christian Science Monitor*, July 12, 2010, http://www.csmonitor.com/World/Asia-Pacific/2010/0712/Why-North-Korea-Cheonan-sinking-gets-wrist-slap-from-UN.

100. "Security Council Condemns Attack on Republic of Korea Naval Ship 'Cheonan,' Stresses Need to Prevent Further Attacks, Other Hostilities in the Region," United Nations Security Council, Department of Public Information, News and Media Division, July 9, 2010, http://www.un.org/News/Press/docs/2010/sc9975.doc.htm.

101. Yoo Jee-ho, "Russian Experts Here to Vet Probe," *Joongang Ilbo*, June 1, 2010, http://joongangdaily.joins.com/article/view.asp?aid=2921236.

102. "China Declines S. Korea Offer to Join Int'l Probe into Sunken Ship," *Kyodo News*, June 10, 2010, http://home.kyodo.co.jp/modules/fstStory/index.php?storyid=506041.

103. "11 N.K. Ships Expelled from the South's Waters Since Passage Ban: Minister," Yonhap, June 11, 2010, http://english.yonhapnews.co.kr/northkorea/2010/06/11/6/0401000000AEN20100611006200315F.HTML.

104. See "Brochure of Torpedo That Sank S. Korean Ship Bears N. Korea's Country Name: Official," Yonhap, June 22, 2010, http://english.yonhapnews.co.kr/news/2010/06/22/73/0200000000AEN20100622002100315F.HTML; and "NK Torpedo Had Quality Assurance Mark in Catalog," *Donga Ilbo*, June 22, 2010, http://english.donga.com/srv/service.php3?bicode=050000&biid=2010062293198.

105. Keiichi Honma, "U.S. Spares N. Korea 'Terror Sponsor' Status," *Yomiuri Shimbun*, June 24, 2010, http://www.yomiuri.co.jp/dy/world/T100623003659.htm.

106. For details of the interview with the anonymous Chinese businessman and of the analysis regarding the poster, see Moon Gwang-lip, "Poster in Pyongyang Recalls the Cheonan," *Joongang Ilbo*, July 15, 2010, http://joongangdaily.joins.com/article/view.asp?aid=2923225; and Sarah Jackson-Han, Jung Young, and Greg Scarlatoiu, "Posters

Show Smashed Ship," *Radio Free Asia*, July 15, 2010, http://www.rfa.org/english/news /korea/poster-07152010143832.html?searchterm=None.

107. For details of the U.S. State Department's sanctions and statements, see "Sanctions Are Going to Hurt," *Joongang Ilbo*, July 24, 2010, http://joongangdaily.joins.com /article/view.asp?aid=2923620.

108. Hwang Doo-hyong, "U.S. Repeats Cheonan Was Sunk by N. Korea's Torpedo: State Dept.," Yonhap, July 28, 2010, http://english.yonhapnews.co.kr/national/2010 /07/29/52/0301000000AEN20100729000400315F.HTML.

109. Hwang Doo-hyong, "Moscow Not to Make Public Probe Outcome on Cheonan's Sinking: Amb. Churkin," Yonhap, August 4, 2010, http://english.yonhapnews.co.kr /national/2010/08/05/26/0301000000AEN20100805000200315F.HTML.

110. "Most South Koreans Skeptical about Cheonan Findings, Survey Shows," *Chosun Ilbo*, September 8, 2010, http://english.chosun.com/site/data/html_dir/2010/09/08 /2010090800979.html.

111. For details of the carefully researched and articulated final results of the JIG investigation released in September 2010, see Kim Deok-hyun, "S. Korea Releases Full Report on Ship Sinking, Reaffirming N. Korea's Responsibility," Yonhap, September 13, 2010, http://english.yonhapnews.co.kr/national/2010/09/13/85 /0301000000AEN20100913004500315F.HTML. For the complete 312-page final report on the sinking of the *Cheonan* released by the JIG, see "Joint Investigation Report on the Attack on the ROK Ship Cheonan," Republic of Korea, Ministry of National Defense, September 14, 2010, http://www.cheonan46.go.kr/95.

112. Jung Sung-ki, "Navy to Focus on Littoral Warfare," *Korea Times*, September 15, 2010, http://www.koreatimes.co.kr/www/news/nation/2010/09/205_73102.html.

113. "Russian TV Blames N. Korea for Cheonan Sinking," *Chosun Ilbo*, September 16, 2010, http://english.chosun.com/site/data/html_dir/2010/09/16 /2010091601080.html.

114. Jung Sung-ki, "Military Investigating Lawmaker for Leaking Secrets," *Korea Times*, October 11, 2010, http://www.koreatimes.co.kr/www/news/nation/2010/10/205_74342.html.

115. "South Koreans Solidly Blame N. Korea for Cheonan Sinking," *Chosun Ilbo*, October 20, 2010, http://english.chosun.com/site/data/html_dir/2010/10/20/2010102000428.html.

116. "80% Believe N. Korea Sank the Cheonan," *Chosun Ilbo*, March 24, 2011, http://english.chosun.com/site/data/html_dir/2011/03/24/2011032401059.html.

117. For more details on the seven rounds of talks between the United Nations Command and North Korean military officers that occurred between July and October 2010, see Park Chan-kyong, "N. Korea Demands to See Evidence on Ship Sinking," AFP, July 15, 2010, http://news.yahoo.com/s/afp/20100715/wl_asia_afp /skoreankoreausmilitary; Song Sang-ho, "UNC, North Korea Discuss Sunken Ship," *Korea Herald*, July 30, 2010, http://www.koreaherald.com/national/Detail.jsp ?newsMLId=20100730000705; Kim Deok-hyun, "U.N. Command, N. Korea End Talks with Little Progress," Yonhap, September 16, 2010, http://english.yonhapnews .co.kr/national/2010/09/16/65/0301000000AEN20100916010500315F.HTML; "DPRK Makes New Proposals on S. Korea Warship Sinking Probe," *Xinhua*, October 5, 2010, http://news.xinhuanet.com/english2010/world/2010-10/05/c_13543618 .htm; and Jung Sung-ki, "UN Command, NK Fail to Set High-Level Military

Meeting," *Korea Times*, October 27, 2010, http://www.koreatimes.co.kr/www /news/nation/2010/10/113_75270.html.

118. Seunghun Lee, "Pieces of the Cheonan Puzzle," *Hankyoreh Daily*, August 5, 2010, http://www.hani.co.kr/arti/english_edition/e_opinion/433660.html.

119. Lee Young-jong and Jeong Yong-joo, "Markings Connect Artillery Shells, Cheonan Torpedo," *Joongang Ilbo*, November 29, 2010, http://koreajoongangdaily.joinsmsn .com/news/article/article.aspx?aid=2928974.

120. Seunghun Lee and J. J. Suh, "Rush to Judgment: Inconsistencies in South Korea's Cheonan Report," Nautilus Institute, Policy Forum 10-039, July 15, 2010, http://www.nautilus.org/publications/essays/napsnet/policy-forums-online /security2009-2010/rush-to-judgment-inconsistencies-in-south-korea2019s -cheonan-report.

121. "Researchers Question Probe into Sinking of S. Korean Naval Ship," Breitbart, July 9, 2010, http://www.breitbart.com/article.php?id=D9GRHFT00&show_article=1.

122. Christine Kim, "Having No Doubt over Ship's Sinking," *Joongang Ilbo*, March 26, 2011, http://joongangdaily.joins.com/article/view.asp?aid=2933970.

123. Hwang Doo-hyong, "Scholar Denounces Progressives for Advocating N. Korea on Cheonan," Yonhap, September 17, 2010, http://english.yonhapnews.co.kr/national /2010/09/17/4/0301000000AEN20100917000800315F.HTML.

124. See Kim So-yeol, "Party Secretary in Cheonan Claim," *Daily NK*, March 27, 2012, http://www.dailynk.com/english/read.php?cataId=nk03700&num=9025.

125. "Int'l Exercise to Be Staged off Busan," *Chosun Ilbo*, June 22, 2010, http://english.chosun.com/site/data/html_dir/2010/06/22/2010062201285.html.

126. "S. Korea Seeks Leading Role in Multinational Drill Slammed by N. Korea: Official," Yonhap, June 20, 2010, http://english.yonhapnews.co.kr/national/2010/06/20 /95/0301000000AEN20100620001500315F.HTML.

127. "S. Korean, U.S. Navies Agree on Closer Cooperation against N. K. Subs," Yonhap, June 16, 2010, http://english.yonhapnews.co.kr/national/2010/06/16/97 /0301000000AEN20100616006900315F.HTML.

128. "S. Korea, U.S. to Hold Naval Drills in Late June," Yonhap, June 18, 2010, http://english.yonhapnews.co.kr/national/2010/06/18/73 /0301000000AEN20100618002100315F.HTML.

129. See Jun Kwanwoo, "U.S., South Korea Start War Games at Sea," AFP, July 25, 2010, http://news.yahoo.com/s/afp/20100725/wl_asia_afp/skoreankoreausmilitary; and Kim Deok-hyun, "S. Korea, U.S. Stage Anti-Submarine Exercises in East Sea," Yonhap, July 26, 2010, http://english.yonhapnews.co.kr/national/2010/07/26/27 /0301000000AEN20100726007900315F.HTML.

130. See Song Sang-ho, "S. Korea to Begin Maritime Exercise in West Sea Today," *Korea Herald*, August 4, 2010, http://www.koreaherald.com/national/Detail.jsp?newsMLId =20100804000757; and "South Korea Prepares against Maritime Intrusion on Day 2 of Naval Exercises," Yonhap, August 6, 2010, http://english.yonhapnews.co.kr/national /2010/08/06/24/0301000000AEN20100806004800315F.HTML.

131. "S. Korea Hosts Maritime Drill to Stop Transfer of WMDs," Yonhap, October 13, 2010, http://english.yonhapnews.co.kr/national/2010/10/13/17 /0301000000AEN20101013000900315F.HTML.

132. Parts of the first portion of this chapter were previously published in Bruce E. Bechtol, Jr., "The Implications of the Cheonan Sinking: A Security Studies Perspective," *International Journal of Korean Unification Studies* 19, no. 2 (2010): 1–40. The author would like to thank the editors and staff of the *International Journal of Korean Unification Studies* for their cooperation, collaboration, and support of this research.

133. For details of the attack on one of the islands near the NLL on November 23, 2010, see Jack Kim and Lee Jae-won, "North Korea Shells South in Fiercest Attack in Decades," Reuters, November 23, 2010, http://www.reuters.com/article /idUSTRE6AM0YS20101123.

134. See "Tactical Details of the Korean Artillery Exchange," STRATFOR Global Intelligence, November 29, 2010, http://www.stratfor.com/memberships/176803 /analysis/20101129_tactical_details_korean_artillery_exchange; and "Military Knew of N. Korean Artillery Move before Attack," *Chosun Ilbo*, November 26, 2010, http://english.chosun.com/site/data/html_dir/2010/11/26/2010112600954.html.

135. Sam Kim, "S. Korean Marines Recount N. Korea's Deadly Shelling of Yeonpyeong," Yonhap, December 14, 2010, http://english.yonhapnews.co.kr/northkorea/2010 /12/14/84/0401000000AEN20101214006800315F.HTML.

136. For exact details of the reports from ROK Marines on the scene and of the South Korean military's reaction to the North Korean artillery attack, see "Seoul Blew Chance to Stop North Korean Provocations," *Chosun Ilbo*, December 7, 2010, http://english.chosun.com/site/data/html_dir/2010/12/07/2010120701039.html; "The Military Needs to Get Faster and More Accurate," *Chosun Ilbo*, December 3, 2010, http://english.chosun.com/site/data/html_dir/2010/12/03/2010120301005 .html; "Military Suggests Counterfire Caused 'Many Casualties' in N. Korea," Yonhap, December 2, 2010, http://english.yonhapnews.co.kr/national/2010/12/02/83 /0301000000AEN20101202009100315F.HTML; and "Yeonpyeong Artillery Warning System 'Was Old and Faulty,'" *Chosun Ilbo*, December 3, 2010, http://english .chosun.com/site/data/html_dir/2010/12/03/2010120300969.html.

137. "5 N. Koreans Confirmed Killed in Yeonpyeong Island Clash," *Korea Times*, December 28, 2010, http://www.koreatimes.co.kr/www/news/special/2011/03/182_78779.html.

138. See "North Korean Newsletter No. 200: Foreign Tips," Yonhap, March 8, 2012, http://english.yonhapnews.co.kr/northkorea/2012/03/07/31/0401000000AEN 20120307008700325F.HTML.

139. Kim Young-jin, "NK Blames Shelling on Lack of Peace Treaty," *Korea Times*, January 11, 2011, http://www.koreatimes.co.kr/www/news/nation/2011/01/113_79508.html.

140. For details regarding the evacuation of the island following the attack, the reaction of the USFK, the state-run media reports from North Korea, the security surrounding the Kim family following the attack, and the internal propaganda regarding the "artillery skills" of Kim Chong-un, see: Im Jeong Jin, "Security Doubled for Kim Jong Il Post-Yeonpyeong," *Daily NK*, December 9, 2010, http://dailynk.com/english /read.php?cataId=nk01500&num=7123; "Yeonpyeong Attack 'Aimed to Bolster Kim Jong-un,'" *Chosun Ilbo*, December 1, 2010, http://english.chosun.com/site/data/html _dir/2010/12/01/2010120100496.html; Choi You-sun, "Pyeongyang Reportedly Spreading Propaganda that Kim Jong-un Orchestrated Attack," *Arirang*, December 1, 2010, http://www.arirang.co.kr/News/News_View.asp?nseq=109785&code

=Ne2&category=2; "USFK Commander Denounces N. Korea's Artillery Attack for Armistice Violation," Yonhap, November 26, 2010, http://english.yonhapnews.co.kr /national/2010/11/26/10/0301000000AEN20101126007000315F.HTML; "Yeonpyeong Island Empty as Repair Efforts Pick up ahead of Joint Drill," Yonhap, November 26, 2011, http://english.yonhapnews.co.kr/national/2010/11/26/68 /0302000000AEN20101126003600315F.HTML; and Jeong Yong-soo and Christine Kim, "Kim and Jong-un Ordered Bombardment: Source," *Joongang Ilbo*, November 25, 2011, http://joongangdaily.joins.com/article/view.asp?aid=2928853.

141. See Lee Won-jean, "North Says Heir Kim Directed Yeonpyeong Shelling," *Joongang Ilbo*, March 16, 2012, http://koreajoongangdaily.joinsmsn.com/news/article/article .aspx?aid=2949998.

142. "N. Korea Deploys More Missiles along West Coast," *Chosun Ilbo*, December 22, 2010, http://english.chosun.com/site/data/html_dir/2010/12/22/2010122200355.html.

143. See "N. Korean Commandos 'Train to Occupy S. Korean Islands,'" *Chosun Ilbo*, January 3, 2011, http://english.chosun.com/site/data/html_dir/2010/12/31/2010123100639 .html; and Kim Se-jeong, "NK Simulates Attack on 5 Western Islands," *Korea Times*, December 30, 2010, http://www.koreatimes.co.kr/www/news/nation/2011/04/116 _78925.html.

144. For detailed information on the submarine exercises that the North Koreans conducted during March 2011, see Kim Su-jeong and Moon Gwang-lip, "Worrying Sub Exercises Seen in North: Sources," *Joongang Ilbo*, April 8, 2011, http://koreajoongangdaily.joinsmsn.com/news/article/article.aspx?aid=2934557.

145. See "Seoul to Change Rules of Engagement with N. Korea," *Chosun Ilbo*, November 26, 2010, http://english.chosun.com/site/data/html_dir/2010/11/26/2010112600956.html.

146. For details about the deployment of Cheonma missiles and President Lee's statements, see Lee Chi-dong, "Lee Orders Fortification of Five Western Border Islands," Yonhap, December 7, 2010, http://english.yonhapnews.co.kr/northkorea/2010/12/07/41 /0401000000AEN20101207005700315F.HTML; and "S. Korea Deploys Missiles on Yeonpyeong Island," Yonhap, December 1, 2010, http://english.yonhapnews.co.kr /national/2010/12/01/44/0301000000AEN20101201008800315F.HTML.

147. "S. Korea to Install Sensors near N. Korea Sea Border," *Island Times*, January 10, 2011, http://islandtimes.us/index.php?option=com_content&view=article&id=6129%3As -korea-to-install-sensors-near-sea-border&Itemid=5.

148. "South Korea Beefs up Offensive Posture against N. Korean Threats: Commander," Yonhap, April 8, 2011, http://english.yonhapnews.co.kr/northkorea/2011/04/08/41 /0401000000AEN20110408005700315F.HTML.

149. "Korea Scales down Defense Ambitions," *Chosun Ilbo*, May 2, 2011, http://english .chosun.com/site/data/html_dir/2011/05/02/2011050200577.html.

150. "Military Rebuilds Shelters on Border Islands with Corrugated Steel Plates," Yonhap, May 9, 2011, http://english.yonhapnews.co.kr/national/2011/05/09/82 /0301000000AEN20110509001400315F.HTML.

151. "[Editorial] Military Reform," *Korea Herald*, December 7, 2010, http://www.koreaherald .com/opinion/Detail.jsp?newsMLId=20101207000554.

152. For details regarding the new Northwest Islands Defense Command, see "S. Korea Sets up Defense Command for Yellow Sea Islands near N. Korea," Yonhap, June 14,

2011, http://english.yonhapnews.co.kr/national/2011/06/14/85/0301000000AEN
20110614004500315F.HTML; and "Marines Recall Yeonpyeong Shelling with New
Perspective," *Korea Times*, November 21, 2011, http://www.koreatimes.co.kr/www/news
/nation/2011/11/117_99175.html.

153. The changes the South Korean military has made to the defenses in the NLL are
significant. For details, see "S. Korea Beefs up Firepower on Frontline Islands," *Donga
Ilbo*, November 24, 2011, http://english.donga.com/srv/service.php3?biid
=2011112453568.

154. Park Seong Guk, "NLL Intrusion Numbers Falling," *Daily NK*, November 16, 2011,
http://www.dailynk.com/english/read.php?catId=nk00100&num=8413.

155. "Massive Military Drill Marks Yeonpyeong Attack Anniversary," *Chosun Ilbo*,
November 23, 2011, http://english.chosun.com/site/data/html_dir/2011/11/23
/2011112300895.html.

156. "NK Issues 'Sea of Fire' Warning against South," *Korea Times*, November 24, 2011,
http://www.koreatimes.co.kr/www/news/nation/2011/11/113_99475.html.

157. For more information on North Korea's illicit and illegal activities, see "Sanctions Are
Going to Hurt," *Joongang Ilbo*.

158. For an example of the types of increased sanctions the United States initiated against
North Korea, see "U.S. Identifies 200 N. Korea-Linked Bank Accounts, 100 of Them
Likely to Be Frozen," Yonhap, July 23, 2010, http://english.yonhapnews.co.kr/news
/2010/07/23/0200000000AEN20100723001200315.HTML.

159. For details on the North Korean NDC statement, see Hyung-jin Kim, "N Korea
Makes Point-by-Point Denial of Ship Sinking," Associated Press, November 2, 2010,
http://hosted.ap.org/dynamic/stories/A/AS_KOREAS_SHIP_SINKS
?SECTION=HOME&SITE=AP&TEMPLATE=DEFAULT.

## 4. Planning for the Unthinkable

1. Parts of this chapter were originally published by the author as "Planning for the
Unthinkable: Countering a North Korean Nuclear Attack and Management of Post-
Attack Scenarios," *Korean Journal of Defense Analysis* 23, no. 1 (March 2011): 1–17. The
author would like to thank the editors and staff of the *Korean Journal of Defense Analysis*.

2. For an excellent summary of North Korea's "nuclear diplomacy," see Emma Chanlett-
Avery and Mi Ae Taylor, "North Korea: U.S. Relations, Nuclear Diplomacy, and
Internal Situation" (Washington, DC: Congressional Research Service, May 26,
2010), http://www.fas.org/sgp/crs/nuke/R41259.pdf.

3. Richard C. Bush, "The Challenge of a Nuclear North Korea: Dark Clouds, Only One
Silver Lining," Policy Paper no. 23 (Washington, DC: Brookings Institution,
September 23, 2010), http://www.brookings.edu/~/media/Files/rc/papers/2010/09
_north_korea_bush/09_north_korea_bush.pdf.

4. Sam Kim, "N. Korea to Use 'Strong Deterrent' in Lieu of Dialogue: Paper," Yonhap,
July 26, 2010, http://english.yonhapnews.co.kr/n_northkorea/2010/07/26/24
/4301000000AEN20100726004800315F.HTML.

5. Yoshihiro Makino, "Pyongyang Touts Nuclear Weapons Progress," *Asahi Shimbun*,
August 2, 2010, http://www.asahi.com/english/TKY201008010215.html.

6. Peter Crail, "Assessing Progress on Nuclear Non-Proliferation and Disarmament: 2009–2010 Report Card" (Washington, DC: Arms Control Association, October, 2010), http://www.armscontrol.org/system/files/ACA_2009-2010_ReportCard.pdf.

7. For details on the nuclear reactor in Syria built with North Korean technology and assistance, see Daveed Gartenstein-Ross and Joshua D. Goodman, "The Attack on Syria's al-Kibar Nuclear Facility," *Focus* 3, no. 1 (Spring 2009), http://www.jewishpolicycenter.org/826/the-attack-on-syrias-al-kibar-nuclear-facility.

8. Daniel Pinkston, "North Korea Conducts Nuclear Test" (Monterey, CA: Center for Nonproliferation Studies, Monterey Institute of International Studies, October 10, 2006), http://cns.miis.edu/pubs/week/pdf/061010_dprktest.pdf.

9. Siegfried S. Hecker, "Report on North Korean Nuclear Program" (Stanford, CA: Center for International Security and Cooperation, Stanford University, November 15, 2006), http://iis-db.stanford.edu/pubs/21266/dprk-report-hecker06.pdf.

10. Hui Zhang, "North Korea's Oct. 9 Nuclear Test: Successful or Failed?," paper presented at the Institute for Nuclear Materials Management Forty-Eighth Annual Meeting, Tucson, Arizona, July 8–12, 2007, http://belfercenter.ksg.harvard.edu/files/NKtest_INMM07_Hui.pdf.

11. See "North Korea Conducts Nuclear Test," BBC News, May 25, 2009, http://news.bbc.co.uk/2/hi/asia-pacific/8066615.stm.

12. Jack Kim, "North Korea Seen Readying for New Nuclear Test," Reuters, May 7, 2009, http://uk.reuters.com/article/idUKTRE54609Q20090507?rpc=401&=undefined&sp=true.

13. See Sam Kim, "N. Korean Nuclear Blast Probably Less Powerful Than Hoped For: Yale Scholar," Yonhap, May 28, 2009, http://english.yonhapnews.co.kr/news/2009/05/28/0200000000AEN20090528007400315.HTML; and Kim Su-jeong and Yoo Jee-ho, "Expert: North's Test Not a Surprise, More to Come," *Joongang Ilbo*, June 1, 2009, http://joongangdaily.joins.com/article/view.asp?aid=2905533.

14. "Statement by the Office of the Director of National Intelligence on North Korea's Declared Nuclear Test on May 25, 2009," Office of the Director of National Intelligence, June 15, 2009, http://www.dni.gov/press_releases/20090615_release.pdf.

15. For analysis on North Korea's third nuclear test, and the data that is known, see Song Sang-ho, "North Korea Conducts 3rd Nuclear Test," *Korea Herald*, February 12, 2013, http://nwww.koreaherald.com/view.php?ud=20130212000883; and Choi He-suk, "Estimates Differ on Size of N.K. Blast," *Korea Herald*, February 14, 2013, http://my.news.yahoo.com/estimates-differ-size-n-k-blast-041003243.html. For information regarding the collection of intelligence and other data during and after the nuclear test, see Mark Hosenball, "Spy Agencies Scrounge for Details on North Korean Nuclear Test," Reuters, February 20, 2013, http://www.reuters.com/article/2013/02/20/us-korea-north-nuclear-usa-idUSBRE91J1CY20130220. For analysis about North Korean efforts to contain the blast so that foreign intelligence agencies could not determine the type of weapon, see Jung-ha Won, "Lack of Data Shrouds Nature of N. Korea Nuclear Test," AFP, February 14, 2013, http://www.google.com/hostednews

/afp/article/ALeqM5gj_QgeYYUBzIqCWhzpOHLJ7ESrLQ?docId=CNG.464e2b
e3b8023ccfe02bede099a1bdce.351.

16. For information on Iranians present at the nuclear test, the payments made to North
Korea for the right to attend the test, and analysis suggesting that the test was of a
miniaturized warhead, see "Report, Iranians at N. Korea Nuclear Test," UPI,
February 15, 2013, http://www.upi.com/Top_News/World-News/2013/02/15/Report
-Iranians-at-N-Korea-nuclear-test/UPI-22931360904909/; "Fears Rise About Iran-
North Korea Nuclear Connection," *NKNews*, February 18, 2013, http://www.nknews
.org/2013/02/fears-rise-about-iran-north-korea-nuclear-connection/; "Iran Paid
Millions for Ringside Seat at N. Korean Nuke Test," *Chosun Ilbo*, February 18, 2013,
http://english.chosun.com/site/data/html_dir/2013/02/18/2013021801176.html;
"Iranian Nuclear Chief Observed Korean Nuke Test," *Jerusalem Post*, February 17, 2013,
http://www.jpost.com/IranianThreat/News/Article.aspx?id=303499; Lee Sang-yong,
"Evidence of Iranian Test Involvement Mounts," *Daily NK*, February 19, 2013,
http://www.dailynk.com/english/read.php?cataId=nk00100&num=10327; "NK
Nuke was Bought and Paid for by a Key End-User: Iran," *Korea Times*, February 20,
2013, http://www.koreatimes.co.kr/www/news/nation/2013/02/511_130797.html; and
Vincent Pry, "Understanding North Korea and Iran," Missile Threat.com, February
26, 2013, http://missilethreat.com/understanding-north-korea-and-iran/.

17. See Mary Beth Nikitin, "North Korea's Nuclear Weapons: Technical Issues," *Congressional
Research Service*, February 12, 2013, http://www.fas.org/sgp/crs/nuke/RL34256.pdf; and
David E. Sanger and Choe Sang-hun, "Defying U.N., North Korea Confirms Third
Nuclear Test," AsianTown.net, February 12, 2013, http://news.asiantown.net/r/28361
/defying-un—north-korea-confirms-third-nuclear-test-prompting-emergency-un
-meeting.

18. "N. Korea 'Has 100 Mobile Missile Launch Platforms,'" *Chosun Ilbo*, February 14, 2013,
http://english.chosun.com/site/data/html_dir/2013/02/14/2013021401237.html.

19. For analysis on the tactics and techniques North Korea uses to launder money and
proliferate materials with a great deal of success, see Jack Kim and Louis Charbonneau,
"North Korea Uses Cash Couriers, False Names to Outwit Sanctions," Reuters,
February 15, 2013, http://news.yahoo.com/north-korea-uses-cash-couriers-false
-names-outwit-013200620.html.

20. Associated Press, "Dispute Imperils North Korea Nuke Talks," Military.com, February 19,
2004, http://www.military.com/NewsContent/0,13319,FL_korea_021904,00.html.

21. See R. Jeffrey Smith and Joby Warrick, "Pakistani Scientist Depicts More Advanced
Nuclear Program in North Korea," *Washington Post*, December 28, 2009,
http://www.washingtonpost.com/wp-dyn/content/article/2009/12/27
/AR2009122701205_pf.html; and "N. Korea Had Enriched Uranium in 2002,"
*Chosun Ilbo*, December 29, 2009, http://english.chosun.com/site/data/html
_dir/2009/12/29/2009122900357.html.

22. "NK Has Built Uranium Enrichment Facilities," *Donga Ilbo*, February 18, 2009,
http://english.donga.com/srv/service.php3?biid=2009021833768.

23. Kim So-hyun, "N. K. Says It Will Start Enriching Uranium," *Korea Herald*, June 15,
2009, http://www.koreaherald.co.kr/NEWKHSITE/data/html_dir/2009/06/15
/200906150033.asp.

24. Selig Harrison, testimony before the United States Congress, House Committee on Foreign Affairs, June 17, 2009, http://foreignaffairs.house.gov/111/har061709.pdf.

25. For more details about North Korea's nuclear weaponization collaboration with Iran, see Larry Niksch, "North Korea's Nuclear Weapons Development and Diplomacy" (Washington, DC: Congressional Research Service, January 5, 2010), http://www.fas.org/sgp/crs/nuke/RL33590.pdf.

26. "DPRK Permanent Representative Sends Letter to President of UNSC," *KCNA*, September 4, 2009, http://www.kcna.co.jp/item/2009/200909/news04/20090904-04ee.html.

27. Kim Hyun, "N. Korea Started Uranium Enrichment before 2002: Seoul Minister," Yonhap, June 15, 2009, http://english.yonhapnews.co.kr/northkorea/2009/06/15/0401000000AEN20090615006200315.HTML.

28. Central Intelligence Agency, Untitled Document Provided to Congress on November 19, 2002, Federation of American Scientists (FAS), November 19, 2002, http://www.fas.org/nuke/guide/dprk/nuke/cia111902.html.

29. For Siegfried Hecker's analysis and the complete report, see his "Special Report: A Return Trip to North Korea's Yongbyon Nuclear Complex" (Stanford, CA: Center for International Security and Cooperation, Stanford University, November 20, 2010), http://www.keia.org/Communications/Programs/Hecker/Hecker%20Program_KEI%20Posted%20Paper.pdf.

30. John M. Glionna, "North Korea Building Light Water Reactor, U.S. Experts Say," *Los Angeles Times*, November 20, 2010, http://www.kentucky.com/2010/11/20/1534141/north-korea-building-light-water.html.

31. See "NK May Have Built Other Uranium Enrichment Facilities," KBS World, December 3, 2010, http://world.kbs.co.kr/english/news/news_In_detail.htm?No=77668.

32. Yoshihiro Makino, "Pyongyang: No Uranium Enrichment Plant Other Than Yongbyon," *Asahi Shimbun*, August 9, 2011, http://www.asahi.com/english/TKY201108080274.html.

33. Julian Ryali, "US Satellite Images Capture New Buildings at North Korea Nuclear Plant," *The Telegraph* (UK), June 14, 2011, http://www.telegraph.co.uk/news/worldnews/asia/northkorea/8574955/US-satellite-images-capture-new-buildings-at-North-Korea-nuclear-plant.html.

34. "US Expert: N. Korea Shouldn't Be Allowed to Test Missiles," *Donga Ilbo*, March 22, 2012, http://english.donga.com/srv/service.php3?biid=2012032283058.

35. For background on the International Atomic Energy Agency (IAEA) report, see George Jahn, "UN: N Korea Nuke Equipment from Black Market," Associated Press, September 2, 2011, http://www.google.com/hostednews/ap/article/ALeqM5hRiVsCmUJglyRcNFTB9Z6vS1ZqNw?docId=e531ec9b77b2409387710ec288575931. For detailed analysis of the IAEA report released in September 2011, see David Albright and Paul Brannan, "ISIS Analysis of IAEA Safeguards Report on the Democratic People's Republic of Korea from September 2, 2011" (Washington, DC: Institute for Science and International Security, September 2, 2011), http://isis-online.org/isis-reports/detail/isis-analysis-of-iaea-safeguards-report-on-the-democratic-peoples-republic-/. For a copy of the actual IAEA Report, see: Report

by the Director General, "Application of Safeguards in the Democratic People's Republic of Korea," United Nations, IAEA, September 2, 2011, http://isis-online.org /uploads/isis-reports/documents/IAEA_DPRK_2Sept2011.pdf.

36. For details on North Korea's nuclear weapons proliferation to Iran, Syria, and Burma, as well as the early collaboration with Pakistan, see Madeline Chambers, "North Korea Supplied Nuclear Software to Iran: German Report," Reuters, August 24, 2011, http://www.reuters.com/article/2011/08/24/us-nuclear-northkorea-iran -idUSTRE77N2FZ20110824; "In Secret DPRK-Iran Pact, Iran Provided $2 Billion to DPRK in Return for Enriched Uranium from North Korea" (in Japanese), *Sankei Shimbun*, February 10, 2011, http://sankei.jp.msn.com/; "U.S. Expresses Concerns over N. Korea's Suspected Arms Trade," Yonhap, June 13, 2011, http://english.yonhapnews .co.kr/national/2011/06/14/13/0301000000AEN20110614000100315F.HTML; "IAEA Reports Syria 'Very Likely' Built Nuclear Facility with North Korea's Assistance," *Arirang*, May 25, 2011, http://www.arirang.co.kr/News/News_View .asp?nseq=116314&code=Ne2&category=2; "N. Korea and Iran 'Sharing Ballistic Missile Technology,'" BBC News, May 14, 2011, http://www.bbc.co.uk/news/world-asia-pacific-13402590; Shaun Waterman, "China Aids N. Korea and Iran with Nuke Advances," *Washington Times*, May 17, 2011, http://www.washingtontimes.com/news /2011/may/17/beijing-aiding-north-korea-and-iran-with-nuke-adva/; Amos Harel, "Israel Fears Iran and North Korea Strengthening Ties," *Haaretz*, July 7, 2011, http://www.haaretz.com/print-edition/news/israel-fears-iran-and-north-korea -strengthening-ties-1.371837; and R. Jeffrey Smith, "Pakistan's Nuclear-Bomb Maker Says North Korea Paid Bribes for Know-How," *Washington Post*, July 6, 2011, http://www.washingtonpost.com/world/national-security/pakistans-nuclear-bomb -maker-says-north-korea-paid-bribes-for-know-how/2010/11/12/gIQAZ1kH1H _story.html.

37. "N. Korea Cannot Make Weapons with Enriched Uranium: Experts," Yonhap, September 4, 2009, http://english.yonhapnews.co.kr/northkorea/2009/09 /04/62/0401000000AEN20090904007400320F.HTML.

38. Bruce E. Bechtol, Jr., *Defiant Failed State: The North Korean Threat to International Security* (Washington, DC: Potomac Books, 2010), 79.

39. See Chang Jae-soon, "S. Korea Keeping Close Watch on N. Korea amid Reports of Nuclear Test Preparations," Yonhap, November 17, 2010, http://english.yonhapnews .co.kr/national/2010/11/17/85/0301000000AEN20101117004500315F.HTML; and Shin Hae-in, "More Reports Confirm Activities at N. K. Nuke Site," *Korea Herald*, November 18, 2010, http://media.daum.net/cplist/view.html?cateid=100000 &cpid=22&newsid=20101118185410925&p=koreaherald.

40. For details of the final preparations for a nuclear test that North Korea appeared to put on hold, see Jennifer Rizzo, "Signs of New Activity at North Korea's Nuclear Test Site," CNN, May 22, 2012, http://security.blogs.cnn.com/2012/05/22/signs-of-new -activity-at-north-koreas-nuclear-test-site/.

41. See David A. Fulghum, "U.S. Experts Weigh North Korean Capabilities," *Aviation Week*, May 28, 2009, http://www.aviationweek.com/aw/generic/story_generic.jsp ?channel=aerospacedaily&id=news/NKOR052809.xml&headline=U.S.%20Experts %20Weigh%20North%20Korean%20Capabilities.

42. See Sharon Squassoni, "North Korea's Nuclear Weapons: How Soon an Arsenal?" (Washington, DC: Congressional Research Service, February 2, 2004), http://www.fas.org/spp/starwars/crs/RS21391.pdf.

43. See "H-5 Light Bomber [Il-28 BEAGLE (ILYUSHIN)]," Global Security.org, July 17, 2006, http://www.globalsecurity.org/military/world/china/h-5.htm; and Rice University, "Democratic People's Republic of Korea," *Military Forces Factsheet—North Korea*, Spring 2010, http://es.rice.edu/projects/Poli378/Korea/Korea.North.html.

44. For analysis on the yield of the North Korean underground nuclear test of 2009, see Jeffery Park, "The North Korean Nuclear Test: What the Seismic Data Says," *Bulletin of the Atomic Scientists*, May 26, 2009, http://www.thebulletin.org/web-edition/features/the-north-korean-nuclear-test-what-the-seismic-data-says.

45. See Matthew Gianni, "Real and Present Danger: Flag State Failure and Maritime Security and Safety," World Wide Fund for Nature, *WWF*, International Transport Workers' Federation, ITF, June, 2008, http://assets.panda.org/downloads/flag_state_performance.pdf.

46. U.S. Marines routinely train with ROK Marines in and around the port of Pohang. See Thomas W. Provost, "Logistics Marines, ROK Marines, Train Together, Side by Side," Marines.com, April 1, 2010, http://www.usmc.mil/unit/mcbjapan/Pages/2010/100402-clr35.aspx.

47. "837th Transportation Battalion," Global Security.org, 2010, http://www.globalsecurity.org/military/agency/army/837transbn.htm.

48. See Thomas M. Magee, "Out of the Ordinary Supply in Korea," *Army Logistician*, March–April 2002, http://www.almc.army.mil/alog/issues/MarApr02/Final.pdf.

49. See "Busan," *Galbijim*, January 19, 2008, http://wiki.galbijim.com/Busan.

50. Hahm Chaibong, "South Korea's Miraculous Democracy," *Journal of Democracy* 19, no. 3 (July 2008), http://www.rand.org/pubs/reprints/2008/RAND_RP1370.pdf.

51. For more information on the U.S. Navy base located in Sasebo, Japan, see CNIC // Commander Fleet Activities Sasebo, http://www.cnic.navy.mil/Sasebo/index.htm.

52. For a review of some of the anecdotal evidence relating to the existence of North Korea's nuclear HEU weaponization program, see Jack Kim, Christine Kim, and Mark Heinrich, "North Korea Looks at New Deal of Its Nuclear Cards," Reuters, August 12, 2009, http://www.reuters.com/article/idUSTRE57B1L920090812.

53. See Joby Warrick and Peter Slevin, "Libyan Arms Design Traced back to China: Pakistanis Resold Chinese-Provided Plans," *Washington Post*, February 15, 2005, http://www.washingtonpost.com/ac2/wp-dyn/A42692-2004Feb14?language=printer; and "U.S. Intelligence Concludes Iran, N. Korea Have Chinese Nuke Warhead Design," East-Asia-Intel.com, August 9, 2006, http://www.east-asia-intel.com/eai/.

54. "North Korean Missile Exports," *The Risk Report* 2, no. 6 (November–December 1996), http://www.wisconsinproject.org/countries/nkorea/north-korea-missile-exports.html.

55. See "North Korea Said to Work at Secret Teheran Site on Iran's Nuclear Warheads," East-Asia-Intel.com, October 3, 2008, http://www.east-asia-intel.com/eai/; "Nuclear Pyongyang Is Helping Iran," Foreign Affairs Committee, National Council of Resistance of Iran, September 23, 2008, http://ncr-iran.org/content/view/5632/107/; Christina Y. Lin, "The King from the East: DPRK-Syria-Iran Nuclear Nexus and Strategic

Implications for Israel and the ROK," Korea Economic Institute, Academic Paper Series 3, no. 7 (October 2008), http://www.keia.org/Publications/AcademicPaperSeries /2008/APS-Lin.pdf; Douglas Frantz, "Iran Closes in on Ability to Build Nuclear Bomb," *Los Angeles Times*, August 4, 2003, http://articles.latimes.com/2003/aug/04/world/fg-nuke4; and AFP, "N Korea May Already Have Nuclear Warheads: Ex-CIA Official," Yahoo!News, September 26, 2008, http://news.yahoo.com/s/afp/20080926/pl _afp/nkoreanuclearweaponsusintelligenc.

56. "Missiles of the World: Nodong-2," Missile Threat.com, The Claremont Institute, 2007, http://www.missilethreat.com/missilesoftheworld/id.83/missile_detail.asp.

57. Kim Tae-hong, "South Korea Needs Precision Strike Capability," *DailyNK*, September 15, 2010, http://dailynk.com/english/read.php?cataId=nk00100&num=6803.

58. "DPRK Ready for Pre-Emptive Attack: Report," *Xinhua*, September 18, 2010, http://news.xinhuanet.com/english2010/world/2010-09/18/c_13517718.htm.

59. For more on the dispersal of North Korean nuclear sites, see Scott Stossel, "North Korea: The War Game," *The Atlantic*, July/August 2005, http://www.theatlantic .com/magazine/archive/2005/07/north-korea-the-war-game/4029/.

60. See Brian Ellison, "North Korean Nuclear Arsenal," Nuclear Files.org, Project of the Nuclear Age Peace Foundation, May 9, 2008, http://nuclearfiles.org/menu/key -issues/nuclear-weapons/issues/capabilities/north-korea-cdi.htm.

61. For more on No Dong facilities in North Korea and possible strike options, see Phillip C. Saunders, "Military Options for Dealing with North Korea's Nuclear Program" (Monterey, CA: James Martin Center for Nonproliferation Studies, Monterey Institute for International Studies, January 27, 2003), http://cns.miis .edu/north_korea/dprkmil.htm.

62. C. Dale Walton and Colin Gray, "The Second Nuclear Age: Nuclear Weapons for the 21st Century," in *Strategy in the Contemporary World*, John Baylis, James Wirtz, Colin Gray, and Eliot Cohen, eds., (New York: Oxford University Press, 2007), 223.

63. Bermudez, "North Korea's Long Reach."

64. U.S. Department of State, "Background Note: North Korea," March 9, 2010, http://www.state.gov/r/pa/ei/bgn/2792.htm.

65. For details on the potential damage the weapons of varying sizes could cause in major cities in South Korea, see Bruce W. Bennett, "Uncertainties in the North Korean Nuclear Threat" (Santa Monica, CA: Rand National Defense Research Institute, 2010), http://www.rand.org/pubs/documented_briefings/2010/RAND_DB589.pdf.

66. Seoul Metropolitan Government, "About Seoul: One-Fourth of the Korean Population," *Seoul of Asia*, 2008, http://english.seoul.go.kr/gtk/about/fact.php?pidx=3.

67. See Jin Hyun-joo, "Seoul Discovers That Environmental Care Can Produce Economic Benefits," *Korea Herald*, October 4, 2005, http://www.citymayors.com /development/seoul_development.html; and "The World's 20 Cities with the Worst Traffic Jams," *World Auto News and Reviews*, 2010, http://allworldcars.com/wordpress /?p=11866.

68. "Non-Combatant Emergency Evacuation Instructions," *United States Forces Korea*, Pamphlet 600-300, April 5, 2007, http://19tsc.korea.army.mil/USFK_Pam_600 -300.pdf.

69. For an excellent example of how U.S. forces on the Korean Peninsula conduct noncombatant evacuation operation exercises, see Adrianna N. Lucas, " Courageous Channel Exercise Tests Non-Combatant Evacuation Readiness," U.S. Army Group Daegu, Installation Management Command, May 28, 2009, http://daegu.korea.army -mil.net/news/articles/5282009115506.asp.

70. See "After the Bomb: Life in the Ruins," AtomicBombMuseum.org, 2006, http://atomicbombmuseum.org/4_ruins.shtml.

71. For an excellent analysis of the environmental issues that would arise following a nuclear attack, see "Recovery from Nuclear Attack," Federal Emergency Management Agency, October 1988, http://www.defconwarningsystem.com/documents/recovery _from_nuclear_attack.pdf.

72. John M. Collins, "Nuclear Bees in North Korea," *Army*, August 2003, http://www.ausa .org/publications/armymagazine/archive/2003/8/Documents/Collins_0803.pdf.

73. See Fred Kaplan, "Quest for Firepower: How to Stop North Korea's Drive for Nukes," *Slate*, July 14, 2003, http://www.slate.com/id/2085595/; and Hans M. Kristensen, "Preemptive Posturing: What Happened to Deterrence?," *Bulletin of the Atomic Scientists* 58, no. 5 (September 1, 2002), http://bos.sagepub.com/content /58/5/54.full.

74. For details on plans reported in the South Korean press to take out North Korean WMD, and how they pertain to South Korea coming under the U.S. nuclear umbrella, see Kwon Ho and Kim Su-jeong, "U.S. Has Plan to Hit WMD in North," *Joongang Ilbo*, February 19, 2011, http://koreajoongangdaily.joinsmsn.com/news/article /article.aspx?aid=2932437.

75. Noah Shachtman, "Inside America's (Mock) Attack on North Korea," *Wired*, May 27, 2009, http://www.wired.com/dangerroom/2009/05/inside-americas-mock-attack -north-korea/.

76. For an excellent analysis of ROK and U.S. intelligence and planning cooperation, see See-Won Byun, "North Korea Contingency Planning and U.S.-ROK Cooperation," (Center for U.S.-Korea Policy, the Asia Foundation, September 2009), http://www .nautilus.org/fora/security/09089TAF.pdf.

77. See Mark Hosenball, "Why Did North Korea Sink the South Korean Ship?," *Newsweek*, May 21, 2010, http://www.newsweek.com/blogs/declassified/2010 /05/21/why-did-north-korea-sink-the-south-korean-ship-.html.

78. See "S. Korea, U.S. to Set up Joint Body to Deter N. Korea's Nuclear Threats," Yonhap, October 8, 2010, http://english.yonhapnews.co.kr/national/2010/10/08 /0301000000AEN20101008008500315.HTML; and Kim Deok-hyun, "S. Korea, U.S. Prepared for 'Instability' in N. Korea," Yonhap, October 8, 2010, http://english .yonhapnews.co.kr/national/2010/10/09/4/0301000000AEN20101009000800315F .HTML.

79. See Sun-won Park, "Strategic Posture Review: South Korea," *World Politics Review*, March 17, 2010, http://www.brookings.edu/articles/2010/0317_korea_park.aspx.

## 5. North Korea and Support for Terrorism

1. For an example of historical cases of North Korean proliferation, see James Cotton, "North Korea's Nuclear and Missile Proliferation and Regional Security," *Current Issues*

*Brief* 1, 1999–2000 (Canberra: Parliament of Australia, Parliamentary Library, August 31, 1999), http://www.aph.gov.au/library/pubs/cib/1999-2000/2000cib01.htm.

2. For a detailed examination of North Korea's proliferation to state actors, see Bechtol *Defiant Failed State*, 49–70.

3. For more background on the role Soviet advisers played in the early history of North Korea, see Andrei Lankov, "Interpreting North Korean History," *Asia Times*, August 18, 2005, http://www.atimes.com/atimes/Korea/GH18Dg02.html.

4. For more analysis on the Soviets' dealings with both China and North Korea, on the military support they provided to both, and on their planning with the North Koreans for the invasion of South Korea, see Kathryn Weathersby, "Soviet Aims in Korea and the Origins of the Korean War: New Evidence from Russian Archives," Cold War International History Project, Woodrow Wilson International Center for Scholars, Working Paper No. 8, November 1993, http://www.wilsoncenter.org/topics/pubs/Working_Paper_8.pdf. For an excellent analysis of the Chinese involvement in the Korean War, see Patrick A. Reiter, "Initial Communist Chinese Logistics in the Korean War," *Quartermaster Professional Bulletin* (Autumn 2004), http://www.quartermaster.army.mil/OQMG/professional_bulletin/2004/Autumn04/Initial_Communist_Chinese_Logistics_in_the_Korean_War.htm.

5. "Soviets Groomed Kim Il-sung for Leadership," *Seoul Times*, November 12, 2009, http://theseoultimes.com/ST/?url=/ST/db/read.php?idx=1937.

6. For more analysis on the purges Kim Il-sung conducted in the late 1950s and the withdrawal of Chinese military forces from North Korea, see Chen Jian, "Limits of the 'Lips and Teeth' Alliance: An Historical Review of Chinese-North Korean Relations," *Asia Program Special Report*, Woodrow Wilson International Center for Scholars, September 2003, http://www.wilsoncenter.org/topics/pubs/asia_rpt115b.pdf.

7. See David Kendall and Ro Ji-woong, "Rebirth of a Nation: From Hermit Kingdom to Global Player," *Korea-Net*, July 8, 2007, http://www.korea.net/news/News/NewsView.asp?serial_no=20070706001&part=112&SearchDay=.

8. For details of the massive subsidies North Korea continued to receive from the Soviet Union throughout the Cold War, see Selig Harrison, *Korean Endgame: A Strategy for Reunification and U.S. Disengagement* (Princeton, NJ: Princeton University Press, 2002), 311.

9. For details on the unusual and formally implemented policy of *juche*, see Grace Lee, "The Political Philosophy of Juche," *Stanford Journal of East Asian Affairs* 3, no. 1 (Spring 2003), http://www.stanford.edu/group/sjeaa/journal3/korea1.pdf.

10. See "Overview of Korea," *14th ILO Asian Regional Meeting*, 2006, http://www.mol2006busan.org/tour1.php.

11. For more analysis on how the Soviet Union financed proxy states that in turn trained and/or supplied Marxist movements or terrorist groups, see Nikos Passas, "Terrorism Financing Mechanisms and Policy Dilemmas," in *Terrorism Financing and State Responses: A Comparative Perspective*, ed. Jeanne K. Giraldo and Harold A. Trinkunas (Stanford, CA: Stanford University Press, 2007), 27–28.

12. Daryl M. Plunk, "North Korea: Exporting Terrorism?," Asian Studies Backgrounder no. 74 (Washington, DC: Heritage Foundation, February 25, 1988), http://www.heritage.org/research/asiaandthepacific/asb74.cfm.

13. Barry Rubin, "North Korea's Threats to the Middle East and the Middle East's Threats to Asia," in "Asia Book," *The Middle East Review of International Affairs*, 2005, http://meria.idc.ac.il/books/brkorea.html.

14. "Hezbollah a North Korea–Type Guerilla Force," *Intelligence Online* 529 (August 25–September 7, 2006), http://www.oss.net/dynamaster/file_archive/060902 /26241feaf4766b4d441a3a78917cd55c/Intelligence%20Online%20on%20Hezbolllah.pdf.

15. Philip C. Wilcox, U.S. coordinator for counterterrorism, U.S. Department of State, "U.S. Department of State 96/04/30 Briefing: Amb. Wilcox on Patterns of Global Terrorism, 1995," Office of the Coordinator for Counterterrorism, U.S. Department of State, Washington, DC, April 30, 1996, http://dosfan.lib.uic.edu/ERC/arms /cterror_briefing/960430cterror.html.

16. Stéphane Courtois and Mark Kramer, "Communism and Terrorism," in *The Black Book of Communism: Crimes, Terror, Repression*, ed. Mark Kramer (Cambridge, MA: Harvard University Press, 1999), 356–57.

17. See "World: Drama of the Desert: The Week of the Hostages," *Time*, September 21, 1970, http://www.time.com/time/magazine/article/0,9171,942267-2,00.html.

18. See Yoel Sanno, "Talks Aside, North Korea Won't Give up Nukes," *Asia Times*, March 2, 2004, http://www.atimes.com/atimes/Korea/FC02Dg04.html.

19. Portions of the first four sections of this chapter were earlier published in an article titled "North Korea and Support to Terrorism: An Evolving History," *Journal of Strategic Security* 3, no. 2 (2010): 45–54. The author would like to thank and acknowledge Jeremy Tamsett, editor in chief of the *Journal of Strategic Security*.

20. "How N. Korea Goes about Exporting Arms," *Chosun Ilbo*, March 10, 2010, http://english.chosun.com/site/data/html_dir/2010/03/10/2010031000953.html.

21. For details on instances North Korean merchant ships have been caught reflagging their vessels, see Gianni, "Real and Present Danger."

22. See Carl Anthony Wege, "The Hizbollah–North Korean Nexus," *Small Wars Journal*, January 23, 2011, http://smallwarsjournal.com/blog/journal/docs-temp/654-wege.pdf.

23. Moon Chung-in, "[Outlook] The Syrian Nuke Connection," *Joongang Ilbo*, November 26, 2007, http://joongangdaily.joins.com/article/view.asp?aid=2883146.

24. "Hizballah Acquires CW," *Montreal Middle East Newsline*, July 14, 2008.

25. Anshel Pfeffer, "IDF Reveals Intel on Huge Hezbollah Arms Stockpile in Southern Lebanon," *Haaretz*, July 8, 2010, http://www.haaretz.com/print-edition/news/idf -reveals-intel-on-huge-hezbollah-arms-stockpile-in-southern-lebanon-1.300656.

26. See Associated Press, "N. Korea to Mass-Produce Syria-Provided Missile," *Product Design & Development*, June 2, 2009, http://www.pddnet.com/news-ap-n-korea-to -mass-produce-syria-provided-missile—060209/.

27. "VOA: N. Korea Supplied WMD to Hezbollah," KBS World, December 3, 2011, http://world.kbs.co.kr/english/news/news_In_detail.htm?No=86476.

28. "North Korea 'Helped Syria Build Missile Factory,'" *Chosun Ilbo*, November 28, 2011, http://english.chosun.com/site/data/html_dir/2011/11/28/2011112800692.html.

29. Richard Beeston, Nicholas Blanford, and Sheera Frenkel, "Embattled Syrian Regime Still Sending Missiles to Lebanese Militants," *The Times* (UK), July 15, 2011, http://www.iiss.org/whats-new/iiss-in-the-press/july-2011/embattled-syrian-regime -still-sending-missiles-to-lebanese-militants/.

30. "Hezbollah a North Korea–Type Guerilla Force."

31. Lenny Ben-David, "Mining for Trouble in Lebanon," *Jerusalem Post*, October 29, 2007, http://www.jpost.com/servlet/Satellite?cid=1192380684296&pagename=JPost %2FJPArticle%2FPrinter.

32. Ali Nouri Zadeh, "Iranian Officer: Hezbollah Has a Commando Naval Unit," *Asharq Alawsat*, July 29, 2006, http://www.asharq-e.com/news.asp?section=1&id=5801.

33. Nicholas Blanford, "A Secure, Undisclosed Location," *Foreign Policy*, November 11, 2011, http://www.foreignpolicy.com/articles/2011/11/11/a_secure_undisclosed_location.

34. See "Hezbollah Training in North Korea," *The Intelligence Summit*, April 25, 2007, http://intelligence-summit.blogspot.com/2007/04/hezbollah-training-in-north -korea.html.

35. See Fact Sheet: Designation of Iranian Entities and Individuals for Proliferation Activities and Support for Terrorism," United States Treasury Department, October 25, 2007, http://www.treas.gov/press/releases/hp644.htm.

36. Larry Niksch, "North Korea: Terrorism List Removal?" (Washington, DC: Congressional Research Service, July 10, 2008), http://www.dtic.mil/cgi-bin /GetTRDoc?AD=ADA484792

37. For details regarding many of the activities that the IRGC conducts in support of Hezbollah, see Anthony H. Cordesman, "Iran's Support of the Hezbollah in Lebanon" (Washington, DC: Center for Strategic and International Studies, July 15, 2006), http://csis.org/files/media/csis/pubs/060715_hezbollah.pdf.

38. See Jonathan Spyer, "Behind the Axis: The North Korean Connection," *Jerusalem Post*, May 22, 2010, http://www.jpost.com/Features/FrontLines/Article.aspx?id=176027; and "How N. Korea Goes about Exporting Arms."

39. Lakna Paranamanna, "N. Korea Aided LTTE: Rohan," *Daily Mirror*, October 2, 2010, http://www.highbeam.com/doc/1P3-2162161861.html.

40. Bertil Lintner, "North Korea: Coming in from the Cold," *Far Eastern Economic Review*, October 25, 2001, http://www.asiapacificms.com/articles/northkorea/.

41. Roger Davies, "Sea Tigers, Stealth Technology, and the North Korean Connection," *Jane's Intelligence Review*, March 2001, http://www.lankalibrary.com/pol/korea.htm.

42. "Tigers North Korean Link Bared?," *Lanka Newspapers.com*, March 5, 2007, http://www.lankanewspapers.com/news/2007/3/12823.html.

43. Niksch, "North Korea: Terrorism List Removal?"

44. For the meager details regarding the reports that North Korea was making an arms deal with Al Qaeda, see Jung Jae-jung and Moon Gwang-lip, "Afghan Rebels Got Missiles from North: Wikileaks," *Joongang Ilbo*, July 28, 2010, http://joongangdaily .joins.com/artic.sp?aid=2923820; "North Korea 'Sold Missiles to Taliban,'" *Chosun Ilbo*, July 28, 2010, http://english.chosun.com/site/data/html_dir/2010/07/28 /2010072800299.html; and Kang Hyun-kyung, "Are Koreas in Standoff over Terror War?," *Korea Times*, July 28, 2010, http://www.koreatimes.co.kr/www/news/nation /2010/07/113_70354.html.

45. Mark Hilliard, "Ex-IRA Chief Sean Garland Could Be Tried in Republic of Ireland over Korean Forgery Plot," *Belfast Telegraph*, January 28, 2012, http://www.belfasttelegraph .co.uk/news/local-national/republic-of-ireland/exira-chief-sean-garland-could-be -tried-in-republic-of-ireland-over-korean-forgery-plot-16110182.html.

46. For details regarding the North Korean manufacturing and distribution of American counterfeit "super notes," see Bill Gertz, "N. Korea General Tied to Forged $100 Bills," *Washington Times*, June 2, 2009, http://www.washingtontimes.com/news /2009/jun/02/n-korea-general-tied-to-forged-100-bills/?page=all#; Gregory Elich, "North Korea and the Supernote Enigma," *Global Research*, May 7, 2008, http://www.globalresearch.ca/index.php?context=va&aid=8919; and Justin Mitchell and Catherine Jiang, "Tracking the North Korean Supernote," *Asia Sentinel*, March 7, 2007, http://www.asiasentinel.com/index.php?option=com_content&task=view &id=408&Itemid=31.

47. For details of the sanctions that both the Clinton and Bush administrations initiated, see Karin Lee and Julia Choi, "North Korea: Economic Sanctions and U.S. Department of Treasury Actions, 1955–September 2007" (Washington, DC: National Committee on North Korea, January 18, 2007), http://www.google.com /url?q=http://www.ncnk.org/resources/publications/NCNK_Economic_Sanctions _Current&sa=U&ei=-DMFT6mPDOnKsQLy6fGQCg&ved=0CBIQFjAB&usg =AFQjCNHFgoqEQijq9G0nZASFJI3tWuRFSQ.

48. See "Obama Extends Sanctions on North Korea," *RIA Novosti*, June 24, 2011, http://en.rian.ru/world/20110624/164808376.html.

49. For more details on the Proliferation Security Initiative, see Myung Jin Kim, "South Korea–North Korea Relations: Influence of the PSI on North Korea," *Strategic Insights* 5, no. 7 (September 2006), http://www.nps.edu/Academics/centers/ccc/publications /OnlineJournal/2006/Sep/kimSep06.html.

50. See "Proliferation Security Initiative," *United States Department of State*, http://www.state .gov/t/isn/c10390.htm.

51. Joby Warrick, "Arms Smuggling Heightens Iran Fears," *Washington Post*, December 3, 2009, http://www.washingtonpost.com/wp-dyn/content/article/2009/12/02 /AR2009120203923.html.

52. Barak Ravid, "Israel to UN: North Korea Arms Proliferation Destabilizing the Middle East," *Haaretz*, July 23, 2010, http://www.haaretz.com/news/diplomacy -defense/israel-to-un-north-korea-arms-proliferation-destabilizing-the-middle -east-1.303720.

53. See Ingrid Melander and Renee Maltezou, "Greece Searches Ship for Arms: Source," Reuters, September 28, 2010, http://www.reuters.com/article/2010/09/28/us-greece -korea-syria-idUSTRE68R2TP20100928; and AFP, "Greece Seized North Korea Chemical Weapons Suits," *Defense News*, November 16, 2011, http://www.defensenews .com/story.php?i=8275708.

54. "NATO Intercepts Military Cargo Ship Bound for Eritrea—UN," *Sudan Tribune*, May 11, 2011, http://www.sudantribune.com/NATO-intercepts-military-cargo,38864.

55. For details on many of the issues UNSC 1874 addressed, see "Iran Bought Masses of N. Korean Arms," *Chosun Ilbo*, December 4, 2009, http://english.chosun.com/site /data/html_dir/2009/12/04/2009120400315.html.

56. See Yonhap, "U.S. Identifies 200 N. Korea-Linked Bank Accounts"; "Hong Kong Looks for Secret N. Korean Accounts," *Chosun Ilbo*, August 5, 2010, http://english .chosun.com/site/data/html_dir/2010/08/05/2010080500646.html; "Switzerland to Look into N. Korean Bank Accounts," *Chosun Ilbo*, August 2, 2010, http://english.chosun

.com/site/data/html_dir/2010/08/02/2010080200459.html; and "Luxembourg to Help Track N. Korean Bank Accounts," *Chosun Ilbo*, July 29, 2010, http://english.chosun .com/site/data/html_dir/2010/07/29/2010072900283.html.

57. "Sanctions Information as Important as Enforcement," *Daily NK*, August 4, 2010, http://www.dailynk.com/english/read.php?cataId=nk03500&num=6659.

58. Kim Yong-hun, "Report Explains Sanctions Decisions," *DailyNK*, August 6, 2010, http://www.dailynk.com/english/read.php?cataId=nk00100&num=6667.

59. "Continuation of the National Emergency with Respect to North Korea," *The White House, Office of the Press Secretary*, June 23, 2011, http://www.federalregister.gov /articles/2011/06/24/2011-16100/continuation-of-the-national-emergency-with -respect-to-north-korea.

60. For details of the sanctions imposed and the individuals and entities targeted under the 2010 executive order, see Daniel Dombey, "US Steps up North Korea Sanctions," *Financial Times*, August 30, 2010, http://www.ft.com/intl/cms/s/0/b7cc6b56-b46a -11df-8208-00144feabdc0.html#axzz1icoZ9ag4; and Robert Burns, "Obama Expands Sanctions against North Korea," Associated Press, August 30, 2010, http://www.msnbc.msn.com/id/38921932/ns/world_news-asia_pacific/t/obama -expands-sanctions-against-north-korea/.

61. Executive Office of the President, "Continuation of the National Emergency."

62. Hwang Doo-hyong, "U.S. Imposes Fresh Sanctions on N. Korea, Iran, Syria for WMD: State Dept," Yonhap, May 25, 2011, http://www.oananews.org/node/184213.

63. See "27 N. Korean Entities, 5 Individuals Targeted by U.S. Sanctions," Yonhap, September 21, 2011, http://english.yonhapnews.co.kr/national/2011/09/21/35 /0301000000AEN20110921009500315F.HTML.

64. See Bill Gertz, "North Korean Elite Linked to Crime," *Washington Times*, May 24, 2010, http://www.washingtontimes.com/news/2010/may/24/north-korea-elite-linked-to -crime/print/.

65. Office Number 39 and the individuals in it are the most vital aspect of North Korea's proliferation activities. See Lee Young-jong, "Will Sanctions Target Kim's Room 39?," *Joongang Ilbo*, August 4, 2010, http://koreajoongangdaily.joinsmsn.com/; and "Elusive Manager of Kim Jong-il's Slush Fund Pops up Again," *Chosun Ilbo*, December 15, 2010, http://english.chosun.com/site/data/html_dir/2010/12/15/2010121501150.html.

66. "North Korean Dollar Earners 'Absconding,'" *Chosun Ilbo*, December 17, 2010, http://english.chosun.com/site/data/html_dir/2010/12/17/2010121700494.html.

67. See Hwang Doo-young's "N. Korea Avoids Being Listed as U.S. State Sponsor of Terrorism: State Dept.," Yonhap, August 5, 2010, http://english.yonhapnews.co.kr /national/2010/08/06/0301000000AEN20100806000200315.HTML; and Hwang Doo-young, "U.S. Not to Relist N. Korea for Lack of Evidence of Terrorism: State Dept.," Yonhap, November 18, 2010, http://english.yonhapnews.co.kr/national /2010/11/18/91/0301000000AEN20101118000700315F.HTML.

## 6. Conclusion

1. For more perspectives regarding how the succession process in North Korea was rushed following Kim Jong-il's stroke in 2008, see L. Gordon Flake, "Breaking the Cycle of North Korean Provocations," Testimony Before the United States Senate,

Committee on Foreign Relations, March 1, 2011, http://www.foreign.senate
.gov/imo/media/doc/Flake_Testimony.pdf.

2. See Joon Seok Hong, "Political Succession in North Korea," *Freeman Spogli Institute for International Studies: Spice Journal,* Fall 2011, http://iis-db.stanford.edu/docs/592 /North_Korea.pdf.

3. See Jae-Cheon Lim, *Kim Jong-il's Leadership of North Korea* (London: Routledge Books, 2008), 79–89.

4. See Yun Duk-min, "North Korea's Power Succession and Changes in Leadership," *Korea Focus,* August 24, 2010, http://www.koreafocus.or.kr/design2/layout/content _print.asp?group_id=103254.

5. For some excellent examples of the changes North Korea's government was forced to make following the end of the Cold War, see Robert Sutter, "China and North Korea after the Cold War: Wariness, Caution, and Balance," *International Journal of Korean Studies* 14, no. 1 (Spring 2010), http://www.icks.org/publication/pdf/2010-SPRING -SUMMER/3.pdf.

6. For in-depth and detailed results of a poll conducted in the United States approximately a week following Kim Jong-il's death, see "Even after Kim's Death, North Korea Remains a Threat for Americans," *Angus Reid Public Opinion,* December 27, 2011, http://www.angus-reid.com/wp-content/uploads/2011/12/2011.12.27 _Korea_USA.pdf.

7. For an assessment of North Korea's military, including its size and its relationship with Kim Chong-un, see Susan Seligson, "The World Watches North Korea," *BU Today,* January 11, 2012, http://www.bu.edu/today/2012/the-world-watches-north -korea/.

8. For an analysis of the role that North Korea's military plays in government and society, see Daniel L. Byman and Jennifer Lind, "Keeping Kim: How North Korea's Regime Stays in Power," *International Security,* Belfer Center Policy Brief, July 2010, http://belfercenter.ksg.harvard.edu/files/byman-lind-policybrief-final.pdf.

9. For analysis that reflects a view that the DPRK fears an attack by South Korea and/or the United States, see Guillermo Pinczuk, "Building Multi-Party Capacity for a WMD Free Korea: Security Assurances" Institute for Foreign Policy Analysis, March 16, 2005, http://www.ifpa.org/pdf/shanghai/Security-Assurance-Briefing.pdf.

10. For a definition of this model for determining a military threat, see Melissa Applegate, *Preparing for Asymmetry: As Seen through the Lens of Joint Vision 2020* (Carlisle, PA: Strategic Studies Institute, 2001), http://www.au.af.mil/au/awc/awcgate/ssi /preparng.pdf.

11. Kongdan Oh and Ralph Hassig, "Military Confrontation on the Korean Peninsula," *Joint Forces Quarterly* 64 (First Quarter 2012), http://www.ndu.edu/press/lib/pdf/jfq -64/JFQ-64_82-90_Oh-Hassig.pdf.

12. See Gen. Walter L. Sharp, commander, United Nations Command, Republic of Korea–United States Combined Forces Command, and commander, U.S. Forces, Korea, Statement for the Record to the United States Senate Armed Services Committee, April 12, 2011, http://armed-services.senate.gov/statemnt/2011 /04%20April/Sharp%2004-12-11.pdf.

13. See Kim Min-seok and Yoo Jee-ho, "North Adopts New War Invasion Strategy: Source," *Joongang Ilbo*, April 27, 2010, http://joongangdaily.joins.com/article /view.asp?aid=2919725.

14. For analysis regarding North Korea's ultimate goal of regime survival, see Samuel Kim, "North Korea's Nuclear Strategy and the Interface between International and Domestic Politics," *Asian Perspective* 34, no. 1 (2010), http://www.asianperspective .org/articles/v34n1-c.pdf.

15. For analysis that examines North Korea' s aggressive behavior and the long-term goal of unifying the Korean Peninsula by force, see Gordon Toon, "The Enigma of the Korean Peninsula: An Examination of North Korea and Relevant Security Implications," *Global Security Studies* 1, no. 2 (Summer 2010), http://globalsecuritystudies .com/Toon%20Korea%20TWO.pdf.

16. For examples of acts of terror North Korea carried out against South Korea during the Cold War, see Dan G. Cox, John Falconer, and Brian Stackhouse, *Terrorism, Instability, and Democracy in Asia and Africa* (Lebanon, NH: Northeastern University Press, 2009), 119–21.

17. For an analysis of the North Koreans' cost-benefit analysis in planning for NLL provocations, see Evan Feigenbaum, "Korean Conflict: Could It Escalate?," *East Asia Forum*, December 8, 2010, http://www.eastasiaforum.org/2010/12/08/korean -conflict-could-it-escalate/.

18. For details regarding South Korean and U.S. adjustments to military planning following the NLL provocations in 2010, and the negative reaction of the South Korean populace to China's failure to condemn the events, see Sung-Chool Lee, "The ROK-US Joint Political and Military Response to North Korean Armed Provocations," Center for Strategic and International Studies, *Report of the CSIS Korea Chair*, October 2011, http://csis.org/files/publication/111006_Lee _ROKUSJointResponse_web.pdf.

19. See Martin Fackler and Mark McDonald, "South Korea Reassesses Defenses after Attack," *New York Times*, November 25, 2010, http://www.nytimes.com/2010/11 /26/world/asia/26korea.html.

20. The succession process was in full swing by 2010, and the provocations in the NLL may have been part of the effort to enhance the leadership of the incoming leader, Kim Chong-un. See Jin-ha Kim, "North Korea's Succession Plan: Stability and Future Outlook," Ilmin International Relations Institute, IIRI Working Paper Series 08, December 2010, http://asiasecurity.macfound.org/images/uploads/blog_attachments /wp08_IIRI_Jin-Ha_Kim.pdf.

21. For analysis regarding the possibility of a change in North Korea's nuclear weapons policy following Kim Jong-il's death, see Soo Min Kim, "North Korea after Kim Jong-il," Universal Peace Federation, January 24, 2012, http://www.upf.org/conference/ilckorea -2012/sessions/4202-sm-kim-north-korea-after-kim-jong-il.

22. For a brief analysis of Kim Jong-il's nuclear strategy for dealing with United States, see Graham Allison, "Kim Jong Il: The Great Negotiator," *Power and Policy*, December 20, 2011, http://www.powerandpolicy.com/2011/12/20/kim-jong-il-the-great-negotiator/.

23. See Chaesung Chun, Young-Sun Ha, Dongho Jo, Sung Bae Kim, and Sook-Jong Lee, "Time for the Strategy of Coevolution: How South Korea Can Shape the Future of

the Kim Jong-un Regime," *East Asia Institute, Commentary* no. 24, January 5, 2012, http://www.eai.or.kr/data/bbs/eng_report/20120105211115.pdf.

24. See John Feffer, "Approaching North Korea in the Kim Jong Un Era," *Fair Observer*, January 17, 2012, http://www.fairobserver.com/article/approaching-north-korea-kim-jong-un-era.

25. For more details regarding the U.S. extension of a nuclear umbrella for its ally South Korea, see Jung Sung-ki, "Obama Pledges Nuclear Umbrella for S. Korea," *Korea Times*, June 17, 2009, http://www.koreatimes.co.kr/www/news/nation/2009/06/116_46976.html .

26. The North Koreans likely understand that a nuclear strike would be met with overwhelming military force. See Bennett Ramberg, "Dealing with Nuclear North Korea," *Yale Global*, January 10, 2011, http://yaleglobal.yale.edu/content/dealing-nuclear-north-korea.

27. "CIA: Syrian Reactor Capacity Was 1–2 Weapons per Year," Reuters, April 29, 2008, http://www.ynetnews.com/articles/0,7340,L-3537198,00.html.

28. North Korea has for many years proliferated both ballistic missile technology and nuclear weaponization technology to Iran. See Gerald M. Steinberg, "North Korea and Iran: Will Any Lessons Be Learned?," *Jerusalem Issue Brief* 6, no. 12 (October 11, 2006), http://www.jcpa.org/brief/brief006-12.htm.

29. Associated Press, "Transcript: Worldwide Threat Assessment of the US Intelligence Community for the Senate Select Committee on Intelligence," Associated Press Television News Service, January 31, 2012, http://www.aptnvideo.net/pages/browse/player/player_frameset.jsp?item=210691.

30. For examples of North Korean terrorist acts conducted against the South Koreans in the 1950s and 1960s, see Dick K. Nanto, "North Korea: Chronology of Provocations: 1950–2003" (Washington, DC: Congressional Research Service, March 18, 2003), http://www.fas.org/man/crs/RL30004.pdf.

31. "North Korea: Relations with the Third World," in *A Country Study: North Korea*, Library of Congress, Country Studies, 1993, http://memory.loc.gov/frd/cs/kptoc.html.

32. As the Soviet Union fell apart, subsidies to such countries as North Korea and Cuba ended. See Charles K. Armstrong, "Kim's Nuclear Gamble: Some Historical Perspective," *Frontline*, April 10, 2003, http://www.pbs.org/wgbh/pages/frontline/shows/kim/them/historical.html.

33. For some interesting background data on the ethnic Tamils around the globe who supported the Tamil Tigers financially, see David Rose, "Crouching Tiger, Hidden Raj," *Vanity Fair*, September 30, 2011, http://www.vanityfair.com/politics/features/2011/09/tamil-and-raj-201109.

34. For details about the financial and logistical support that Syria and Iran provide to Hezbollah, see Holly Fletcher, "State Sponsor: Syria," Council on Foreign Relations, Backgrounder, February 2008, http://www.cfr.org/syria/state-sponsor-syria/p9368; and Israel Project, "Iran's Financial and Military Support of Hezbollah," 2009, http://www.theisraelproject.org/site/c.hsJPK0PIJpH/b.2904311/k.D8DF/Irans_Financial_and_Military_Support_of_Hezbollah.htm.

35. For details about Eritrea's support to terrorist groups, see Andrew Manners, "UN Extends Sanctions on Eritrea for Terrorism Support," *Future Directions International*,

December 14, 2011, http://www.futuredirections.org.au/publications/indian
-ocean/29-indian-ocean-swa/336-un-extends-sanctions-on-eritrea-for-terrorism
-support.html.

36. For details regarding the dynastic nature of the regime in North Korea, see Nak-
chung Paik, "The Post Kim Jong-il Era and the 2013 Regime in North Korea," *The
Asia-Pacific Journal: Japan Focus*, January 22, 2012, http://www.japanfocus.org
///events/view/126.

37. David S. Maxwell, "Is the Kim Family Regime Rational and Why Don't the North
Korean People Rebel?," *Foreign Policy Research Institute*, E-Notes, February 2012,
http://www.fpri.org/enotes/2012/201201.maxwell.nkorea.pdf.

38. See Kim Yong-hun, "Nepotism Running Riot in Kim's NK," *DailyNK*, January 11,
2012, http://www.dailynk.com/english/read.php?cataId=nk02900&num=8667.

39. See Scott Snyder, "Kim Jong-un's Dangerous Brother," *The Diplomat*, January 22, 2012,
http://utopic.me/page/13450534I_C/the-diplomat.com/2012/01/22/kim-jong
-un%E2%80%99s-dangerous-brother/.

40. Hyeong Jung Park, "Political Dynamics of Hereditary Succession in North Korea,"
*International Journal of Korean Unification Studies* 20, no. 1 (2011), http://www.kinu.or.kr
/upload/neoboard/DATA03/IJKUS20-1.pdf.

41. Maxwell, "Is the Kim Family Regime Rational?"

42. For more background information on North Korea's "unofficial" open markets that
began during the Kim Jong-il era and that have often been shut down for political or
control reasons, see Ralph C. Hassig and Kongdan Oh, *The Hidden People of North Korea:
Everyday Life in the Hermit Kingdom* (Lanham, MD: Rowman & Littlefield, 2009), 76–78;
and Choe Sang-hun, "North Korea Said to Shut Market in Bid for Control," *New York
Times*, September 19, 2009, http://www.nytimes.com/2009/09/20/world/asia
/20korea.html.

43. See Yonhap, "North Korea's Nominal Head of State Meets with Head of Egyptian
Mobile Service Provider," NK News.org, February 2, 2012, http://nknews.org/2012
/02/n-koreas-nominal-head-of-state-meets-with-head-of-egyptian-mobile-service
-provider/.

44. For details and analysis regarding North Korea's monitoring of its own cell phone
network and the attempted jamming of illicit connections to the Chinese cell phone
network, See Benjamin Ismail, "Frontiers of Censorship: North Korea," *Reporters
Without Borders*, Investigative Report, October 2011, http://fr.rsf.org/IMG/pdf
/rsf_north-korea_2011.pdf.

45. David S. Maxwell, associate director, Center for Peace and Security Studies & Security
Studies Program, Edmund A. Walsh School of Foreign Service, Georgetown
University, e-mail interview by author, February 4, 2012.

46. For analysis of the danger of a potential collapse in North Korea following Kim Jong-
il's death, see Richard Bush, "Kim Jong-il's Death and North Korea's Succession
Process: Q&A with Richard Bush" (Washington, DC: Brookings Institution,
December 19, 2011), http://www.brookings.edu/multimedia/video/2011/1219_bush
_north_korea.aspx

47. See David S. Maxwell, *Catastrophic Collapse of North Korea: Implications for the US Military*
(Ft. Leavenworth, KS: School of Advanced Military Studies, 1996),

http://www.dtic.mil/cgi-bin/GetTRDoc?AD=ADA314274&Location=U2&doc
=GetTRDoc.pdf.

48. For more details on the combined contingency planning for collapse that South Korea
and the United States have engaged in, see Jayshree Bajoria, "North Korea After
Kim," Council on Foreign Relations, Backgrounder, December 19, 2011, http://www
.cfr.org/north-korea/north-korea-after-kim/p17322.

49. Bruce W. Bennett and Jennifer Lind, "The Collapse of North Korea: Military
Missions and Requirements," *International Security* 36, no. 2 (Fall 2011): 84–119.

50. For analysis of the impact of integrating the population of North Korea into a unified,
democratic Korea, see Tara O, "The Integration of North Korean Defectors in South
Korea: Problems and Prospects," *International Journal of Korean Studies* 15, no. 2 (Fall
2011), http://www.icks.org/publication/pdf/2011-FALL-WINTER/8.pdf.

51. See Michael David Dougherty, "The Dirty Little Secret about North Korea," *Business
Insider*, December 19, 2011, http://articles.businessinsider.com/2011-12-19/politics
/30534349_1_nuclear-weapons-humanitarian-crisis-north-korean-state.

52. See Kenji Minemura, "Analysis: Chinese Military on Edge after Death of Kim Jong-il,"
*Asahi Shimbun*, January 23, 2012, http://ajw.asahi.com/article/asia/china
/AJ201201230058.

53. For reporting on China's unwillingness to discuss North Korea's possible collapse
with American officials, see Bill Tarrant and Raju Gopalakrishnan, "Analysis: What's
the Plan if North Korea Collapses?," *News Talk: WSAU.com*, December 23, 2011,
http://wsau.com/news/articles/2011/dec/23/analysis-whats-the-plan-if-north-korea
-collapses/.

# SELECTED BIBLIOGRAPHY

"837th Transportation Battalion." Global Security.Org, 2010. http://www.globalsecurity.org/military/agency/army/837transbn.htm.

*A Country Study: North Korea*. Washington DC: Library of Congress, Country Studies, 1993. http://memory.loc.gov/frd/cs/kptoc.html.

"After the Bomb: Life in the Ruins." AtomicBombMuseum.org, 2006. http://atomicbombmuseum.org/4_ruins.shtml.

"Air Traffic Warned of Rocket Drop Zone." *North Korea Tech*, March 21, 2012. http://www.northkoreatech.org/2012/03/22/air-traffic-warned-of-rocket-drop-zone/.

Albright, David, and Paul Brannan. "ISIS Analysis of IAEA Safeguards Report on the Democratic People's Republic of Korea from September 2, 2011." Washington, DC: Institute for Science and International Security, September 2, 2011. http://isis-online.org/isis-reports/detail/isis-analysis-of-iaea-safeguards-report-on-the-democratic-peoples-republic-/.

Allison, Graham. "Kim Jong Il: The Great Negotiator." *Power and Policy*, December 20, 2011. http://www.powerandpolicy.com/2011/12/20/kim-jong-il-the-great-negotiator/.

Applegate, Melissa. *Preparing for Asymmetry: As Seen through the Lens of Joint Vision 2020*. Carlisle, PA: Strategic Studies Institute, 2001. http://www.au.af.mil/au/awc/awcgate/ssi/preparng.pdf.

Armstrong, Charles K. "Kim's Nuclear Gamble: Some Historical Perspective." *Frontline*, April 10, 2003. http://www.pbs.org/wgbh/pages/frontline/shows/kim/them/historical.html.

"Background Note: North Korea." U.S. Department of State, March 9, 2010. http://www.state.gov/r/pa/ei/bgn/2792.htm.

Bajoria, Jayshree. "North Korea after Kim." Backgrounder. Washington, DC: Council on Foreign Relations, December 19, 2011. http://www.cfr.org /north-korea/north-korea-after-kim/p17322.

Basheer, Margaret. "UN Security Council Condemns North Korea Rocket Launch." Voice of America, April 13, 2012. http://www.voanews.com /content/un-security-council-condemns-north-korea-rocket-launch -147343395/179340.html.

Baylis, John, James Wirtz, Colin Gray, and Eliot Cohen, eds. *Strategy in the Contemporary World.* New York: Oxford University Press, 2007.

Bechtol, Bruce, Jr. *Defiant Failed State: The North Korean Threat to International Security.* Washington, DC: Potomac Books, 2010.

———. "Planning for the Unthinkable: Countering a North Korean Nuclear Attack and Management of Post-Attack Scenarios," *The Korean Journal of Defense Analysis* 23, no. 1 (March 2011): 1–17.

———. "The Cheonan Incident and North Korea's Northern Limit Line Strategy," AEI, Center for Defense Studies, May 25, 2010, http://www .defensestudies.org/?p=2575.

———. "The Implications of the Cheonan Sinking: A Security Studies Perspective," *International Journal of Korean Unification Studies* 19, no. 2 (2010): 1–40.

Ben-David, Alon. "Iran Acquires Ballistic Missiles from DPRK." *Jane's Defence Weekly*, December 29, 2005. http://www.janes.com/security/international _security/news/jdw/jdw051229_1_n.shtml.

Bennett, Bruce W. "Uncertainties in the North Korean Nuclear Threat." Santa Monica, CA: Rand National Defense Research Institute, 2010. http:// www.rand.org/pubs/documented_briefings/2010/RAND_DB589.pdf.

Bennett, Bruce W., and Jennifer Lind. "The Collapse of North Korea: Military Missions and Requirements." *International Security* 36, no. 2 (Fall 2011): 84–119.

Bermudez, Joseph S., Jr. *The Armed Forces of North Korea.* London: I. B. Tauris, 2001.

———. "A History of Ballistic Missile Development in the DPRK: CNS Occasional Paper #2." Monterey, CA: Center for Nonproliferation Studies, Monterey Institute, 1999. http://cns.miis.edu/pubs/opapers/op2/index.htm.

———. "North Korea's Long Reach in Profile." *Jane's Intelligence Review*, November 11, 2003. http://www.janes.com/defence/land_forces /news/idr/idr031111_1_n.shtml.

Blanford, Nicholas. "A Secure, Undisclosed Location." *Foreign Policy*, November 11, 2011. http://www.foreignpolicy.com/articles/2011/11/11/a_secure _undisclosed_location.

Bleiker, Roland. *Divided Korea: Toward a Culture of Reconciliation*. Minneapolis: University of Minnesota Press, 2005.

Boose, Donald W., Jr., Balbina Y. Hwang, Patrick Morgan, and Andrew Scobell, eds. *Recalibrating the U.S.–Republic of Korea Alliance*. Carlisle, PA: Strategic Studies Institute, 2003.

Bush, Richard C. "The Challenge of a Nuclear North Korea: Dark Clouds, Only One Silver Lining." Policy Paper no. 23. Washington, DC: Brookings Institution, September 23, 2010. http://www.brookings.edu/~/media/Files/rc/papers/2010/09_north_korea _bush/09_north_korea_bush.pdf.

———. "Kim Jong-il's Death and North Korea's Succession Process: Q&A with Richard Bush." Washington, DC: Brookings Institution, December 19, 2011. http://www.brookings.edu/multimedia/video/2011/1219_bush _north_korea.aspx.

Byman, Daniel L., and Jennifer Lind. "Keeping Kim: How North Korea's Regime Stays in Power." *International Security*, Belfer Center Policy Brief, July 2010. http://belfercenter.ksg.harvard.edu/files/byman-lind-policybrief -final.pdf.

Byun, See-Won. "North Korea Contingency Planning and U.S.-ROK Cooperation." Center for U.S.-Korea Policy, The Asia Foundation, September 2009. http://www.nautilus.org/fora/security/09089TAF.pdf.

Carpenter, Ted Galen, and Doug Bandow. *The Korean Conundrum: America's Troubled Relationship with North and South Korea*. New York: Palgrave MacMillan, 2004.

Cha, Victor D., and David C. Kang. *Nuclear North Korea: A Debate on Engagement Strategies*. New York: Columbia University Press, 2003.

Chang, Gordon C. *Nuclear Showdown: North Korea Takes on the World*. New York: Random House, 2006.

Chanlett-Avery, Emma, and Mi Ae Taylor. "North Korea: U.S. Relations, Nuclear Diplomacy, and Internal Situation." Washington, DC: Congressional Research Service, May 26, 2010. http://www.fas.org /sgp/crs/nuke/R41259.pdf.

Chen, Jian. "Limits of the 'Lips and Teeth' Alliance: An Historical Review of Chinese-North Korean Relations." *Asia Program Special Report* no. 115. Washington, DC: Woodrow Wilson International Center for Scholars, September 2003. http://www.wilsoncenter.org/topics/pubs/asia_rpt115b.pdf.

Cheon, Seongwhun. "Changing Dynamics of U.S. Extended Nuclear Deterrence on the Korean Peninsula." Special Report. Berkeley, CA: Nautilus Institute for Security and Sustainability, November 10, 2010.

http://www.nautilus.org/publications/essays/napsnet/reports/changing
-dynamics-of-u.s.-extended-nuclear-deterrence-on-the-korean-peninsula.

Choi, Sung-chol, ed. *Understanding Human Rights in North Korea*. Seoul, Korea: Center for the Advancement of North Korean Human Rights, 1997.

Chong, Song-chang. "The Third Conference of North Korea's Workers Party of Korea Representatives and the Establishment of a Succession System for Kim Jong-eun." *Sejong Commentary* no. 196 (in Korean). Seongnam, South Korea: Sejong Institute, September 30, 2010.

Chun, Chaesung, Young-Sun Ha, Dongho Jo, Sung Bae Kim, and Sook-Jong Lee. "Time for the Strategy of Coevolution: How South Korea Can Shape the Future of the Kim Jong-un Regime." *Security Net Commentary* no. 24. Seoul: East Asia Institute, January 5, 2012. http://www.eai.or.kr/data/bbs /eng_report/20120105211115.pdf.

CNIC // Commander Fleet Activities Sasebo website. http://www.cnic.navy .mil/Sasebo/index.htm.

Collins, John M. "Nuclear Bees in North Korea." *Army*, August 2003. http://findarticles.com/p/articles/mi_qa3723/is_200308/ai_n9273177 /pg_7/?tag=content;col.

"Continuation of the National Emergency with Respect to North Korea." *The White House, Office of the Press Secretary*, June 23, 2011. http://www .federalregister.gov/articles/2011/06/24/2011-16100/continuation-of-the -national-emergency-with-respect-to-north-korea.

Cordesman, Anthony H. "Iran's Support of the Hezbollah in Lebanon." Washington, DC: Center for Strategic and International Studies, July 15, 2006. http://csis.org/files/media/csis/pubs/060715_hezbollah.pdf.

Cotton, James. "North Korea's Nuclear and Missile Proliferation and Regional Security." *Current Issues Brief* 1 (1999–2000). Canberra: Parliament of Australia, Parliamentary Library, August 31, 1999. http://www.aph.gov.au /library/pubs/cib/1999-2000/2000cib01.htm.

Cox, Dan G., John Falconer, and Brian Stackhouse. *Terrorism, Instability, and Democracy in Asia and Africa*. Lebanon, NH: Northeastern University Press, 2009.

Crail, Peter. "Assessing Progress on Nuclear Non-Proliferation and Disarmament: 2009–2010 Report Card." Washington, DC: Arms Control Association, October 2010. http://www.armscontrol.org/system/files/ACA _2009-2010_ReportCard.pdf.

Davies, Roger. "Sea Tigers, Stealth Technology, and the North Korean Connection." *Jane's Intelligence Review*, March 2001. http://www.lankalibrary.com/pol/korea.htm.

"Defense White Paper." *Ministry of National Defense, Republic of Korea*, 2010. http://www.mnd.go.kr/.

"Democratic People's Republic of Korea." *Rice University, Military Forces Factsheet: North Korea*, Spring 2010. http://es.rice.edu/projects/Poli378/Korea/Korea .North.html.

Dies, Harry P., Jr. "North Korean Special Operations Forces: 1996 Kangnung Submarine Infiltration." *Military Intelligence Professional Bulletin*, October–December 2004. http://findarticles.com/p/articles/mi_m0IBS /is_4_30/ai_n13822276.

Downs, Chuck. *Over the Line: North Korea's Negotiating Strategy*. Washington, DC: AEI Press, 1999.

"DPRK Jamming GPS Signals, Says Seoul." *North Korea Tech*, May 3, 2012. http://www.northkoreatech.org/2012/05/03/dprk-jamming-gps-signals -says-seoul/.

Dunnigan, James. "North Korea's SS-21 Missiles." *Strategy Page*, May 12, 2005. http://www.strategypage.com/dls/articles/2005512213718.asp.

Eberstadt, Nicholas. *The North Korean Economy: Between Crisis and Catastrophe*. New Brunswick, NJ: Transaction Publishers, 2009.

Elich, Gregory. "North Korea and the Supernote Enigma." *Global Research*, May 7, 2008. http://www.globalresearch.ca/index.php?context=va&aid=8919.

"Even After Kim's Death, North Korea Remains a Threat for Americans." *Angus Reid Public Opinion*, December 27, 2011. http://www.angus -reid.com/wp-content/uploads/2011/12/2011.12.27_Korea_USA.pdf.

"Exclusive: DPRK Satellite to Send Data, Video." *North Korea Tech*, March 20, 2012. http://www.northkoreatech.org/2012/03/20/itu-confirms-dprk -satellite-launch-plans/.

"Exclusive: North Korea's Expected Rocket Trajectory." *North Korea Tech*, March 21, 2012. http://www.northkoreatech.org/2012/03/21/exclusive-north -koreas-expected-rocket-trajectory/.

"Fact Sheet: Designation of Iranian Entities and Individuals for Proliferation Activities and Support for Terrorism." *United States Treasury Department*, October 25, 2007. http://www.treas.gov/press/releases/hp644.htm.

Feffer, John. "Approaching North Korea in the Kim Jong Un Era." *Fair Observer*, January 17, 2012. http://www.fairobserver.com/article/approaching-north -korea-kim-jong-un-era.

Feigenbaum, Evan. "Korean Conflict: Could It Escalate?" *East Asia Forum*, December 8, 2010. http://www.eastasiaforum.org/2010/12/08/korean -conflict-could-it-escalate/.

Flake, L. Gordon. "Breaking the Cycle of North Korean Provocations." Testimony Before the United States Senate, Committee on Foreign Relations, March 1, 2011. http://www.foreign.senate.gov/imo/media/doc /Flake_Testimony.pdf.

Fletcher, Holly. "State Sponsor: Syria." Backgrounder. Washington, DC: Council on Foreign Relations, February 2008. http://www.cfr.org/syria /state-sponsor-syria/p9368.

Fulghum, David A. "U.S. Experts Weigh North Korean Capabilities." *Aviation Week*, May 28, 2009. http://www.aviationweek.com/aw/generic/story _generic.jsp?channel=aerospacedaily&id=news/NKOR052809.xml &headline=U.S.%20Experts%20Weigh%20North%20Korean%20capabilitie.

"Full Text of President Lee's National Address." Yonhap, May 24, 2010. http://english.yonhapnews.co.kr/national/2010/05/24/42 /0301000000AEN20100524003400315F.HTML.

Gartenstein-Ross, Daveed, and Joshua D. Goodman. "The Attack on Syria's al-Kibar Nuclear Facility." *Focus* 3, no. 1 (Spring 2009). http://www .jewishpolicycenter.org/826/the-attack-on-syrias-al-kibar-nuclear-facility.

Gianni, Matthew. "Real and Present Danger: Flag State Failure and Maritime Security and Safety." Oslo/London: World Wide Fund for Nature and International Transport Workers' Federation , June 2008. http://assets.panda.org/downloads/flag_state_performance.pdf.

Giraldo, Jeanne K., and Harold A. Trinkunas, eds. *Terrorism Financing and State Responses: A Comparative Perspective*. Stanford, CA: Stanford University Press, 2007.

"GPS Jammers in Action." *Strategy Page*, September 13, 2011. http://www.strategypage.com/htmw/htecm/20110913.aspx

Green, Chris. "Q&A Reveals Cheonan Disaster Details." *DailyNK*, May 20, 2010. http://www.dailynk.com/english/read.php?cataId=nk00100&num =6395.

Gregson, Wallace "Chip." "Statement for the Record by Wallace 'Chip' Gregson, Assistant Secretary of Defense for Asian & Pacific Security Affairs, Department of Defense." Submitted to the Senate Armed Services Committee, September 16, 2010. http://armed-services.senate.gov/statemnt /2010/09%20September/Gregson%2009-16-10.pdf.

Gwertzman, Bernard. "North Korea's Uncertain Succession." Interview with Scott Snyder. Washington, DC: Council on Foreign Relations, December 19, 2011. http://www.cfr.org/north-korea/north-koreas-uncertain -succession/p26858.

"H-5 Light Bomber [Il-28 BEAGLE (ILYUSHIN)]." Global Security.Org, July 17, 2006. http://www.globalsecurity.org/military/world/china/h-5.htm.

Haggard, Stephan, and Marcus Noland. "Hunger and Human Rights: The Politics of Famine in North Korea." Washington, DC: U.S. Committee for Human Rights in North Korea, 2005. http://www.hrnk.org/download /Hunger_and_Human_Rights.pdf.

Hahm, Chaibong. "South Korea's Miraculous Democracy." *Journal of Democracy* 19, no. 3 (July 2008). http://www.rand.org/pubs/reprints/2008 /RAND_RP1370.pdf.

Han, Sarah Jackson, Jung Young, and Greg Scarlatoiu. "Posters Show Smashed Ship." *Radio Free Asia*, July 15, 2010. http://www.rfa.org/english/news/korea /poster-07152010143832.html?searchterm=None.

Harrison, Selig. *Korean Endgame: A Strategy for Reunification and U.S. Disengagement.* Princeton, NJ: Princeton University Press, 2002.

———. Testimony before the United States Congress. House Committee on Foreign Affairs, June 17, 2009. http://foreignaffairs.house.gov/111 /har061709.pdf.

Hassig, Ralph C., and Kongdan Oh. *The Hidden People of North Korea: Everyday Life in the Hermit Kingdom.* Lanham, MD: Rowman & Littlefield, 2009.

Hecker, Siegfried S. "Report on North Korean Nuclear Program." Stanford, CA: Center for International Security and Cooperation, Stanford University, November 15, 2006. http://iis-db.stanford.edu/pubs /21266/dprk-report-hecker06.pdf.

———. "Special Report: A Return Trip to North Korea's Yongbyon Nuclear Complex." Stanford, CA: Center for International Security and Cooperation, Stanford University, November 20, 2010. http://www.keia.org /Communications/Programs/Hecker/Hecker%20Program_KEI%20Posted %20Paper.pdf.

Herman, Steve. "North Korea Warned of Deeper Isolation Should Provocations Continue." *Voice of America*, May 21, 2012. http://www.voanews.com/articleprintview/781384.html.

Hong, Joon Seok. "Political Succession in North Korea." *Freeman Spogli Institute for International Studies: Spice Journal* (Fall 2011). http://iisdb.stanford.edu /docs/592/North_Korea.pdf.

Hwang, Jang-yop. "Testimonies of North Korean Defectors." Republic of Korea, National Intelligence Service, January 1999. http://www.fas.org /irp/world/rok/nis-docs/index.html.

Im, Jeong Jin. "Military-First, but Still No Heating on Bases." *DailyNK*, January 24, 2011. http://www.dailynk.com/english/read.php?cataId=nk01500 &num=7290.

———. "People's Army Starts Kim Jong-eun Campaign." *DailyNK*, October 6, 2010. http://www.dailynk.com/english/read.php?cataId=nk01500&num =6876.

———. "Security Doubled for Kim Jong Il Post Yeonpyeong." *DailyNK*, December 9, 2010. http://dailynk.com/english/read.php?cataId =nk01500&num=7123.

"Investigation Result on the Sinking of ROKS 'Cheonan.'" Republic of Korea, Ministry of National Defense, May 20, 2010. http://www.globalsecurity .org/military/library/report/2010/100520_jcmig-roks- cheonan/100520_jcmig-roks-cheonan.pdf.

"Iran's Financial and Military Support of Hezbollah." *The Israel Project*, 2009. http://www.theisraelproject.org/site/c.hsJPKoPIJpH/b.2904311/k.D8DF /Irans_Financial_and_Military_Support_of_Hezbollah.htm.

Ismail, Benjamin. "North Korea: Frontiers of Censorship." Investigation Report. Paris: Reporters Without Borders, October 2011. http://fr.rsf.org/IMG/pdf/rsf_north-korea_2011.pdf.

Joint Civilian-Military Investigative Group. "Investigation Result on the Sinking of ROKS 'Cheonan.'" Republic of Korea, Ministry of National Defense, May 20, 2010. http://www.mnd.go.kr/mndEng_2009 /WhatsNew/RecentNews/.

Joint Communiqué. "The 42nd U.S.-ROK Security Consultative Meeting." *U.S. Defense News*, October 8, 2010. http://www.defense.gov/news /d20101008usrok.pdf.

Kendall, David, and Ro Ji-woong. "Rebirth of a Nation: From Hermit Kingdom to Global Player." *Korea-Net*, July 8, 2007. http://www.korea.net /news/News/NewsView.asp?serial_no=20070706001&part=112 &SearchDay=.

Kerr, Paul. "North Korea Increasing Weapons Capabilities." *Arms Control Today*, December 2005. http://www.armscontrol.org/act/2005_12 /Dec-NKweapons.asp.

Kihl, Young Whan, and Hong Nack Kim, eds. *North Korea: The Politics of Regime Survival*. Armonk, NY: M. E. Sharp, 2006.

Kim, Capt. Duk-Ki, Republic of Korea Navy. "The Republic of Korea's Counter-Asymmetric Strategy: Lesson from ROKS Cheonan and Yeonpyeong Island." *Naval War College Review* 65, no. 1 (Winter 2012). http://www.usnwc.edu/getattachment/8e487165-a3ef-4ebc-83ce -0ddd7898e16a/The-Republic-of-Korea-s-Counter-asymmetric-Strateg.

"Kim Far Behind in Succession Stakes." *DailyNK*, June 29, 2011. http://dailynk.com/english/read.php?cataId=nk00100&num=7891.

Kim, Jin-ha. "North Korea's Succession Plan: Stability and Future Outlook." IIRI Working Paper Series 08. Seoul: Ilmin International Relations Institute, December 2010. http://asiasecurity.macfound.org/images /uploads/blog_attachments/wp08_IIRI_Jin-Ha_Kim.pdf.

Kim, Myung Jin. "South Korea–North Korea Relations: Influence of the PSI on North Korea." *Strategic Insights* 5, no. 7 (September 2006). http://www.nps.edu /Academics/centers/ccc/publications/OnlineJournal/2006/Sep/kimSep06 .htm.

Kim, Samuel. "North Korea's Nuclear Strategy and the Interface between International and Domestic Politics." *Asian Perspective* 34, no. 1 (2010). http://www.asianperspective.org/articles/v34n1-c.pdf.

Kim, Soo Min. "North Korea after Kim Jong-il." Address to the International Leadership Conference, Universal Peace Federation, Seoul, January 24, 2012. http://www.upf.org/conference/ilckorea-2012/sessions/4202 -sm-kim-north-korea-after-kim-jong-il.

Kim, So-yeol. "Cloak and Dagger on the Pyongyang Streets?" *DailyNK*, January 24, 2011. http://www.dailynk.com/english/read.php?cataId=nk00400 &num=7288.

———. "Party Secretary in Cheonan Claim." *DailyNK*, March 27, 2012. http://www.dailynk.com/english/read.php?cataId=nk03700&num=9025.

———. "The Rise and Rise of Choi Hyong-rae." *DailyNK*, April 11, 2012. http://www.dailynk.com/english/read.php?cataId=nk00100&num=9095.

Kim, Sung Chull. *North Korea under Kim Jong Il: From Consolidation to Systemic Dissonance.* New York: State University of New York Press, 2006, 89–91.

Kim, Tae-hong. "Google Earth Torpedoes North Korean Lie." *DailyNK*, June 1, 2010. http://www.dailynk.com/english/read.php?cataId=nk00100&num =6444.

———. "South Korea Needs Precision Strike Capability." *DailyNK*, September 15, 2010. http://dailynk.com/english/read.php?cataId=nk00100&num=6803.

Kim, Yong-hun. "Kim Jong-nam Standing on the Highway." *DailyNK*, September 22, 2011. http://www.dailynk.com/english/read.php?cataId=nk00100 &num=8203.

———. "Lee Myung-su Covers Many Security Bases." *DailyNK*, April 8, 2011. http://dailynk.com/english/read.php?cataId=nk00400&num=7548.

———. "Nepotism Running Riot in Kim's NK." *DailyNK*, January 11, 2012. http://www.dailynk.com/english/read.php?cataId=nk02900&num=8667.

———. "Report Explains Sanctions Decisions." *DailyNK*, August 6, 2010. http://www.dailynk.com/english/read.php?cataId=nk00100&num=6667.

———. "There Is Still a Possibility of Uprising in North Korean Society." *DailyNK*, July 21, 2011. http://www.dailynk.com/english/read.php?num =7967&cataId=nk00300.

Klingner, Bruce. "New North Korean Missile Unit Reflects Growing Missile Threat." Web memo 2831. Washington, DC: Heritage Foundation, March 11, 2010. http://www.heritage.org/Research/Reports/2010/03/New -North-Korean-Missile-Unit-Reflects-Growing-Missile-Threat.

Kramer, Mark, ed. *The Black Book of Communism: Crimes, Terror, Repression.* Cambridge, MA: Harvard University Press, 1999.

Kristensen, Hans M. "Preemptive Posturing: What Happened to Deterrence?" *Bulletin of the Atomic Scientists* 58, no. 5 (September 1, 2002). http://bos.sagepub.com/content/58/5/54.full.

Kwak, Tae-hwan, and Seung-ho Joo, eds. *The United States and the Korean Peninsula in the 21st Century.* Aldershot Hampshire, UK: Ashgate, 2006.

Kwon, Ho-Youn, ed. *Divided Korea: Longing for Reunification.* Chicago: North Park University Press, 2004.

Lee, Beom-ki, and Lee Seok-young. "Younger Men Taking over Security World." *DailyNK*, June 21, 2011. http://www.dailynk.com/english/read .php?cataId=nk01500&num=7853.

Lee, Grace. "The Political Philosophy of Juche." *Stanford Journal of East Asian Affairs* 3, no. 1 (Spring 2003). http://www.stanford.edu/group/sjeaa/journal3 /korea1.pdf.

Lee, Karin, and Julia Choi. "North Korea: Economic Sanctions and U.S. Department of Treasury Actions, 1955–September 2007." Washington, DC: National Committee on North Korea, January 18, 2007. http://www.google.com/url?q=http://www.ncnk.org/resources /publications/NCNK_Economic_Sanctions_Current&sa=U&ei =-DMFT6mPDOnKsQLy6fGQCg&ved=0CBIQFjAB&usg =AFQjCNHFgoqEQijq9GonZASFJI3tWuRFSQ.

Lee, Myung-bak. "Opening Remarks by President Lee Myung-bak at a Meeting with Top Commanders of the ROK Armed Forces, May 04, 2010." Office of the President, Republic of Korea, May 4, 2010. http://english.president .go.kr/pre_activity/speeches/speeches_view.php?uno=3119&board_no =E03.

Lee, Seok Young. "AWOL and Hungry Soldiers Making Trouble." *DailyNK*, September 21, 2011. http://www.dailynk.com/english/read.php?cataId =nk01500&num=8197.

Lee, Seunghun, and J. J. Suh. "Rush to Judgment: Inconsistencies in South Korea's Cheonan Report." Nautilus Institute, Policy Forum 10-039, July 15, 2010. http://www.nautilus.org/publications/essays/napsnet/policy-forums

-online/security2009-2010/rush-to-judgment-inconsistencies-in -south-korea2019s-cheonan-report.

Lee, Suk Bok. *The Impact of U.S. Forces in Korea.* Washington, DC: National Defense University Press, 1987.

Lee, Sung-Chool. "The ROK-US Joint Political and Military Response to North Korean Armed Provocations." Report of the CSIS Korea chair. Washington, DC: *Center for Strategic and International Studies,* October 2011. http://csis.org/files/publication/111006_Lee_ROKUSJointResponse _web.pdf.

Lee, Sung-jin. "Cheonan Sinking Rumor Proudly Circulating in North Korea." *DailyNK,* April 27, 2010. http://www.dailynk.com/english/read.php?cataId =nk01500&num=6286.

Lim, Jae-Cheon. *Kim Jong-il's Leadership of North Korea.* London: Routledge Books, 2008.

Lin, Christina Y. "The King from the East: DPRK-Syria-Iran Nuclear Nexus and Strategic Implications for Israel and the ROK." Korea Economic Institute, Academic Paper Series 3, no. 7 (October 2008). http://www .keia.org/Publications/AcademicPaperSeries/2008/APS-Lin.pdf.

Lintner, Bertil. "North Korea: Coming in from the Cold." *Far Eastern Economic Review,* October 25, 2001. http://www.asiapacificms.com/articles /northkorea/.

Lucas, Adrianna N. "Courageous Channel Exercise Tests Non-Combatant Evacuation Readiness." U.S. Army Group Daegu, Installation Management Command, May 28, 2009. http://daegu.korea.army-mil.net/news/articles /5282009115506.asp.

Magee, Thomas M. "Out of the Ordinary Supply in Korea." *Army Logistician,* March–April, 2002. http://www.almc.army.mil/alog/issues/MarApr02 /Final.pdf.

Malone, Kelly J. "Preemptive Strikes and the Korean Nuclear Crisis: Legal and Political Limitations on the Use of Force." *Pacific Rim Law & Policy Journal* 12, no. 3 (2003). http://digital.law.washington.edu/dspace-law/bitstream /handle/1773.1/744/12PacRimLPolyJ807.pdf?sequence=1.

Manners, Andrew. "UN Extends Sanctions on Eritrea for Terrorism Support." *Future Directions International,* December 14, 2011. http://www.futuredirections.org.au/publications/indian-ocean/29-indian- ocean-swa/336-un-extends-sanctions-on-eritrea-for-terrorism -support.html.

Maxwell, David S. *Catastrophic Collapse of North Korea: Implications for the U.S. Military.* Ft. Leavenworth, KS: School of Advanced Military Studies, 1996.

http://www.dtic.mil/cgi-bin/GetTRDoc?AD=ADA314274&Location =U2&doc=GetTRDoc.pdf.

———. E-mail interview with author, February 4, 2012.

———. "Is the Kim Family Regime Rational and Why Don't the North Korean People Rebel?" *Foreign Policy Research Institute*, E-Notes, February 2012. http://www.fpri.org/enotes/2012/201201.maxwell.nkorea.pdf.

McCreary, John. "Nightwatch: 11 February 2009." *AFCEA Intelligence*, February 11, 2009. http://nightwatch.afcea.org/NightWatch_20090211.htm.

———. "Nightwatch: 20120417." *Nightwatch*, April 16, 2012. http://www.kforcegov.com/NightWatch/NightWatch_12000074.aspx.

Minnich, James M. *The Denuclearization of North Korea: The Agreed Framework and Alternative Options Analyzed*. Milton Keynes, UK: Lightning Source, 2003.

"Missiles of the World: Nodong-2." Missile Threat.com, Claremont Institute, 2007. http://www.missilethreat.com/missilesoftheworld/id.83/missile _detail.asp

Mitchell, Justin, and Catherine Jiang. "Tracking the North Korean Supernote." *Asia Sentinel*, March 7, 2007. http://www.asiasentinel.com/index.php ?option=com_content&task=view&id=408&Itemid=31.

Mok Yong-jae. "No Sign of End to GPS Jam." *DailyNK*, May 14, 2012. http://www.dailynk.com/english/read.php?cataId=nk00100&num=9225.

———. "North Korea's 'Princelings' Unveiled." *DailyNK*, April 18, 2011. http://www.dailynk.com/english/read.php?cataId=nk00400&num=7587.

Monsourov, Alexandre Y., ed. *Bytes and Bullets: Information Technology, Revolution, and National Security on the Korean Peninsula*. Honolulu: Asia Pacific Center for Security Studies, 2005. http://www.apcss.org/Publications/Edited %20Volumes/BytesAndBullets/CH13.pdf.

Moore, Gregory J. "America's Failed North Korea Nuclear Policy: A New Approach." *Asian Perspective* 32, no. 4 (2008). http://www.asianperspective.org /articles/v32n4-b.pdf.

Nanto, Dick K. "North Korea: Chronology of Provocations: 1950–2003." Washington, DC: Congressional Research Service, March 18, 2003. http://www.fas.org/man/crs/RL30004.pdf.

Niksch, Larry. "North Korea: Terrorism List Removal?" Washington, DC: Congressional Research Service, July 10, 2008.

———. "North Korea's Nuclear Weapons Development and Diplomacy." Washington, DC: Congressional Research Service, January 5, 2010. http://www.fas.org/sgp/crs/nuke/RL33590.pdf.

"Non-Combatant Emergency Evacuation Instructions." United States Forces Korea, Pamphlet 600-300, April 5, 2007. http://19tsc.korea.army.mil /USFK_Pam_600-300.pdf.

"N. Korea: US Breaking Deal Over Rocket." *Voice of America*, March 31, 2012. http://voznews.com/edition/n-korea-us-breaking-nuclear-deal-over -rocket-general-news.

"North Korea Begins Launch Pad Preparations for April Rocket Launch: A 38 North Exclusive." 38 North, March 29, 2012. http://38north.org/2012/03 /tongchang0329/.

"North Korea Downsizes To Remain Competitive." *Strategy Page*, December 30, 2010. http://www.strategypage.com/htmw/htlead/articles/20101230.aspx.

"North Korea Said to Work at Secret Teheran Site on Iran's Nuclear Warheads." East-Asia-Inte.com, October 3, 2008. http://www.east-asia -intel.com/eai/.

"North Korea: Suspicious Minds." *Frontline*, January 2003. http://www.pbs.org/frontlineworld/stories/northkorea/facts.html#03.

"North Korea's Nuclear-Capable Missiles." *The Risk Report* 2, no. 6 (November– December 1996). http://www.wisconsinproject.org/countries/nkorea /nukemiss.html.

"North Korean Missile Exports." *The Risk Report* 2, no. 6 (November–December 1996). http://www.wisconsinproject.org/countries/nkorea/north-korea -missile-exports.html.

"North Korean Nuclear Arsenal." Nuclear Files,Org, Project of the Nuclear Age Peace Foundation, May 9, 2008. http://nuclearfiles.org/menu/key -issues/nuclear-weapons/issues/capabilities/north-korea-cdi.htm.

"Nuclear Pyongyang is Helping Iran." *Foreign Affairs Committee, National Council of Resistance of Iran*, September 23, 2008. http://ncr-iran.org/content /view/5632/107/.

O, Tara. "The Integration of North Korean Defectors in South Korea: Problems and Prospects." *International Journal of Korean Studies* 15, no. 2 (Fall 2011). http://www.icks.org/publication/pdf/2011-FALL-WINTER/8.pdf.

Oberdorfer, Don. *The Two Koreas: A Contemporary History*. New York: Basic Books, 2001.

Oh, Kongdan. "The Death of Kim Jong-il." *Analysis*. Washington, DC: Brookings Institution, December 19, 2011. http://www.brookings.edu /opinions/2011/1219_north_korea_oh.aspx.

Oh, Kongdan, and Ralph Hassig. "Military Confrontation on the Korean Peninsula." *Joint Forces Quarterly* 64 (First Quarter 2012). http://www.ndu.edu /press/lib/pdf/jfq-64/JFQ-64_82-90_Oh-Hassig.pdf.

O'Hanlon, Michael, and Mike Mochizuki. *Crisis on the Korean Peninsula: How to Deal with a Nuclear North Korea*. Washington, DC: Brookings Institution Press, 2003.

Olsen, Edward A. *Korea, the Divided Nation*. Westport, CT: Praeger Publishers, 2005.

"One Fourth of the Korean Population." *Seoul of Asia*, 2008. http://english.seoul.go.kr/gtk/about/fact.php?pidx=3.

"Overview of Korea." 14th ILO Asian Regional Meeting, 2006. http://www.mol2006busan.org/tour1.php.

Paik, Nak-chung. "The Post Kim Jong-il Era and the 2013 Regime in North Korea." *The Asia-Pacific Journal: Japan Focus*, January 22, 2012. http://www.japanfocus.org///events/view/126.

Pan, Esther. "North Korea's Capitalist Experiment." Backgrounder. Washington, DC: Council on Foreign Relations, June 8, 2006. http://www.cfr.org/publication/10858/.

Park, Hyeong Jung. "Political Dynamics of Hereditary Succession in North Korea." *International Journal of Korean Unification Studies* 20, no. 1 (2011). http://www.kinu.or.kr/upload/neoboard/DATA03/IJKUS20-1.pdf.

Park, In-ho. "South Korea Refutes North Korean Refutations of Investigation Results." *DailyNK*, May 31, 2010. http://www.dailynk.com/english/read.php?cataId=nk00100&num=6439.

Park, Jeffrey. "The North Korean Nuclear Test: What the Seismic Data Says." *Bulletin of the Atomic Scientists*, May 26, 2009. http://www.thebulletin.org/web-edition/features/the-north-korean-nuclear-test-what-the-seismic-data-says.

Park, Seong Guk. "NLL Intrusion Numbers Falling." *DailyNK*, November 16, 2011. http://www.dailynk.com/english/read.php?cataId=nk00100&num=8413.

Park, Sun-won. "Strategic Posture Review: South Korea." *World Politics Review*, March 17, 2010. http://www.brookings.edu/articles/2010/0317_korea_park.aspx.

Park, Sung-kook. "Tasks of the General Bureau of Reconnaissance." *DailyNK*, May 7, 2010. http://www.dailynk.com/english/read.php?cataId=nk02900&num=6341.

Pinczuk, Guillermo. "Building Multi-Party Capacity for a WMD Free Korea: Security Assurances." Institute for Foreign Policy Analysis, March 16, 2005. http://www.ifpa.org/pdf/shanghai/Security-Assurance-Briefing.pdf.

Pinkston, Daniel. "North Korea Conducts Nuclear Test." Monterey, CA: Center for Nonproliferation Studies, Monterey Institute of International Studies, October 10, 2006. http://cns.miis.edu/pubs/week/pdf/061010_dprktest.pdf.

————. "North Korea's Foreign Policy towards the United States." *Strategic Insights* 5, no. 7 (September 2006). http://cns.miis.edu/other/pinkston _strategic_insights_sep06.pdf.

Plunk, Daryl M. "North Korea: Exporting Terrorism?" Asian Studies Backgrounder no. 74. Washington, DC: Heritage Foundation, February 25, 1988. http://www.heritage.org/research/asiaandthepacific/asb74.cfm.

Pocock, Chris. "UAV Crash in Korea Linked to GPS Jamming." *Aviation International News Online*, June 1, 2012. http://www.ainonline.com/aviation-news/ain-defense-perspective/2012-06-01/uav-crash-korea-linked-gps -jamming.

Power, John. "Should S. Korea Increase Its Missile Range?" *Asia One*, April 24, 2012. http://www.asiaone.com/News/AsiaOne+News/Asia/Story /A1Story20120424-341667.html.

"Proliferation Security Initiative." United States Department of State. http://www.state.gov/t/isn/c10390.htm.

Ramberg, Bennett. "Dealing with Nuclear North Korea." *Yale Global*, January 10, 2011. http://yaleglobal.yale.edu/content/dealing-nuclear-north-korea.

"Recovery from Nuclear Attack." *Federal Emergency Management Agency*, October 1988. http://www.defconwarningsystem.com/documents/recovery_from _nuclear_attack.pdf.

Reiter, Patrick A. "Initial Communist Chinese Logistics in the Korean War." *Quartermaster Professional Bulletin*, Autumn 2004. http://www.quartermaster .army.mil/OQMG/professional_bulletin/2004/Autumn04/Initial _Communist_Chinese_Logistics_in_the_Korean_War.htm.

Report by the Director General. "Application of Safeguards in the Democratic People's Republic of Korea." United Nations, IAEA, September 2, 2011. http://isis-online.org/uploads/isis-reports/documents/IAEA_DPRK _2Sept2011.pdf.

Rubin, Barry. "North Korea's Threats to the Middle East and the Middle East's Threats to Asia." In "Asia Book," *The Middle East Review of International Affairs*, 2005. http://meria.idc.ac.il/books/brkorea.html.

"Sanctions Information as Important as Enforcement." *Daily NK*, August 4, 2010. http://www.dailynk.com/english/read.php?cataId=nk03500 &num=6659.

Saunders, Phillip C. "Military Options for Dealing with North Korea's Nuclear Program." Monterey, CA: James Martin Center for Nonproliferation Studies, Monterey Institute for International Studies, January 27, 2003. http://cns.miis.edu/north_korea/dprkmil.htm.

Scobell, Andrew, and John M. Sanford. *North Korea's Military Threat: Pyongyang's Conventional Forces, Weapons of Mass Destruction, and Ballistic Missiles*. Strategic

Studies Institute Monograph. Carlisle, PA: U.S. Army War College, April 2007. http://www.strategicstudiesinstitute.army.mil/pdffiles/PUB771.pdf.

Seligson, Susan. "The World Watches North Korea." *BU Today*, January 11, 2012. http://www.bu.edu/today/2012/the-world-watches-north-korea/.

Shachtman, Noah. "Inside America's (Mock) Attack on North Korea." *Wired*, May 27, 2009. http://www.wired.com/dangerroom/2009/05/inside -americas-mock-attack-north-korea/.

Sharp, Gen. Walter L., commander, United Nations Command, Republic of Korea–U.S. Combined Forces Command; and commander, U.S. Forces Korea. Statement for the Record to the United States Senate Armed Services Committee, April 12, 2011. http://armed-services.senate.gov /statemnt/2011/04%20April/Sharp%2004-12-11.pdf.

Shin, Joo-hyun. "North Korean Submarine Helmsman Breaks 14-Year Silence." *DailyNK*, June 1, 2010. http://www.dailynk.com/english/read.php?cataId =nk02500&num=6445.

Snyder, Scott. "Kim Jong-un's Dangerous Brother." *The Diplomat*, January 22, 2012. http://utopic.me/page/134505341_C/the-diplomat.com/2012/01/22 /kim-jong-un%E2%80%99s-dangerous-brother/.

Squassoni, Sharon. "North Korea's Nuclear Weapons: How Soon an Arsenal?" Washington, DC: Congressional Research Service, February 2, 2004. http://www.fas.org/spp/starwars/crs/RS21391.pdf.

"Statement By the Office of the Director of National Intelligence on North Korea's Declared Nuclear Test on May 25, 2009." Office of the Director of National Intelligence, June 15, 2009. http://www.dni.gov/press_releases /20090615_release.pdf.

Steinberg, David I., ed. *Korean Attitudes toward the United States: Changing Dynamics.* Armonk, NY: M. E. Sharpe, 2005.

Steinberg, Gerald M. "North Korea and Iran: Will Any Lessons Be Learned?" *Jerusalem Issue Brief 6*, no. 12 (October 11, 2006). http://www.jcpa.org /brief/brief006-12.htm.

Stossel, Scott. "North Korea: The War Game." *The Atlantic*, July/August 2005. http://www.theatlantic.com/magazine/archive/2005/07/north-korea-the -war-game/4029/.

Sutter, Robert. "China and North Korea after the Cold War: Wariness, Caution, and Balance." *International Journal of Korean Studies* 14, no. 1 (Spring 2010). http://www.icks.org/publication/pdf/2010-SPRING-SUMMER/3.pdf.

"Syria Improves It's SCUD D Missile With Help From North Korea." *Geostrategy-Direct*, February 22, 2006. http://www.geostrategy-direct.com /geostrategy%2Ddirect/.

"Tactical Details of the Korean Artillery Exchange." *STRATFOR*, November 29, 2010. http://www.stratfor.com/memberships/176803/analysis/20101129 _tactical_details_korean_artillery_exchange.

Tarrant, Bill, and Raju Gopalakrishnan. "Analysis: What's the Plan if North Korea Collapses?" *News Talk: WSAU.Com*, December 23, 2011. http://wsau.com/news/articles/2011/dec/23/analysis-whats-the-plan-if -north-korea-collapses/.

"The Naval Clash on the Yellow Sea on 29 June 2002 Between South Korea and North Korea: The Situation and ROK's Position." *Ministry of National Defense, Republic of Korea*, July 1, 2002. http://www.globalsecurity.org /wmd/library/news/rok/2002/0020704-naval.htm.

Thielmann, Greg. "Long-Range Ballistic Missile Development: A Tale of Two Tests." Arms Control Association Threat Assessment Brief. Washington, DC: Arms Control Association, May 10, 2012. http://www.armscontrol.org /files/TAB_Long-Range-Ballistic-Missile-Development-A-Tale-of-Two -Tests.pdf.

Toon, Gordon. "The Enigma of the Korean Peninsula: An Examination of North Korea and Relevant Security Implications." *Global Security Studies* 1, no. 2 (Summer 2010). http://globalsecuritystudies.com/Toon%20Korea %20TWO.pdf.

"Transcript: Worldwide Threat Assessment of the US Intelligence Community for the Senate Select Committee on Intelligence." Associated Press Television News Service, January 31, 2012. http://www.aptnvideo.net/pages /browse/player/player_frameset.jsp?item=210691.

"Untitled Document Provided to Congress on November 19, 2002." (UNCLASSIFIED) *Central Intelligence Agency*, November 19, 2002. http://www.fas.org/nuke/guide/dprk/nuke/cia111902.html.

Vick, Charles P. "Has the No-Dong B/Shahab-4 Finally Been Tested in Iran for North Korea?" Global Security.org, May 2, 2006. http://www.globalsecurity .org/wmd/library/report/2006/cpvick-no-dong-b_2006.htm.

———. "Taep'o-dong 2 (TD-2), NKSL-X-2." Global Security.org, March 20, 2007. http://www.globalsecurity.org/wmd/world/dprk/td-2.htm.

Wall, Mike. "North Korea's Rocket Technology Explained: An Observer's Guide." SPACE.com, April 2, 2012. http://www.space.com/15130-north -korea-rocket-missile-technology.html.

Wallace, Robert Daniel. *Sustaining the Regime: North Korea's Quest for Financial Support*. Lanham, MD: University Press of America, 2007.

Weathersby, Kathryn. "Soviet Aims in Korea and the Origins of the Korean War, 1949–1950: New Evidence from Russian Archives." Cold War International History Project, Working Paper no. 8. Washington, DC:

Wilson International Center for Scholars, November 1993. http://www.wilsoncenter.org/topics/pubs/Working_Paper_8.pdf.

Wege, Carl Anthony. "The Hizbollah–North Korean Nexus." *Small Wars Journal*, January 23, 2011. http://smallwarsjournal.com/blog/journal/docs -temp/654-wege.pdf.

Wilcox, Philip C., U.S. coordinator for counterterrorism, U.S. Department of State. "U.S. Department of State 96/04/30 Briefing: Amb. Wilcox on Patterns of Global Terrorism, 1995." Office of the Coordinator for Counterterrorism, U.S. Department of State, Washington, DC, April 30, 1996. http://dosfan.lib.uic.edu/ERC/arms/cterror_briefing /960430cterror.html.

Xiang, Ah. "Communists and the Japanese Invasion of Manchuria." *Republican China*, September 20, 2011. http://republicanchina.org/COMMUNISTS -AND-JAPAN-INVASION-MANCHURIA.v0.pdf.

Yun, Duk-min. "North Korea's Power Succession and Changes in Leadership." *Korea Focus*, August 24, 2010. http://www.koreafocus.or.kr/design2/layout /content_print.asp?group_id=103254.

Zadeh, Ali Nouri. "Iranian Officer: Hezbollah Has a Commando Naval Unit." *Asharq Alawsat*, July 29, 2006. http://www.asharq-e.com/news.asp?section =1&id=5801.

Zhang, Hui. "North Korea's Oct. 9 Nuclear Test: Successful or Failed?" Paper presented at the Institute for Nuclear Materials Management Forty-Eighth Annual Meeting, Tucson, Arizona, July 8–12, 2007. http://belfercenter .ksg.harvard.edu/files/NKtest_INMM07_Hui.pdf.

# INDEX

Page numbers followed by *f* indicate illustrations.

# ABOUT THE AUTHOR

Bruce E. Bechtol, Jr., is associate professor of political science at Angelo State University and a retired marine. He was formerly on the faculty at the Marine Corps Command and Staff College (2005–2010) and the Air Command and Staff College (2003–2005). Dr. Bechtol served as an adjunct visiting professor at the Korea University Graduate School of International Studies (2006–2007). He was an intelligence officer at the Defense Intelligence Agency from 1997 until 2003, eventually serving as the senior analyst for Northeast Asia in the Intelligence Directorate (J2) on the Joint Staff in the Pentagon. He formerly sat on the editorial review board of the *East Asian Review* from 2005 to 2009 and served as editor of the *Defense Intelligence Journal* from 2004 to 2005. He is currently on the editorial advisory board of the *Korea Observer* (2011–present). He is the current president of the International Council on Korean Studies, and serves on the board of directors of the Council on U.S.-Korean Security Studies. He is the author of *Defiant Failed State: The North Korean Threat to International Security* and *Red Rogue: The Persistent Challenge of North Korea*, and he is the editor of *Confronting Security Challenges on the Korean Peninsula* and *The Quest for a Unified Korea: Strategies for the Cultural and Interagency Process*. He is also the author of more than thirty articles in peer-reviewed journals.